Foreign Economic Liberalization

Foreign Economic Liberalization

Transformations in Socialist and Market Economies

EDITED BY

András Köves
and Paul Marer

Westview Press
BOULDER, SAN FRANCISCO, AND OXFORD

Copyright © 1991 by Westview Press, Inc.

Published in 1991 in the United States of America by Westview Press, Inc., 5500 Central Avenue, Boulder, Colorado 80301, and in the United Kingdom by Westview Press, 36 Lonsdale Road, Summertown, Oxford OX2 7EW

A CIP catalog record for this book is available from the Library of Congress. ISBN 0-8133-8198-3.   ISBN 0-8133-8199-1 (pbk).

Printed and bound in the United States of America

The paper used in this publication meets the requirements of the American National Standard for Permanence of Paper for Printed Library Materials Z39.48-1984.

10   9   8   7   6   5   4   3   2   1

Contents

Tables and Figures

Tables

Figures

Acknowledgments

This book is based in large part on the papers and formal discussions originally presented at the Conference on Attempts at Liberalization: Hungarian Economic Policy and International Experience, held in Budapest in November, 1989. The Conference brought together specialists on economic systems and economic policy as well as on international trade from Hungary and from all over the world. Among the 300 participants were members of the academic community from various universities, colleges, and research institutes, as well as representatives of the business world, the banking community, governments, and international organizations. The Conference was generously supported by the United Nations Development Program, the Ministry of Trade of Hungary, the National Bank of Hungary, the Commercial and Credit Bank of Budapest, the Hungarian Credit Bank, and the Hungarian Economic Association. The Conference was organized by the KOPINT-DATORG Institute for Economic and Market Research and Informatics in Budapest. Special thanks are due to János Deák, General Director of KOPINT-DATORG, for his advice and support. Several universities and other institutions also made contributions by providing released time and covering travel expenses for their staff members. We express our appreciation to all these organizations.

The editors are deeply grateful to the formal participants in the Conference, especially to Rezső Nyers, Chairman of the Committee on Economic Reform of the Hungarian Government at the time of the Conference, and to those who served as chairpersons: Hasan Ersel of the Central Bank of the Republic of Turkey, László Szamuely of the KOPINT-DATORG Institute, Ed A. Hewett of the Brookings Institution, Professors Jeffrey D. Sachs of Harvard University and Rolf J. Langhammer of the Kiel Institute of World Economics.

For helping to plan the Conference and subsequently working on the volume, Judit Berényi, Katalin Nagy, Klára Ungár, Katalin Tamon and many other members of the KOPINT-DATORG Institute deserve special acknowledgment and thanks.

A somewhat expanded version of this book will appear later this year in Hungarian, published by Közgazdasági és Jogi Könyvkiadó and KOPINT-DATORG in Budapest. The Hungarian version includes additional chapters and, in some cases, the longer versions of several of the chapters. For example, whereas this English version makes only sparing references to the literature in other languages, the Hungarian volume offers a more comprehensive compilation of the literature in Hungarian and other languages.

Many individuals contributed considerable time and effort to enable the editors to blend into a cohesive volume the revised versions of some of the Conference contributions and the additional papers and comments solicited subsequently. In particular, we wish to thank our contributors who were gracious enough to put up with our numerous suggestions for revisions. We owe much to the editing of Elizabeth Marer, and to Melanie Kearns at Indiana University, who typed the manuscript and then prepared it, through several stages, for camera-ready copy, undertaking much of the work on very short notice. Susan McEachern at Westview Press was most helpful with her suggestions and for seeing the work through its various stages of publication.

The publication of this book was made possible by a grant from the National Council for Soviet and East European Research, which provided released time to the U.S. co-editor. We also acknowledge a publication preparation grant from the Indiana Center for Global Business of the School of Business of Indiana University, and thank its director, Professor Lawrence S. Davidson, for the Center's timely contribution.

András Köves
Paul Marer

About the Contributors

Bela Balassa	Professor of Political Economy, Johns Hopkins University; Consultant, The World Bank
Joseph Y. Battat	Institutional Development Officer, Foreign Investment Advisory Service, The World Bank
Armeane M. Choksi	Director, Country Department I, Latin America and the Caribbean Region, The World Bank
László Csaba	Principal Economist, Institute for Economic, Market Research and Informatics, Budapest
Guillermo de la Dehesa	Chief Executive Officer, Banco Pastor, Madrid
János Gács	Head of Research Department, Institute for Economic, Market Research and Informatics, Budapest
Nadav Halevi	Professor of Economics, Hebrew University, Jerusalem
András Inotai	Economist, Trade Policy Division, The World Bank
Béla Kádár	Minister of International Economic Relations of the Government of Hungary, Budapest
András Köves	Deputy Director, Institute for Economic, Market Research and Informatics, Budapest
Rolf J. Langhammer	Chief of Research Division, Kiel Institute of World Economics, Kiel
Kamilla Lányi	Principal Economist, Institute for Economic, Market Research and Informatics, Budapest
Neng Liang	Assistant Professor of International Business, Loyola College, Baltimore

Paul Marer	Professor of International Business, Indiana University, Bloomington
Michael Michaely	Lead Economist, Brazil Department, The World Bank; Aron and Michael Chilewich Emeritus Professor of International Trade, Hebrew University, Jerusalem
András Nagy	Head of Department, Institute of Economics, Hungarian Academy of Sciences, Budapest
Gábor Obláth	Head of Research Department, Institute for Economic, Market Research and Informatics, Budapest
Demetris Papageorgiou	Chief, Trade, Finance and Industry, Brazil Department, The World Bank
Yung Chul Park	Professor of Economics, Korea University, Seoul
Dwight H. Perkins	Director, Harvard Institute for International Development, Harvard University, Cambridge
William R. Rhodes	Senior Executive-International, Citibank, New York
Jeffrey Sachs	Galen L. Stone Professor of International Trade, Harvard University, Cambridge
Károly Attila Soós	Principal Economist, Institute of Economics, Hungarian Academy of Sciences; Chairman, Committee on the Budget, Hungarian National Assembly, Budapest
Márton Tardos	Principal Economist, Institute of Economics, Hungarian Academy of Sciences; Vice Chairman, Economic Committee, Hungarian National Assembly, Budapest
Masaru Yoshitomi	Director, Economic Research Institute, Economic Planning Agency, Government of Japan, Tokyo

Introduction and Overview

Introduction

András Köves and Paul Marer

How This Book Came About

In November 1989, a Conference on "Attempts at Liberalization: Hungarian Economic Policy and International Experience," was held in Budapest. Leading experts from around the world participated. The Conference had a threefold purpose. One was to assess the theories, strategies, and postwar experiences of foreign economic liberalization of countries around the world. The second was to discuss the problems of reform and transformation—especially of foreign trade, investment, and finance—of the countries of Central and Eastern Europe and China. The third purpose was to consider which theories and experiences of economic liberalization in market economies are relevant, perhaps with modifications, for the further liberalization or transformation of Hungary and the other socialist or formerly socialist countries.

This volume traces its origins to the Budapest conference, but it is not a proceedings. It contains fewer than half of the papers presented, practically all of them revised to take into account developments during 1990 and the arguments advanced by the other participants at the Conference and in their contributions to this volume.

Main Themes and Contributions

The unifying theme of the book is experiences and options of foreign economic liberalization in countries that differ in size, resource endowment, level of development, extent of market imperfections, and political conditions. This book, the editors hope, will make a lasting contribution to the literature on this topic. There are few works that bring together in one place—specifically but succinctly—the postwar experiences with liberalization of a large number of market economies. At the same time, the book also helps inform the policy debates of (and for) the socialist and ex-socialist countries around the globe on strategies of liberalization and systemic transformation. The issues raised and the options examined will remain current not only for the socialist world, as more and more of these countries try to become market economies, but also for all nations that desire a greater integration into the global economy and seek an improved understanding of the domestic preconditions and policies that will promote this.

About half of the contributions focus on the experiences of market economies. Several of the chapters are by leading experts—from the World Bank, academia, research institutes, and the private sector—who try to synthesize the wealth of cross-country experiences of liberalization attempts and outcomes. Other essays in the section describe the liberalization experiences, respectively, of Spain, Israel, Japan, Korea, Taiwan, and Mexico, written by leading experts and policy makers from these countries. The authors not only describe but also reflect on what they have learned from the record, and on the relevance of the experiences of the individual economies for the transforming socialist and ex-socialist countries.

In the next section, six chapters discuss Hungary's liberalization experiences and policy options. For more than twenty years that country has been in the forefront of economic reforms in the communist world. The contributors describe what has been accomplished during the last two decades, assess the economic and political legacies inherited by Hungary's new government formed after democratic elections in 1990, present detailed discussions of the policy options, and make policy recommendations. The editors worked closely with the authors to ensure little overlap among the chapters. Although the focus is on Hungary, the issues and policy tradeoffs for that country are generally applicable, or will be applicable at some point in the future, for all of the countries of Central and Eastern Europe.

In the next section, four contributions spell out the main similarities and differences among the countries of Central and Eastern Europe. Jeffrey Sachs summarizes developments there and offers his policy recommendations, with an emphasis on Poland. Soós looks at the link between economic liberalization and stabilization; Tardos evaluates alternative approaches to privatization and how they affect other aspects of domestic and foreign economic liberalization. Csaba's essay enumerates the constraints and driving forces of system change throughout the region.

The editors decided not to include separate chapters on other countries in the region. Because most of them still lag behind Hungary's economic liberalization, a description of their individual experiences would have covered much of the same ground as the earlier experiences of Hungary, which are well documented here. Somewhat unique, of course, is the experience and situation in Poland, dealt with in some detail by Sachs. The GDR, which as far as policy options are concerned is fully a special case, is not discussed separately; nor is much said about the special features and situations of Yugoslavia or the USSR. The volume concludes with an essay about China's experiences in opening up its economy through 1989.

Synopses of the Individual Contributions

The book is "tied together" by the editors' introductory essay (Chapter 1), which contrasts economic liberalization in market economies and in the countries of Central and Eastern Europe. The chapter discusses, in concrete terms, why and how foreign economic liberalization must be an integral part of the economic transformation that has gotten under way in the countries of Central and Eastern Europe. It contrasts the different approaches taken by Hungary and Poland and examines the relevance of the liberalization experiences of the developing and newly industrializing countries for Central and Eastern Europe.

Market-Economy Experiences

The contributions in this part of the book focus on the generalizable experiences of the developing countries and their implications for Eastern Europe. In Chapter 2, Choksi, Michaely and Papageorgiou tell us about the lessons of successful postwar trade liberalizations in 19 market economies, summarizing the findings and conclusions of a seven-volume study (not published as yet at the time of writing) sponsored by the World Bank. They focus on the transition process, that is, on how countries move from a distorted trade regime towards a more liberal one. They find that reforms can work, regardless of initial conditions, if certain rules are followed: a non-inflationary macroeconomic policy, proper reform sequencing, a rapid dismantling of quantitative restrictions, a credible pre-announcement of further measures, and (where appropriate), substantial currency depreciation.

In Chapter 3, Langhammer sketches his understanding of the basic principles of trade liberalization and then focuses on the domestic and external obstacles that can derail it. He examines the experiences of a large number of developing and newly industrializing countries and makes recommendations on how to overcome constraints, such as vested interests attempting to block economic policies by political action.

In Chapter 4, Balassa compares the economic policies and performances during 1963-1987 of two groups of newly industrializing countries: four economies in the Far East (Singapore, Hong Kong, Korea, and Taiwan) versus four in Latin America (Argentina, Brazil, Chile, and Mexico). He not only documents in concrete terms the superior performance of the Far Eastern countries—a fact that is well known in general—but he also identifies the main policy factors he believes are responsible for the differences in the East Asian versus the Latin American performances. Two of the important external economic policy choices, according to Balassa, are foreign trade strategies and external borrowing. These interact with two other important variables, the domestic savings ratios and the efficiency of investment, to help determine economic performance. Balassa's essay quantifies the levels and trends in these variables and thus provides the larger context in which foreign economic strategies have their impacts.

Liang, Marer, and Battat recommend an alternative to the conventional bipolar classification of trade strategies: inward- vs. outward-oriented (Chapter 5). The authors show, theoretically as well as empirically, that in many cases import substitution and export promotion can co-exist, under various arrangements, for example, as integral parts of a "protected export promotion" strategy. They show that the foreign trade outcomes of the small and medium-sized centrally planned economies (CPEs) appear to have similarities with the "de facto import promotion" strategies of many third world countries. However, they note, it does not appear possible to apply to the CPEs a similar empirical measurement of trade strategies that they use for developing countries with more market-oriented systems.

András Inotai describes and illustrates with examples the global trend toward more liberal rules on foreign direct investment (FDI). He then shows the relationship between trade liberalization and FDI liberalization, and concludes with policy recommendations for the countries of Central and Eastern Europe (Chapter 6).

Turning to the liberalization experiences of certain individual market economies, Spain's is presented first. Many believe that Spain's highly successful liberalization example is the most directly relevant for the countries of Central and Eastern Europe because this medium-sized and relatively poor European country has moved successfully from a highly authoritarian political and autarkic economic system to political democracy, a market economy, and membership in the European Community. Spain's experience is presented succinctly but in very concrete terms by Guillermo de la Dehesa, the country's former minister of economics and finance. He concludes by offering both technical and political advice to decision makers in Central and Eastern Europe (Chapter 7).

Somewhat in contrast to Spain stands the experience of Israel, where the liberalization process has been much more protracted and less successful. The main reasons for this are that, until 1977, the government was led by the Labor Party which had a "socialist" ideological orientation (although in terms of growth, the last years of the labor government were especially dynamic); the huge economic burdens and political-economic uncertainties that Israel faces, given its special situation; and the economic policy mistakes that are easy to identify by hindsight. Nevertheless, even Israel has succeeded in liberalizing almost fully its trade, but not its capital account. Halevi offers the conclusion that the most important policy relevant for foreign economic liberalization is properly to determine the exchange rate to support the liberalization effort (Chapter 8).

The chapter on Japan tries to answer two frequently asked questions that are of special relevance for Eastern Europe: (1) to what extent is Japan's economic success attributable to the active role that its government has played in the economy, and (2) how was it possible that long-persisting and pervasive protectionism did not impede sustained improvements in efficiency and export-competitiveness of the private sector? Both questions are answered thoughtfully and in specific detail by Yoshitomi, Director of the Research Institute of Japan's Economic Planning Agency (Chapter 9). He says that intense domestic competition for greater market shares among private corporations in Japan, together with a set of not easily replicable Japanese institutions and practices, including government-business relations, is a large part of the answer to both questions. Among the essay's many insights, Yoshitomi explains, for example, why and how Japan protected its economy during the 1950s and 1960s, and how its strategy of "protected export promotion" has worked in practice. The chapter details the growing domestic and international pressures on Japan to liberalize its foreign economic relations and spells out how the country is responding.

Park contrasts the evolution of the postwar foreign economic strategies of Taiwan and Korea (Chapter 10). He shows that, in both countries, import-substitution and export-promotion have co-existed, in patterns that have certain similarities with those of Japan. Domestic market protection was accorded to many producers until they developed into efficient exporters. The governments' incentive systems were structured in such a way that if import-substituting firms failed to meet the export-performance test within a reasonable time frame, they could not prosper.

In a rather striking policy change, Mexico began to liberalize around 1985. In 1990, in response to developments in Central and Eastern Europe, Mexico's leaders decided to speed up the implementation of the country's liberalization program in order to enhance the attractiveness of Mexico in competing with Eastern Europe and other parts of the world for increasingly scarce risk capital. The main aspects of Mexico's policy turn are described in fascinating detail by Rhodes, a senior executive of one of the largest U.S. multinational banks, who has negotiated for many years with debtor governments in Latin America and Eastern Europe. Rhodes then calls attention to the growing global shortage of capital, shows the relationship between a country's liberalization program and obtaining funds from foreign commercial banks, and concludes with observations about prospective investors comparing the business environments in Latin America and Eastern Europe (Chapter 11).

Hungary's Experiences and Policy Options

Hungary has had more than two decades of economic reform experience whose lessons are of interest. The country remains in the forefront of domestic and foreign economic liberalization and system transformation, so that reports on where these processes stand, and on the current policy debates, are instructive. Six articulate economists discuss local developments, placing them in regional and international contexts.

Köves demonstrates convincingly why the trade and financial arrangements that were still in place in the CMEA in 1990 must be changed (Chapter 12). One reason is that the existing trade and settlement systems are simply not sustainable under the changed economic and political circumstances in the USSR and the countries of Eastern Europe. Of equal importance is that the arrangements prevailing are incompatible with the process of marketization and foreign economic liberalization to which most of the countries of Central and Eastern Europe are committed. Köves then outlines the pros and cons of each of the main alternative arrangements for reforming or transforming the CMEA system, details where the negotiations between the Soviet Union and Hungary stood as of July 1990, and recommends the establishment, with Western help, of a safety net to help finance for Hungary the large though temporary deterioration in its convertible-currency balance of payments that will result from the change in intra-CMEA arrangements. Köves concludes by discussing the interest of the West in the success of Hungary's precedent-setting initiative to transform intra-CMEA relations.

The details of Hungary's more than two-decades-long experience with trade liberalization vis-à-vis market economies is discussed by Gács (Chapter 13). Focusing on trade strategy, the institutions that conduct foreign trade, and on export and import controls, he concludes that between 1968 and 1989, three important steps were taken by the authorities: in 1968 they abolished compulsory plan (including trade) directives; in the early 1980s they weakened and by the late 1980s gave up the monopoly of foreign trade; and in 1989 introduced a three-year program to liberalize four-fifths of convertible-currency imports. Based on a well-documented assessment of how trade was actually conducted during these 23 years, Gács concludes that so far the reforms did not add up to comprehensive trade liberalization. This is because access to imports has continued to be determined only in part by the purchasing power of the prospective importers and by the price of the importables (including tariffs and the exchange rate); a more important role has been played by administrative practices, often hidden from view. During this entire period, Hungary's reformed economic system as well as economic policies had reinforced each other to protect domestic producers across the board.

The essay by Lányi (Chapter 14) is a no-holds-barred and well-documented indictment of the visible and invisible regulations that, according to the author, have strangled Hungary's foreign trade ever since the introduction of the "New Economic Mechanism" in 1968. She enumerates the jungle of compulsory and advisory, published and confidential, written and unwritten, general and case-by-case series of rules and regulations that have tied the hands and sapped the initiatives of Hungary's producing and trading enterprises. She ventures the hypothesis that many of the regulations were invented by the authorities as a counterforce to the 1968 reforms, to prevent firms from exercising those very powers of decision that the reform supposedly had granted to them.

Whereas the two preceding essays focused mainly on the past, Obláth's contribution bridges the past and the future (Chapter 15). Building on the findings of Gács, Lányi, and others, Obláth's essay notes that ever since 1968, one of the major aims of Hungary's foreign economic diplomacy was to "sell" the country's economic reforms and to convince the West that Hungary's system was not much different from those of market economies. The fact that Hungary more or less succeeded in this has now become counterproductive: "If the image of the Hungarian economic system is built upon a fiction—and especially if both the Hungarian government and the West have interests in maintaining this fiction—then neither the policies of opening up nor the necessary forms of assistance can be designed in an economically rational way." Obláth discusses in what sense the perceptions about Hungary's trading system are fictional and then notes the consequences. He concludes with a set of policy recommendations. Their essence is the conversion of quantitative and other types of restrictions into tariffs, a selective and temporary increase in the level of tariffs, and a program to liberalize imports.

Next, Nagy summarizes the main lessons of import-liberalization in the developed and developing countries and assesses their relevance for Hungary (Chapter 16). He stresses the importance of the differences in the motivation of state-owned versus private enterprises. He notes that in Hungary the former is still the dominant form of ownership, a situation that cannot be expected to change in the near future. Nagy argues that as long as enterprises are not cut off from the umbilical cord of the state, are not subject to the control of private or public owners of capital, and competition does not exert a sufficiently strong pressure on them to improve efficiency, all liberalization and decentralization attempts tend to be dangerous. He concludes with a set of policy recommendations on the dos and don'ts of trade liberalization under Hungary's current economic and political system.

Even broader in sweep is the next chapter by Béla Kádár, a scholar who in 1990, just after he completed this essay, became Minister of International Economic Relations in Hungary's new government. Kádár discusses the broad strategy of economic liberalization (Chapter 17). He notes that the economic legacies of the old system and the prevailing political situation limit greatly the new government's room for manoeuver. The economic legacies include a nascent but still undeveloped market, weak competition, absence of real owners of the means of production, a low level of efficiency, non-market relations in the CMEA, and a population nurtured in a paternalistic environment. These add up to an economy in which market-type policy instruments will not be very effective. Moreover, the domestic population and Hungary's foreign partners both expect the economic transformation to be politically non-violent. This means that it would not be wise for the new government to pursue policies, however economically rational, that ignore the domestic thresholds of tolerance. The strategic priority of economic liberalization, in Kádár's view, must be programs that encourage an export-oriented structural transformation (which require, among other measures, liberalizing the import of foreign capital), improve the efficiency of state-owned enterprises (which means hardening their budget constraints, deregulation, and increased competition), and privatize in ways that make economic sense but proceed at a pace that is politically acceptable to the population. Only after significant progress has been achieved in these areas can Hungary move in large steps to further liberalize prices, wages, and imports, reduce taxes, and introduce a convertible currency.

Eastern Europe and China

The last five essays continue to discuss economic liberalization and transformation issues but in ways that are less Hungary-specific. Jeffrey Sachs reviews why past attempts at reform in Eastern Europe were generally not successful and then outlines a program of rapid market transformation (Chapter 18). The main elements of his program are: let prices find market-clearing levels, based on free trade and convertibility with the West; move trade with the Soviet Union on a market basis; remove restrictions on the private sector; privatize state-owned firms and impose tougher discipline on enterprises that remain state owned; and assure macroeconomic stability through restrictive monetary and fiscal policies. Except for revamping and reorienting trade with the Soviet Union and privatizing state-owned enterprises, both of which will take time (he discusses privatization options in some detail), the pace of the rest of the transition program should be decisive and rapid. Next, Sachs assesses the stabilization-cum-liberalization program that Poland introduced in January 1990, concluding that its achievements are substantially greater than its problems. He stresses that 1990 statistics on the decline of production and the standard of living and on the increases in unemployment are biased as measures of the effectiveness of the program. Sachs concludes with strong recommendations on the kind of assistance the West should provide to promote liberalization and transformation of the countries of Central and Eastern Europe.

Soós's essay takes up one of the main issues raised by Sachs: the relations between economic liberalization and stabilization (Chapter 19). Soós argues that during the early phase of the transition, while the economic systems of these countries still retain many of their old features and markets remain undeveloped, liberalization should not proceed too quickly. Rapid liberalization can easily lead to economically and politically unmanageable problems. One such problem is inflation, which cannot be controlled effectively by tight monetary policy as long as the banking system does not function effectively, bankruptcy is not a real threat, the supply responsiveness of firms is weak, and much of domestic production cannot compete readily with imports on a price basis because foreign goods are in a different "class" than domestic import substitutes. The essence of the inherited economic system is that it was driven by the authorities (and not by the market) via direct or indirect central controls; that much of production is highly concentrated (monopolistic or oligopolistic), so that their lobbies are strong and effective; and that managers have insufficient pressures, incentives, and experience to respond quickly and effectively to market signals. The basic problem, of course, is the absence of real owners with an interest in maximizing the rate of return on capital, and the absence of competition. It is typical that early on during the system change, the old, hierarchical mode of control is dismantled but the new, horizontal system of market relations does not yet function. If, in such a situation, wages, prices, the exchange rate and imports are liberalized too quickly, Soós argues, then inflation—which is difficult to control—will accelerate and the trade balance deteriorate, which most of these countries cannot afford to finance. His policy conclusions are that measures that would push up inflation or worsen the balance of payments should be applied cautiously or postponed until systemic reforms have made sufficient progress. He recommends that the focus should be on decisive actions to transform the economic system.

Márton Tardos takes up another of the main issues raised, among others, by Sachs: privatization (Chapter 20). He argues persuasively that privatization should be as high a priority task as economic stabilization and that the two policies must reinforce each other. Nevertheless, privatization will not be popular. Even though it will improve society's economic situation in the long run, it will also increase differences in income and wealth during implementation, which will generate social opposition. Tardos then spells out the implications for organizing privatization and for managing the political process of economic liberalization during transition.

Csaba picks up the theme of the pace of liberalization and system transformation (Chapter 21). He enumerates a series of objective constraints that, whether we like it or not, are likely to make the pace slower than would appear to be desirable, especially for outside observers and policy advisors. The constraints are political and social as well as economic. Among the former are the temptation of the new governing political parties to "manage" the economy; the desire of the large fiscal, monetary, and other bureaucracies to maintain their discretionary powers; the vested interests of many participants in the unofficial economy to retain an overregulated and noncompetitive system in which they have learned to earn monopoly profits; and the anti-market sentiments of much of the population, conditioned as they have been to associate "marketization" with price increases and growing income inequalities rooted in "profiteering." Among the economic constraints are the legacies of the old systems, such as their gross neglect of the infrastructure and the environment; absence of the right kind of social safety net, which must now be created; and the huge foreign debt-service obligations of several of the countries. In combination, these factors limit the availability of domestic capital and the incentives for foreign capital to invest in these countries. This will inevitably slow the pace of economic growth. This is one of the factors that will constrain the pace of economic liberalization and transformation; there are objective political and social reasons also. To be sure, the picture is not all gloomy; there are also driving forces that promote liberalization and systemic change, which are enumerated.

The concluding contribution, by Dwight Perkins, is on China (Chapter 22). The author reviews China's decade-long (1979-89) experience with reforms in the industrial and foreign economic sectors, identifies the pressures for reversal that culminated in the events of June 1989 at Tiananmen Square, and speculates about future policy options. This concise essay touches on many of the points raised by the preceding contributions, and thus provides an opportunity to pinpoint important similarities as well as differences between China and the countries of Central and Eastern Europe. Reforms in China were prompted, as in Eastern Europe, by the leadership's dissatisfaction with economic performance. There were large differences among the leaders and their advisors on what reform model to follow. Some were notably impressed by the market-oriented and export-led models of South Korea and Taiwan; others, wanting less radical tinkering with the bureaucratic command system, argued that Hungary's reform experience was the most relevant for China. The outcome—a sort of compromise—was continuously shaped by the pragmatic results of the reform experiments and by domestic politics. The main similarity between China and Hungary was that in both countries the introduction of economy-wide reforms (in 1968 in Hungary and in 1979 in China) was driven by the success of earlier reforms in agriculture and that in both countries the reforms significantly modified but did not abandon central planning. The main similarity between China and the East Asian countries was their stress on export promotion and the successes achieved, although the economic systems and the instruments used were of course different. Nevertheless, one major element of China's reform was the decision early on to open up the economy to foreign trade and investment. The steps taken are detailed in the chapter.

It is striking to find that (except for the retention of directive central planning for a share of industrial production) China not only undertook all the foreign economic reforms that Hungary did through 1989, but that China did considerably more. This means that in terms of opening up its economy to foreign trade and investment, until June 1989, China was ahead of all the countries of Central and Eastern Europe, not to speak of the USSR. It is not surprising, therefore, that China's export achievements were notable also. Between 1978 and 1988, China's total exports rose from $10 to $48 billion, at an average annual rate of 17%. Of the $38 billion increase, $29 billion was accounted for by a rise in manufactures exports, a performance not far below that of South Korea and Taiwan during the same period and well above the average of the developing countries.

A major difference between China and the countries of Central and Eastern Europe, Perkins points out, is the positive (but difficult to quantify) influence on China's exports of the tens of millions of overseas Chinese in Southeast Asia, Hong Kong, Taiwan, and North America, many of whom are among the world's most knowledgeable traders.

The whole world is aware of China's dramatic policy turn that is symbolized by tanks crushing demonstrators in Tiananmen Square on June 4, 1989. As to the economic causes of the policy reversal, Perkins notes that the kind of soft budget constraint on enterprises and the fundamental institutional weaknesses of the banking system that several contributors to this volume stress for the countries of Eastern Europe (e.g.,the chapters by Obláth, Nagy, Kádár, Soós, and Tardos) had caused "free" market prices in China to rise and inflation to accelerate, which then brought a very strong backlash.

Looking to the future, Perkins concludes:

> Eliminating the strains of China's recent reforms through greater controls will bring about tensions of other kinds: slower growth in output, exports, and employment. With a workforce that is growing by fifteen million new entrants a year and a rural population where many more tens of millions are redundant, China can ill afford a slow growth policy. China thus faces a major dilemma: . . . [Will] the inevitable compromise between market forces and bureaucratic commands arise out of thoughtful debate and purposeful experimentation or [will it] be imposed by officials determined to hold on to bureaucratic power without challenge and without much concern for the economic costs to the nation."

Conclusions

The contributions that focus on economic liberalization in a large variety of developing and by now developed market economy countries add up to a very persuasive case that increased marketization and opening up to import competition and to FDI are essential components of an economy's sustainably good performance. Theoretical arguments and empirical evidence also suggest that, under certain conditions, temporary and selective protectionism can be a policy instrument to promote economic growth as well as manufactured exports.

This is a very important message that must also be heeded by the reforming (mostly ex-socialist) "to-be-market economies." But the fact they are not yet market economies, that—after generations of communist rule—market imperfections are so much greater, so much more fundamental, than in practically all of the developing countries, raises a fundamental issue: what is the proper scope and sequencing of foreign economic liberalization? Most of the contributions, explicitly or implicitly, are debating this issue.

The debate is complex and has many aspects that are country specific. But at the core is one overriding issue. A rapid move toward marketization generates strong pressures for open inflation that are very difficult (some say impossible) to control with instruments that are market-conforming. There are a set of institutional and other reasons for this: the budget constraints on firms are still not entirely hard; the state, as the dominant owner of the means of production, is unable effectively to exercise ownership functions; the highly monopolized structure of much of production; and a banking system that functions exceedingly poorly. These add up to an economic environment in which competition is largely absent. The argument that competition should be strengthened by rapidly opening up the economy to import competition and foreign investment runs into objections. One is that import liberalization and making the country attractive for foreign investors would require a very large depreciation of the exchange rate. This would feed inflation that, together with the rapid sale of the "national patrimony" to foreigners, simply cannot be politically managed. The only way out of this "Catch 22" situation, according to several of the contributors, is that marketization and foreign economic liberalization must go hand-in-hand with systemic reforms. The essence of such reforms is rapid privatization, basic reforms in the system of financial intermediation, and creating the rules and conditions of domestic competition. But in each of these areas it is also exceedingly difficult to proceed quickly, to some extent for economic but more for political reasons.

1

Economic Liberalization in Eastern Europe and in Market Economies

András Köves and Paul Marer

During 1989-90, several of the nations that used to be called "socialist" or centrally planned economies (CPEs) have made a fundamental commitment to transform their traditional or reformed but still centrally directed economic systems into market economies. The GDR, Poland, Czechoslovakia, and Hungary have certainly embarked on such a road. There is a good possibility that other CPEs or former CPEs will join them during the 1990s. An essential condition of successful transformation is integrating more fully into the world economy. This requires, first and foremost, liberalizing their domestic economies by promoting competition and thereby gaining sustained economic efficiency and improving the standard of living.

This essay offers a conceptual framework for foreign economic liberalization, summarizes the literature on the topic, discusses the experiences of selected market economies, and tries to persuade why and how liberalization should proceed in the countries of Central and Eastern Europe. Since all the contributions deal with one or another aspect of these issues, this introductory essay effectively integrates the contributions.

Definitions

Economic liberalization is defined here broadly, as reducing the role of government in microeconomic decisions, increasing reliance on the price mechanism rather than controls, and increased integration into the world economy. Foreign economic relations that must be liberalized encompass relations among the CMEA countries, imports, exports, foreign direct

We acknowledge the helpful comments of Gábor Obláth and László Szamuely on a draft of this essay.

investment, and the convertibility of the currency. Owing to the close interconnectedness between liberalizing a country's foreign economic relations and compatible reforms in its domestic economy, one cannot discuss one without the other.

In the countries that are already market economies and if the focus is only on trade, liberalization is defined as moving toward a neutral trade regime, i.e., one that provides equal incentives to domestic sales and exports. Liberalization can take the following forms: moving from quotas and non-tariff-barriers to tariffs, lower tariffs, and making the exchange rate more realistic (which in almost all cases means a real, as opposed to just nominal, depreciation).

The focus of this essay is on liberalizing foreign economic relations in the countries of Central and Eastern Europe, i.e., the GDR, Czechoslovakia, Poland, Hungary, Romania, and Bulgaria. Yugoslavia is not included because the authors do not know enough about its history and country-specific features. The Soviet Union and China face a somewhat different set of problems than the countries located in Central and Eastern Europe, owing to differences in their economic and political circumstances, including size. China's experiences are summarized in the contribution in this volume by Perkins.

Liberalization in Central and Eastern Europe in Comparative International Perspective

The problems of economic liberalization in Central and East Europe are in certain respects similar, but in important respects quite different from those of the non-socialist countries, whether more or less developed. The question of economic liberalization appears in countries where there is an unusually large degree of state participation in economic decisions. This means some combination of state ownership of the means of production and control/regulation of economic activities. One of its manifestations is a high degree of attempted insulation of the domestic economy from external influences. The majority of the world's countries belong in this category.

A further *similarity*, especially with developing countries, is that liberalization is often triggered by or has to begin in the midst of substantial macroeconomic instability, whose main features are a budget deficit that cannot be financed fully by savings, loose or ineffective monetary policy, substantial open or repressed inflation, and the resulting severe pressures on the balance of payments. Substantial weakening of a country's international creditworthiness may also be a feature. This raises the issue: should economic liberalization accompany or follow macroeconomic stabilization? Central and Eastern Europe, as well as many developing countries, also have in common the fact that many essential market institutions, such as financial intermediaries, are underdeveloped. This is a consequence, broadly speaking, of a country's low level of development and/or the nature of its economic system.

One of the key *differences* between the countries of Central and Eastern Europe and the rest of the world is the scope of the state's participation in the economy. This region is comprised of countries where industrial production and foreign trade were practically full state monopolies and even retail trade and services were operated by the state or state-enterprise-like cooperatives (e.g., in Czechoslovakia, the GDR, Romania). Even in Hungary, where since the 1960s reforms have unleashed a significant growth in private activities, until the late 1980s about 90 per cent of the means of production were controlled by the state and foreign trade remained a state monopoly. A consequence of this is that liberalization is more difficult and has further to go than in most developing countries.

In Central and Eastern Europe, not only was foreign trade a state monopoly but, on average, about half of it was conducted with other state-trading countries, under the auspices of the CMEA. This has meant, in practice, a strategic orientation toward the Soviet Union, under fundamentally different principles and institutional arrangements than trade is conducted with or between market economies. As a consequence, the degree of insulation of these economies from international markets was much greater than even those developing countries that have, or have had, highly illiberal trade regimes. Moreover, while in the developing countries trade restrictions typically take the form of *explicit* quotas and like measures, in the CPEs the quotas tend to be *implicit* and arise from the very nature of the economic system.

International Politics and Economic Liberalization

The introduction of the CPE system was the consequence of developments in international politics after World War II. Postwar arrangements then had remained, in essence, unchanged for more than four decades. To be sure, this did not prevent several countries from undertaking economic reforms, even though international politics, entrenched domestic interests, and policy failures did limit how far liberalization could actually proceed and what it could accomplish.

Dramatic political and economic developments in the USSR and in Soviet-East European relations (changes that were perhaps also influenced by developments in certain countries in Central and Eastern Europe) have triggered the disintegration of the postwar political systems in Central and Eastern Europe. That, in turn, has irrevocably altered the nature of East-West relations. This means that the political constraints that were in place for more than four decades have eroded or been fully lifted. As a consequence, new political opportunities have opened up in relations with the West.

It is in this sudden and dramatic political context that the questions of economic liberalization must be addressed. Until the late 1980s, economic liberalization in Central and Eastern Europe could proceed only in small steps; today there is a much wider choice among economic liberalization strategies, and economic considerations can be given greater weight in choosing among them. For this reason, from the point of view of the industrial countries, the responsibility is not only to allow liberalization, but also to actively assist the countries of Central and Eastern Europe in their historic transformation. From this point of view, the "environment" for Central and Eastern Europe is favorable, which partly compensates for the fact that economic liberalization in this region is taking place in an international environment that is more highly competitive and thus more difficult to succeed in than at any time since World War II.

A number of scholars (among them Béla Kádár in this volume) have noted that in many of the economically successful developing countries, economic liberalization has preceded political liberalization. In fact, the former has usually created the preconditions for the latter. Whether one assumes a "natural progression" from economic to political liberalization, it should be noted that in the countries of Central and Eastern Europe, political change is preceding fundamental economic liberalization. This may have implications for the timing and sequencing of economic liberalization programs.

Motives for Liberalization

The countries of Central and Eastern Europe wish to create a well-functioning market economy. An essential precondition for it is liberalizing their foreign economic relations. This means several things. Of decisive importance is transforming the institutional arrangements and practices of trade and finance among the countries of the Council for Mutual Economic Assistance (CMEA)[1] so as to make them comparable with a market-type economic system.

Another key aspect of liberalization is import competition, needed to improve relative prices and the operation of the price system. In the small and medium-sized economies of this region, foreign economic competition must be relied upon, especially in view of the high concentration of domestic production, with only a small share of the work force being employed by small and medium-sized firms. Import liberalization vis-à-vis market economies is also essential to provide technology and products as well as management and marketing know-how, and to expand manufactures exports which requires the timely availability of high-quality and competitively priced inputs.

In traditional or even in modified CPEs, import competition does not exist, initially as much for political as for systemic reasons—i.e., the strong desire to avoid excessive dependence. This pressures the authorities toward rather extreme versions of attempted import substitution, which is reinforced by basic features of the economic system, such as those that view any displacement of existing or planned production by imports as "disturbance" to be avoided. Furthermore, given the difficulty of finding exportables, imports are "controlled" to safeguard the balance of payments. In the absence of meaningful prices and profits, neither enterprises nor the authorities are motivated to seeks gains from trade through comparative advantage; the motive for imports is to overcome supply bottlenecks.

Increased domestic competition, successful restructuring, and a steady growth of exports require the elimination of these economies' large anti-export bias, and a substantial inflow of foreign direct investment (FDI). To promote FDI, a country needs liberal FDI rules and regulations as well as domestic economic conditions that are conducive for it. Until recently, these countries had a schizophrenic attitude toward FDI. Recognizing that, worldwide, FDI has become an important avenue to import technology, marketing, and management know-how, the laws on joint ventures were a bit liberalized. But until recently, joint ventures had more public relations than macroeconomic significance.

Also important is to build an effective link between the domestic and foreign economies via a convertible currency. Although striving for convertibility was for many years a slogan in some of these countries, meaningful convertibility was not in the cards, again essentially for systemic reasons. Introducing convertibility while cost and price ratios remained arbitrary would have given rise to a wide dispersion of profitability among enterprises, which would have been incompatible with a centrally planned or directed economy. Full convertibility also means that access to goods, services, and assets are controlled by those who possess the currency; this, too, would have been incompatible with a centrally directed system.

In sum, two interrelated considerations make foreign economic liberalization essential. One is to help "marketize" these economies; the other, to capture the potentially large static and dynamic gains from trade that the small and medium sized economies of Central and East Europe have inadvertently foregone while their economies remained centrally directed. Even though Poland, Hungary, and even China have, over the years, modified in varying degrees their economic systems (for example, while foreign trade had remained a monopoly, a growing number of enterprises did receive foreign trading rights), those steps did not go sufficiently far to yield large gains from trade.[2]

Strategies of Liberalization

Relations between Foreign Economic Relations, Macrostabilization, and System Change

The majority of Central and East European countries are at or near an economic crisis: growth has slowed or stopped, the balance of payments constraint has become binding for several countries, and shortages have increased, in some countries dramatically, as has inflation. In Central and Eastern Europe, these problems are laid at the doorstep of a poorly functioning economic system. To be sure, smaller or greater mistakes in economic policy have also contributed to an economy in fundamental disequilibrium.

There is a consensus that macroeconomic stability is a necessary but not sufficient condition of sustainable improvements in economic performance. Two issues that are often discussed separately should be considered simultaneously. One is how to handle the often large disequilibrium inherited at the time the system transformation begins (i.e., Poland). The other is that the steps needed as part of the transformation (e.g., allowing prices to be market determined and reducing subsidies) generates inflationary pressures which must be managed. Both of these require stabilization policies, which means some combination of monetary, fiscal, industrial and social policies. However, as long as the economic system remains fundamentally unchanged, traditional policies of stabilization will not "set things right" nor will bring about sustained improvements in economic performance, for reasons detailed later.

An equally important factor is that under the prevailing economic system, the responses of economic agents, such as financial intermediaries and enterprises, to standard stabilization policies will be weaker or different than those of their counterparts in market economies. For example, the supply responses of enterprises that have no real owners will not be as adaptive as economic textbooks suggest.

The conclusion is that economic stabilization cannot be handled separately from system change. And since foreign economic liberalization is a key component of both macroeconomic stabilization and system change, all these strategies must also be linked. For example, stabilization policies should include, import liberalization in order to improve the price system and control inflation, while increased FDI is necessary to help improve (along with other actions) the balance of payments. Of course, the statement that stabilization, system change, and liberalization are not fully separable does not provide practical advice to policymakers who must grapple with concrete issues.

Alternative Approaches in Central and Eastern Europe

Two main alternative approaches to economic liberalization can be discerned, one based on the program adopted and partly implemented in Poland (the Balcerowicz program) and the other whose outlines are emerging in various discussions in Hungary. The essence of the Balcerowicz program that is being implemented as of January 1, 1990 is rapid internal and external liberalization within the context of a shock-therapy stabilization program, but without (during its first six months) large-scale privatization, as noted in the chapter by Sachs. The key elements of stabilization were the rapid elimination of the budget deficit through large cuts in subsidies and other kinds of spending; the closure of unprofitable enterprises, thereby abandoning job security; a very tight monetary policy, initially involving large interest rate increases to restrain credit demand and to create incentives for saving; and restricting wage increases to a fraction of the rate of inflation. The key elements of economic liberalization were the virtual elimination of all price controls (leaving administered prices only in energy and housing) and introducing the domestic current-account convertibility of the *zloty*.

An alternative approach (which, for simplicity, we call the consensus program for Hungary) considers gradual liberalization an essential companion of system transformation as well as economic stabilization. To be sure, one needs to spell out the content of the programs as well as the recommended sequencing and pace of their implementation. Our views on this are detailed in the next section. Here we wish to focus on the reasons why Hungary and Poland may justifiably require different approaches to liberalization, and on the main strategic differences and implications of the alternative approaches.[3]

Poland and Hungary had fundamentally different political and economic situations at the points of inception of their programs, following democratic elections. (In Poland, the elections were held in June 1989 and the program began in January 1990; in Hungary the elections were held in March-April 1990 and the Antall government promised to introduce a comprehensive three-year recovery program as of January 1991.) Specifically:

1. The Mazowiecki government came into power with broad public support, giving it an implicit mandate to introduce even a deeply unpopular program. By contrast, the Antall government has not enjoyed such a broad-based political support so that the political feasibility of introducing and sustaining a shock-therapy program was much weaker.

2. The economy that Poland's new government had inherited was in deep crisis, suffering from hyperinflation, immense shortages of goods and

services in the consumer and production sectors, a dual and highly segmented (*zloty*/dollar) currency system, and a dismal rating of international creditworthiness. In this situation, something drastic had to be done and shock therapy seemed both unavoidable and the only approach that held out the hope that the situation would improve. The economy of Hungary, while facing huge difficulties, was in much better shape: inflation, although accelerating, was still considerably less during the first half of 1990 than the rate of inflation in Poland *after* the introduction of the program (174 percent during January-June 1990). Although there were and are spot-shortages in Hungary, their scope and extent could not be compared with the practically empty shelves in the stores (selling for *zloty*) just before the program was introduced in Poland. While Poland had to reschedule its foreign debt and has been unable to pay the interest on it fully, Hungary has been able to preserve its external creditworthiness throughout. In sum, there was much less of an economic justification for countenancing the concentrated pain and social tension that precedes and follows the introduction of a Polish-type program (e.g., by allowing at once most prices to be market-clearing and imposing draconian controls on the money supply, spending, and wages).

3. A further significant difference between Hungary and Poland is their past histories of economic reform. After 1968, but especially during 1987-89, Hungary has made significant (though far from adequate) progress in modifying its economic system (e.g., having eliminated compulsory plan directives more than two decades ago and introducing such foreign economic liberalization measures as encouraging joint ventures with foreigners, securing the de facto partial convertibility of its currency, and moving toward import liberalization). By contrast, the progress in Poland through 1989 had been much more modest. To be sure, throughout the period, Poland has had a predominantly private (though highly regulated) agriculture and in recent years it allowed small private business ventures by foreigners of Polish origin (the Polonia firms). Thus, having already travelled on the reform road part way, Hungary had less pressure to introduce a bold short-term liberalization cum stabilization program.

The juxtaposition of Hungary and Poland brings into sharp relief a point of fundamental importance, namely, that in spite of the many systemic similarities, there are also highly significant political, economic, and social differences among the countries at the time when their programs of economic stabilization, system change, and liberalization are being discussed or introduced. It is fashionable today to state that market socialism is not a viable economic system. As a broad proposition, we also believe this to be true. But the other side of the coin is that the implementation of market-oriented reforms represents important preparation for the introduction of a real market economy, which is possible only after the political transformation has been carried out. It is worth noting that only in Hungary has there been a reasonably comprehensive and sustained program of economic liberalization before the recent dramatic political developments had taken place in Central and Eastern Europe. Hungary has accumulated a set of positive and negative experiences, a foundation on which it can build a more comprehensive program. Elsewhere in the region, such experiences are not yet available. One of the lessons of Hungary's reform experience is how poorly market-type instruments and institutions function in an economy where the means of production are predominantly state owned, especially as long as producers are large and are protected from competition and the rules and institutions of the market remain undeveloped.

This is the reason for the emphasis on ownership reform in the economic program proposals of the joint Hungarian-International Blue Ribbon Commission:

> There are no proven means to motivate producers toward efficiency, customer satisfaction and innovative behavior in societies where the state owns most assets and does not allow genuine markets to develop. . . . The fundamental objective of transforming ownership is the wholesale transfer of most state assets to new owners, who, with the rights of ownership and their interest in dividends and capital gains, will improve the utilization of those assets.[4]

The Commission then recommends that privatization should proceed as rapidly as economic and political conditions allow, so that in three years at least one-third and in five years at least one-half of presently state-owned enterprises should be in private hands.

In summary, the strategy of the "consensus program" for Hungary is the simultaneous and economy-wide introduction of programs of economic stabilization, liberalization, and system change, each having a series of sequential steps which should be implemented (depending on the point of view of the recommender), rapidly or gradually.

Are the Experiences of Market Economies Relevant in Eastern Europe?

The contributions in this volume suggest that the answer is yes, though with certain modifications. Based on a World Bank study of 19 countries during 36 episodes of liberalization, summarized in this volume in the chapter by Choksi et al., political stability has been found to be the single most essential ingredient of successful liberalization in market economies. This is because political stability is needed for the introduction of a "strong" program (which Choksi et al. define rather precisely) and to sustain it consistently for a minimum of six years (and thus typically over the course of at least two governments). Other studies also confirm that stop-and-go policies or "weak" programs cause great harm because of the importance of expectations. As Langhammer states in his chapter, "The cost of economic liberalization tends to increase with the level of expectations of private agents that the reforms will fail."

What does economic theory say about the trade-policy aspects of liberalization? Conventionally, trade policies are defined in a bipolar spectrum, with inward-orientation at one end and outward-orientation at the other. This is based on a common view that incentives for the export and import-competing sectors are negatively correlated. Yet, it is well-known that Japan, Taiwan, and South Korea have employed and to some extent are still employing strong import protection measures, yet their export performance has been stellar. Another paradox that calls into question the conventional bipolar classification is the co-existence in some countries during some periods—in Latin America as well as in Eastern Europe—of a high degree of anti-export bias with sustained large increases in imports.

One contribution in the volume proposes a new classification and interpretation of trade strategies, one that divides the economy into three sectors—exportables, importables, and nontradables (Liang et al.). Moreover, it focuses not so much on the conventional economy-wide "degree of protection" but more on the "pattern of protection," i.e., whether trade policy attempts to protect all three or only one or two of the sectors and, within a sector, all producers or only some of them, and whether protection is permanent or temporary. The authors note that several highly successful countries have pursued just such a policy of "protected export promotion." The central idea is to protect for a time certain branches on the home market while at the same time giving their firms a carrot as well as a stick to export and to compete internationally. The trick is for the government to distinguish between "momentary" and "long-run" comparative advantage, the former being determined by a country's existing factor proportions, the latter by parameters such as the propensities to save, rates of labor force expansion, and the growth in education. Several of the country studies in this volume confirm and provide the details of how such policies were pursued, for example, by Japan (in the chapter by Yoshitomi) as well as by South Korea and Taiwan (in the chapter by Park).

Spain's recent liberalization experience is notably relevant for the countries of Central and Eastern Europe. Spain, too, was isolated, economically as well as politically, for the first two postwar decades under Franco. His motto that "Spain is different" parallels the earlier attempts of the CMEA countries trying to maintain economic and political "independence from capitalist Europe." Because most Spaniards wanted to be West Europeans explains why, after Franco, all political parties from communist to conservative voted in favor of joining the EC. That, in turn, required adoption of a market economy, including rapid liberalization of foreign economic relations, whose details are summarized here by one of its architects, de la Dehesa (Chapter 7). For the countries of Central and Eastern Europe, too, economic liberalization may be "driven" by their desire to associate in some way with the EC and thus to join or rejoin Western Europe.

Components of Economic Liberalization

Revamping the CMEA

The institutional mechanism of intra-CMEA relations still in effect in 1990 is not compatible with a decentralized, market-driven, open economy toward which the Central and East European nations wish to progress. Given the large share of the CMEA countries in their external relations, removing the CMEA constraint is perhaps the most important act of liberalization. It must consist of discontinuing the state-trading system, which has domestic as well as inter-country (intra-CMEA) aspects. This kind of systemic change should be differentiated from changing the pricing and currency of settlement, which may or may not be a part of changing the CMEA system. This is because the pricing and currency of settlement can be altered without modifying existing state-trading arrangements.

In view of the fact that at the end of June 1990, the Soviet Union abrogated its long-standing agreements to settle intra-CMEA transactions in transferable rubles, it appears certain that the large majority, if not all, of the members of the CMEA will move to current world market pricing and convertible-currency settlement as of the beginning of 1991. Negotiations will be conducted during the second half of 1990 concerning the details of the new bilateral agreements. What is uncertain is whether the states' obligations to deliver and purchase certain specific products will remain in force, explicitly or (perhaps under a new name) in substance. In the latter case, the possibility of domestic liberalization will remain constrained, as explained in the chapter by Köves.

The transition to the prospective new pricing, settlement, and trading system will create, in and of itself, a major shock to the economies of the Central and East European countries, for several reasons. One is that their terms of trade would deteriorate substantially, though in varying extent, during the first few years, as the overpricing of manufactures exports is eliminated, since the East Europeans are net exporters of manufactures in trade with the Soviets. This will have an adverse short-term impact on the convertible balance of payments. Furthermore, it would force their firms to compete with suppliers from the rest of the world on the CMEA market, too.

Different CMEA countries (and experts in the countries) have different views on the tradeoff between the short-term cost and long-term gains of transition to the new arrangements. For example, the majority of Hungarians involved in the debate hold the view that a quick transition would be preferable because, in the event, they are hoping that it would be possible to negotiate an adequate "safety net" with the Soviets. (This hope might have had some foundation in early 1989 but today it seems to be less well founded, economically as well as politically. A more realistic but also far from assured option would be help from the West.) Furthermore, they stress the problematic nature of a gradual transition. One is that the Soviets would not likely to be willing or able to manage intermediate solutions since their main interest is to improve the terms of trade. In exchange for securing this benefit, they may be willing to agree to accept a fundamental change in the system of trading. Moreover, in the debates in Hungary great stress is placed on the need to change the expectations and attitudes of Hungarian enterprises concerning the continued availability of "soft" and subsidized export markets in the CMEA countries.

Liberalizing Imports

International experience unequivocally shows that the key step of import liberalization is transforming a system of explicit and implicit quotas to tariffs and exchange-rate based "controls" on imports. This is of decisive importance in Central and Eastern Europe where quantitative restrictions were pervasive since only they were compatible with centrally planned or directed systems. Considering that the Central and East European countries are small and medium-sized economies, and that creating workable domestic competition will take time, import liberalization is all the more important in order to bring about competition, to promote exports, and to help control inflation. Moving toward a more liberal foreign trade regime is not incompatible with the introduction or maintenance of selective and temporary protection via policies that promote intelligent import substitution, since such policies can promote exports and increase a country's world market orientation, as is elaborated theoretically as well as through case studies in the chapters by Liang et al., Park, Yoshitomi, Obláth, and Kádár. The protection that these authors describe and implicitly endorse is fundamentally different, in terms of its objectives as well as instruments, from that practiced by the Central and East European countries during the past 40 years and which has insulated them from the world economy, in spite of their increased trade dependence. A point worth noting is that the increased foreign trade participation ratios (exports plus imports as percent of GDP) of these economies cannot be taken as indications of increased openness, as in market economies, but simply as the unintended outcomes of their economic systems and policies, as noted in the chapter by Gács.

Import liberalization will be much easier to implement in countries that, over the years, have introduced significant reforms in foreign trade by weakening and eventually disbanding the state's monopoly of foreign trade, by granting foreign trading rights to a growing number of business entities and by abandoning the monopolization of production and trade of various economic activities.[5] Hungary has made notable strides toward import liberalization. The concept was an integral part of the NEM introduced in 1968. There were practical steps in that direction during the NEM's early years, until the balance of payments constraint gave renewed strength to those advocating administrative, "hands-on," case-by-case controls, as noted in Gács's chapter. As part of the new wave of reform, in 1989 Hungary introduced a three-year program of import liberalization. Under it, two-thirds of imports from outside the CMEA were liberalized by 1990. Substantial import liberalization is also a part of the Balcerowicz program. The situation of the GDR is self-explanatory. Czechoslovakia also plans to be moving in this direction soon.

Decontrolling Exports

The control of exports is as much a basic feature of a CPE as is the control of imports. Who can and should produce for export, who is authorized to make what deals, the terms and condition of foreign trade transactions, the channels of sourcing and disposition of output are all controlled. Therefore, the decentralization of exports is as important as the liberalization of imports. Although it may seem strange that in economies where the promotion of exports is crucial and has been given a great deal of lip service, export decontrol could be an issue. This is so, nonetheless, owing to a number of system-specific features of the CPEs that discriminate against exports.

To begin with, there is discrimination against small producers by the system generally and also by the foreign trade organizations (FTOs) that prefer large-volume deals and thus choose to deal mainly with large enterprises. Further, export competition among domestic enterprises has until now been discouraged.

Formal and informal controls on economic activities, such as giving supply responsibilities to specific firms on the domestic or CMEA markets, are basic features of central planning, as are "profile restrictions" on producers that prohibit them from entering into certain lines of production. Of course, the greatest source of systemic anti-export bias that needs to be eliminated is the pervasive administrative controls on imports.

Promoting Foreign Direct Investment

International experience has shown that at some stage of development a relatively open system of FDI becomes an essential part of increased openness and integration into the world economy, by promoting the crossborder flow of technology, know-how, marketing, management, foreign trade, and finance. Whether a Central or East European country has entirely prohibited (as some have) or permitted (as others have) FDI under limited circumstances, in all these economies the participation of foreign capital was marginal at best through 1989. This contrasts with countries of similar size and level of development in Western Europe and other parts of the world, where foreign capital has played a central role. Foreign capital is attracted to a country with a clear, fair, and stable legal, regulatory and tax framework as well as a domestic political and economic environment that are conducive to foreign investors.

During 1989-90, the extensive worldwide publicity that political and economic developments in this part of the world have received, as well as the desire of business firms of benefitting from various bilateral and multilateral assistance programs offered to the Central and East European countries by the West, were the equivalent in their impact to that of a huge marketing effort on behalf of these countries. Many firms in the industrial countries have began to consider seriously—and often for the first time— investment opportunities in Central and Eastern Europe, in some cases considering this part of the world as one of the last "virgin" territories for expansion, hoping to participate in the coming "boom"; others are simply responding to competitive pressures. Prospects that intra-CMEA transactions may soon be settled in a convertible currency have made investing in one of the smaller member countries of the CMEA more attractive because it would make it possible to use such investment as a bridgehead to penetrate the large Soviet and CMEA market.

A special reason that a Central or East European country may be attractive to foreign investors is the opportunity to participate in the privatization as bidders, under the privatization programs that are getting under way in these countries. More generally, the more advanced a country is in having introduced market-oriented reforms and the greater the political stability, the more attractive it is for foreign firms. All the more so in light of the shortage of private capital in these countries. However, the shortage of domestic capital both encourages and also limits foreign participation because it makes it more difficult to find domestic partners and viable projects.

Rapid increase in foreign participation faces a number of economic and political constraints. One is that during these initial stages of transformation, the countries are not yet well prepared to effectively receive the hordes of inquiries and visits from foreign investors. Legal, accounting, and regulatory procedures are not yet well established and are frequently changing, as is noted by Inotai in Chapter 6.

The attitudes of the host countries toward FDI is generally positive, although not without concerns and reservations. Some are against the unrestricted selling of the "national patrimony," others are worried about the sale price and whether the locals can compete on equal basis. In none of these countries is yet fully clear who has what rights to initiate and conclude sales to foreign (the same for domestic) investors, who is to receive the proceeds, and to what purposes the proceeds can be put.

The policy implication of these dilemmas is the debate that is now getting under way in all of these countries on whether foreign investors should receive national, preferential, or discriminatory treatment. It is highly likely that the mixture of these three kinds of policy approaches will not be uniform throughout the region.

Moving Toward Currency Convertibility

There are many different kinds of convertibility. One should identify which concept is being discussed by or recommended to policymakers. The basic distinction is between resident and non-resident convertibility. Each group can be further divided into the enterprise and the household sectors. Most important, we believe, is that domestic enterprises should be able to acquire foreign currency readily (if they have the domestic-currency cover) to import the goods and services needed. This is a critically important aspect of liberalization because it enhances competition, improves or keeps in check relative prices, and provides a necessary though not sufficient condition for export competitiveness.

Poland, Hungary, and of course the GDR have nearly achieved this type of de facto convertibility already in 1990 because the bulk of their imports has been liberalized (meaning that for those goods, domestic enterprises can obtain the foreign currency readily). Czechoslovakia has announced its intention to move in this direction. To be sure, even if imports were fully liberalized, one cannot speak of full resident convertibility for the enterprise sector as long as the export earnings of firms must continue to be surrendered. The usual justification is the precarious status of the balance of payments and, especially, that practically all of these countries' foreign debt is an obligation of the state.[6] If a country wishes to attract FDI, it must provide the convertibility of its currency to non-residents, for their earnings on those investments (a current-account item) as well as the repatriation of capital (a capital-account item). We thus conclude that the most important kinds of convertibility to strive for are: (1) resident convertibility, for the import-side of the current account and for the enterprise sector and (2) non-resident convertibility for selected current- and capital-account transactions, also for the enterprise sector.

As far as the household sector is concerned, convertibility for non-resident tourists should be granted, and has been done in practically all of the countries for some time, for reasons that are self evident. At this stage it is less feasible and important to provide the same privilege for residents also. Although full convertibility of the domestic currency for households is very important politically (and of course this is what the person on the street means by convertibility), postponing it is quite justified economically if the country faces severe balance of payments pressures and the danger of capital flight.

For the household sector, liberalization means unrestricted foreign travel and unrestricted access to foreign currency. Free travel has now been assured by Hungary, Poland, Czechoslovakia and of course the GDR (and most of the other CPEs and ex-CPEs in Europe have been moving in this direction). But generous access to foreign currency (at all or at affordable rates) is still not assured in any of these countries (except of course the GDR), owing to the pent-up demand for travel and the status of the balance of payments. As the example of Hungary during 1988-89 showed, when travel restrictions were lifted and the duty-free allowance increased as political concessions to the population, there followed a surge of "shopping tourism" to Western Europe and capital flight, with dire consequences for the balance of payments. For this reason, the foreign-currency allowance of duty free per person was reduced and duty-free privileges were tightened in 1990.

One way to achieve and maintain resident convertibility for both the enterprise and household sectors is to allow the exchange rate to be fully market determined. This brings us to various arguments concerning alternative exchange rate regimes. A country wishing to liberalize has two basic options: to allow the exchange rate to be fully market determined, letting it float, or to fix the exchange rate and to maintain it for a time at a given level. There are also various in-between options. The main advantages of a floating rate are that the authorities need not maintain large reserves and that a single exchange rate will prevail throughout the economy and for all transactions. At the same time, a floating rate has a number of disadvantages. One is that under the conditions that typically prevail in the Central and East European countries during the early stages of transformation, the market will tend to assign an extremely low value to the currencies of these countries. That, in turn, means a substantial cheapening of a country's goods, services, and assets to foreigners (as well as strong open inflationary pressures). The reasons are the huge pent-up demand by residents for the foreign goods, services, and assets that foreign exchange can now buy (the demand may be large in part owing to the monetary overhang in the economy), political and economic uncertainties (including the expected acceleration of inflation) that tend to trigger capital flight, the unavailability to residents of certain kinds of safe financial and real investment opportunities in their own country, and of course their economies' weak export competitiveness and heavy import dependence.

Inflationary pressures caused by a large depreciation of the currency (and by other factors) are much more difficult to keep at bay in the ex-CPEs than in market economies. Among the reasons are that in the former, the monetary system is as yet underdeveloped: the commercial banking system has been set up only recently and is as yet oligopolistic in its structure and practices; the banks have inherited a great deal of nonperforming assets which they are not in a position to collect or to write off; and payment discipline of enterprises is as yet weak, in part because there is no institution that would have an interest to exert pressure by initiating bankruptcy proceedings. One consequence is the unchecked creation of a great deal of "quasi money" as a growing volume of inter-enterprise bills remain unsettled. Hence the reason that the inflationary impact of a large depreciation is of great concern, especially in light of the other factors that are generating inflation during the early stages of the transformation process.[7]

Given the economic, social and political problems that a large depreciation of the currency is likely to involve, and the uncertainties about the extent and timing of its benefits, policymakers and even many experts tend to shy away from recommending this course of action, except when the situation is desperate, as in Poland.

The other option is to set a fixed exchange rate. Its advantage is that, at least in theory, the authorities are in a better position to manage the problems just enumerated. Its disadvantage is that fixed rates are not possible to maintain without economic policies that support it, as well as in the absence of substantial reserves. An intermediate option, for example, would be frequent but small adjustments in the exchange rate, e.g., like a crawling peg system.

In any event, a basic issue here is where to set the exchange rate and what kind of exchange rate policy to pursue. Poland, as part of its program of stabilization and economic liberalization, decided on a very substantial devaluation of its exchange rate, making it possible to have a uniform rate throughout the economy, and it pledged to maintain that rate for some time. Hungary also has a fixed exchange rate regime but its official rate values the forint significantly higher than the rate prevailing on the parallel (grey) market.[8] Around mid-year 1990, the official rate coexisted with a substantial trade surplus and a modest current-account deficit that were considered acceptable by Hungary's foreign lenders, from the point of view of maintaining a reasonable equilibrium in the balance of payments. Of course, periodic devaluations will be required to compensate for the inflation differential between Hungary and its main trade partners; a more substantial devaluation may be required if some domestic or external shock would significantly worsen the external balance. At the time of writing (July 1990), it is too early to evaluate whether the exchange rate regimes and policies of Poland and Hungary are appropriate for achieving their intended objectives, or even whether they can be maintained.

Conclusions

One of the legacies of central planning in Central and Eastern Europe is that changes in prices, profits, and therefore also in the exchange rate cannot be assumed to have the same decisive economic impact as comparable changes would have in a well-functioning market economy. As long as the locus of property rights is not clearly defined because most productive assets are not in private hands, and as long as the market mechanism functions very imperfectly (in part for the reason just mentioned), one must be careful about making market-economy-like behavioral assumptions. The actions of individuals as managers, entrepreneurs, savers, providers of labor services, and consumers may not be similar to their counterparts in full-fledged market economies. Therefore, market-economy-type policy instruments may be less effective or may have to be applied more bluntly (e.g., exchange rate devaluations greater, monetary policy tighter) than in a market economy with clear property relations. This is why ownership and other reform issues are linked so closely with foreign economic liberalization.

Notes

1. The CMEA's full members included the USSR, Bulgaria, Czechoslovakia, the GDR, Hungary, Poland, Romania, Mongolia, Cuba, and Vietnam. Postwar developments in the CMEA through 1980 are detailed in Paul Marer and J. M. Montias, eds., *East European Integration and East-West Trade* (Bloomington: Indiana University Press, 1980). Developments in the 1980s are discussed in Jozef M. van Brabant, *Economic Integration in Eastern Europe: A Reference Book* (Hertfordshire: Harvester Wheatsheaf, 1989).

2. Although foreign economic liberalization was envisioned as a component of Hungary's New Economic Mechanism introduced in 1968, both systemic factors and the status of its balance of payments had hindered its practical realization. A policy of attempted import substitution was maintained, which is best implemented by monopoly FTOs; each transaction had to be licensed. There was little incentive to allow imports that could displace domestic producers.

3. One may consider the proposal of János Kornai for Hungary a third alternative. His proposal is a "one-stroke surgery" for stabilization and the simultaneous introduction of full currency convertibility. One feature of the Kornai program is preferential treatment of the private sector, simultaneously imposing restrictive measures (on credits, imports, wages) on the state sector. See János Kornai, *The Road*

to a Free Economy: Shifting from a Socialist System, the Example of Hungary (New York: Norton, 1990). Intense debates in Hungary on Kornai's proposal focus on the advisability of a Polish-type shock therapy in Hungary; if not, a series of issues arise concerning the dispreferential treatment of state-owned enterprises in Kornai's program. Since for a number of practical reasons the state sector will continue to play a major economic role, the question is how to improve its performance: by restricting its activities or by gradual liberalization, while trying to impose on them economic conditions that apply to the private sector also.

4. *Hungary in Transformation to Freedom and Prosperity: Economic Program Proposals of the Joint Hungarian-International Blue Ribbon Commission* (Indianapolis: Hudson, 1990), pp. 21, 26.

5. A comprehensive and comparative review of these and other kinds of reforms in the foreign trading systems of the CMEA countries can be found in Ivan Szegvári, "Külkereskedelmi nyitás: a szocialista országok reformfolyamata" [Foreign Trade Liberalization: Reform Processes of the Socialist Countries], *Gazdaság*, No. 4, 1990.

6. It appears that the requirement to surrender export proceeds could be abolished if the country had a well-functioning foreign-currency market and flexible exchange rates.

7. This statement is not intended to suggest that tight monetary and fiscal policies should be rejected, only that they are more difficult to apply than in market economies, so there is greater need to combine them with other policy measures.

8. In July 1990, the discrepancy between the official and the grey market rates was about 50 percent; in Poland during 1989, the discrepancy was several hundred percent.

PART TWO

Market-Economy Experiences

2

The Design of Successful Trade Liberalization Policies

Armeane M. Choksi, Michael Michaely, and Demetris Papageorgiou

The view that a liberal trade regime promotes economic growth and efficiency has won wide acceptance in recent years. The reason is simple. Many developing countries—for a variety of reasons, and in a variety of different circumstances—have moved from highly restrictive trade regimes toward policies that cause fewer economic distortions, and the results of these reforms speak for themselves. But whereas most economists now agree that trade liberalization works, until recently much less was known about the transition process; *viz.*, how liberalization works and how a country could move from a distorted trade regime toward a more liberal one.

This has been an important gap in our understanding. Without a detailed grasp of the processes of liberalization, economists lacked answers to questions of pressing interest to policymakers. Above all, they were unable to say with much confidence whether some approaches to liberalization were more likely to succeed than others.

Specifically, what sort of initial conditions favor a lasting commitment to reform? Should reform programs be strong and sudden, or moderate and gradual? Should reforms be attempted in a certain sequence? Is a stable political background essential for success, or merely desirable? What role should the exchange rate play? Where does macroeconomic policy fit in?

Ignorance of transition processes meant that economists had little to say about the detailed design of trade liberalization. But lack of knowledge has also obscured another set of issues, distinct from the first, though related to it and paramount in importance to policymakers—namely, what are the costs of liberalization? Liberal trade regimes may be good for growth in the longer term, but what about the short term? Do reform programs harm

This essay should not be taken as necessarily reflecting the views of the World Bank.

TABLE 2.1   Episodes of Trade Liberalization

Latin America		Asia and Pacific		Mediterranean	
Argentina 1	(1967-70)	Indonesia 1	(1950-51)	Greece 1	(1953-55)
Argentina 2	(1976-80)	Indonesia 2	(1966-72)	Greece 2	(1962-82)
Brazil	(1965-73)	Korea 1	(1965-67)	Israel 1	(1952-55)
		Korea 2	(1978-79)	Israel 2	(1962-68)
				Israel 3	(1969-77)
Chile 1	(1956-61)	New Zealand 1	(1951-56)	Portugal 1	(1970-74)
Chile 2	(1974-81)	New Zealand 2	(1962-81)	Portugal 2	(1977-80)
		New Zealand 3	(1982-84)		
Colombia 1	(1964-66)	Pakistan 1	(1959-65)	Spain 1	(1960-66)
Colombia 2	(1968-82)	Pakistan 2	(1972-78)	Spain 2	(1970-74)
				Spain 3	(1977-80)
Peru	(1979-80)	Philippines 1	(1960-65)	Turkey 1	(1970-73)
		Philippines 2	(1970-74)	Turkey 2	(1980-84)
Uruguay	(1974-82)	Singapore	(1968-73)	Yugoslavia	(1965-67)
		Sri Lanka 1	(1968-70)		
		Sri Lanka 2	(1977-79)		

Periods of liberalization are in parentheses.
Source: Compiled by the authors.

output at first? Does freer trade (especially in the form of lower import barriers) cause a deterioration in the balance of payments, and if so, over what time period? And since the goal of reform is to shift resources from inefficient to efficient uses, what are the implications for employment and for the distribution of income?

A World Bank study under our direction, which has just been completed, has shed some new light on these questions.[1] The research was broad in scope, analyzing the course of liberalization in 19 countries during 36 distinct episodes of reform (see Table 2.1). The study covered, by and large, every attempt at significant trade reform undertaken by developing countries since World War II until as recently as 1984, depending on the country. The results are encouraging, and in some cases surprising.

This chapter highlights the major findings of the synthesis volume (Volume 7) of this study, presented under two headings. First, we shall discuss the attributes of a sustainable policy of trade liberalization. Following that, we shall describe the short-term impact of liberalization.

The Episodes of Liberalization

The study defines trade liberalization broadly. The benchmark is the idea of neutrality. A completely neutral trade regime is one that provides equal incentives to domestic sales and to exports. Thus, in principle, a trade regime with government intervention, but one that manages to provide equal incentive to exports and domestic sales, is a neutral one, as is a completely free trade regime with no government intervention. A program of reform that moves a country's trade system closer to this paradigm is regarded as a liberalization; policies that move it further away are regarded as a reversal of liberalization. Broadly, trade liberalization can take one of two forms: changes in price (lower tariffs, for instance), and changes in the form of intervention (such as a shift to tariffs from import quotas).

To provide a short-hand measure of liberalization, a "liberalization index" for each country was constructed. Year-by-year during the periods studied, a value was assigned ranging from one (for the highest possible degree of trade intervention) to 20 (complete trade liberalization). These indices are based partly on objective quantitative criteria (i.e., rates of effective protection, actual tariff rates, real exchange rates, etc.) and partly on judgement. They cannot be used to compare the level of liberalization across countries. But they do give a good qualitative impression of the course of reform and the change in the policy regime over time. They also make it possible to be more precise about the beginning and ending of each liberalization episode in each country.

Even this broad-brush measure reveals big differences in approach. Reforms in some countries were much more gradual than in others. In many cases, reforms came in more than one phase. (The various episodes will be denoted as follows: Chile 1 for its first program, Chile 2 for the next, and so on.) Sometimes the later episodes of liberalization were built on measures taken earlier; in others, they had to make up ground lost in the meantime. So it is clear at the outset that "liberalization" means something different for each country, and indeed for each distinct episode of reform within any given country.

The challenge, nonetheless, was to look beyond the specific and find the regularities among these diverse experiences. These might then be used to draw conclusions for policy. As a first step, Table 2.2 provides a summary description of the core content of the 36 programs, together with a ruling on their fate: "sustained," "partially sustained," and "collapsed."

One of the most striking regularities was that QRs were relaxed in all but seven of the 36 episodes.[2] The exceptions were Brazil, Greece 2, Israel 3, New Zealand 3, Philippines 2, Portugal 1, and Turkey 1. In many of these cases, QRs had been either insignificant to begin with or mostly removed in earlier episodes.

TABLE 2.2 Policy Elements of Trade Liberalization

	Major Relaxation of QRs?	Reduction of Tariffs?	Devaluation?	Preannounce-ment?
Sustained				
Chile 2	Yes	Yes	Yes	Yes
Greece 1	Yes	Yes	Yes	No
Greece 2	No	Yes	No	Yes
Indonesia 2	Yes	No	Yes	No
Israel 1	Yes	No	Yes	No
Israel 2	Yes	No	Yes	Yes
Israel 3	No	Yes	No	Yes
Korea 1	No	No	No	No
Korea 2	No	Yes	No	Yes
New Zealand 2	No	No	No	No
New Zealand 3	No	No	No	No
Singapore	Yes	No	No	Yes
Sri Lanka 2	Yes	No	Yes	No
Turkey 2	Yes	No	Yes	Yes
Uruguay	Yes	Yes	No	Yes
Partially Survived				
Colombia 2	No	No	Yes	No
Pakistan 1	No	No	Yes	No
Pakistan 2	No	Yes	Yes	No
Philippines 1	Yes	No	Yes	Yes
Philippines 2	No	No	Yes	No
Portugal 2	No	Yes	Yes	Yes
Spain 1	Yes	Yes	Yes	Yes
Spain	No	Yes	No	Yes
Spain 3	No	Yes	Yes	No
Collapsed				
Argentina 1	No	Yes	Yes	No
Argentina 2	No	Yes	Yes	Yes
Brazil	No	Yes	No	No
Chile1	No	No	Yes	No
Colombia 1	No	No	No	No
Indonesia 1	No	No	No	No
New Zealand 1	No	No	No	No
Peru	No	Yes	No	Yes
Portugal 1	No	No	No	Yes
Sri Lanka 1	No	No	Yes	No
Turkey 1	No	No	Yes	No
Yugoslavia	No	Yes	Yes	Yes

Source: Compiled by the authors.

Often, trade liberalization formed part of a broader economic stabilization package. A currency devaluation and a contractionary fiscal policy were elements in almost all such cases. Tight monetary policy was less commonly part of the formula, and in still fewer cases a formal prices-and-incomes policy played a role. Among the episodes of liberalization, some mixed trade reform with expansionary fiscal policy: Israel 2, New Zealand 3, Peru, Spain 3, Sri Lanka 2, and Turkey 1.

In six of the episodes, the liberalization package was introduced in one go; in the others a sequence of measures was involved. In about half of these, some sort of plan for the sequence was set out at the beginning. In several other cases, a vaguer commitment to further steps was made. In the rest, liberalization was a continuing process with no pre-announced course.

Evidently, to extract policy lessons for the survivability of trade liberalization from the 36 episodes of reform, it is necessary to look beyond a mere listing of the measures undertaken. The links between survival and a range of other factors—the intensity of the reforms, the path of the real exchange rate, macroeconomic policy, the ordering of the different elements of reform, the initial circumstances of their introduction, and the political background during their implementation—are all examined in greater detail below.

Attributes of Sustained Liberalizations

Strong or Weak Reforms?

Some reforming countries have been much bolder than others, radically altering their trade regimes within a comparatively short span of time, rather than chipping away at reform over a period of many years. Which works better, radicalism or gradualism?

To answer this question, it is necessary to be a bit more precise about what "radicalism" and "gradualism" mean. The study judges the intensity of liberalization according to two criteria: the scale of the reforms, and the pace at which they are introduced. The study therefore classified the 36 episodes according to whether they were "strong" or "weak," and "fast" or "slow." Each country's classification is based on its index of liberalization; so this measurement of intensity is subject to the same caveats as the indices themselves. The most extreme cases are easy enough to place. Most people would agree that Chile 2 and Greece 1 were strong programs, and that Turkey 1 and Pakistan 2 were weak. Intermediate cases are much harder to assign.

One of the study's most important findings is that strong programs lasted better than weak ones. Table 2.3 shows that 19 episodes were strong and 17 weak. Five of the strong programs (26 percent) collapsed, whereas seven of the weak ones (41 percent) collapsed. If anything, these figures

TABLE 2.3   Attributes of Trade Liberalization

	Strong or Weak?	Sustained?
Argentina 1	Weak	No
Argentina 2	Strong	No
Brazil	Strong	No
Chile 1	Strong	No
Chile 2	Strong	Yes
Colombia 1	Weak	Partially
Colombia 2	Strong	Partially
Greece 1	Strong	Yes
Greece 2	Weak	Yes
Indonesia 1	Weak	No
Indonesia 2	Strong	Yes
Israel 1	Strong	Yes
Israel 2	Strong	Yes
Israel 3	Strong	Yes
Korea 1	Weak	Yes
Korea 2	Weak	Yes
New Zealand 1	Weak	No
New Zealand 2	Weak	Yes
New Zealand 3	Weak	Yes
Pakistan 1	Weak	Partially
Pakistan 2	Weak	Partially
Peru	Strong	No
Philippines 1	Strong	Partially
Philippines 2	Weak	Partially
Portugal 1	Weak	No
Portugal 2	Weak	Partially
Singapore	Strong	Yes
Spain 1	Strong	Partially
Spain 2	Weak	Partially
Spain 3	Strong	Partially
Sri Lanka 1	Weak	No
Sri Lanka 2	Strong	Yes
Turkey 1	Weak	No
Turkey 2	Strong	Yes
Uruguay	Strong	Yes
Yugoslavia	Strong	No
Summary	Strong	Weak
Sustained	10	5
Collapsed	5	7
Partially Sustained	4	5
TOTAL	19	17

Source: Compiled by the authors.

understate the superiority of the strong reforms. The study defined episodes of liberalization to exclude those that collapsed within two years. If these unsuccessful cases had been included in the table, they would have fallen overwhelmingly into the weak category. The golden rule of sustainable reform appears to be: bold is best.

How far is duration itself linked to long-term sustainability? In other words, is there a critical period beyond which, if the program has stayed in place, its longer-term survival is then assured? The study found that six years appears to be a watershed of sorts. If a liberalization program lasts that long, it is very likely to last indefinitely. This might be because a six-year span often involves a transition from one government to the next. A change of government presumably poses one of the sternest tests of any liberalization episode: if the program survives in the new political environment, it therefore stands a good chance of enduring into the long term. In addition, a new set of vested interests is usually created under a more efficient trade regime, which provides the needed political resistance to the reversal of the process of reform.

Another question is whether the fate of earlier episodes of reform influences the success of later attempts. Of the 13 countries whose first episode collapsed or was only partially sustained, 11 made further efforts at reform. Five of these second attempts (Chile, Indonesia, New Zealand, Sri Lanka, and Turkey) were sustained. Another five (Colombia, Pakistan, the Philippines, Portugal, and Spain) were partially sustained. That leaves only one collapse on the second attempt: Argentina.

This is a striking result. The supposed "Latin American pattern" of repeated failed attempts at trade reform is in fact true only of Argentina. A closer look at the five countries that followed a failed or only partially successful first attempt with a fully successful second one is also revealing. Four of the five successful second attempts were strong. Compare this with the six countries that followed a first failure or partial success with another attempt. Five of the six disappointing second attempts were weak.

This suggests that an earlier failure makes it all the more important for the second attempt to be strong—which seems plausible. A history of failure undermines the credibility of reform. Other things being equal, a later package may have to be stronger to be credible.

More generally, a country's earlier history of trade-distorting policies is also likely to affect the credibility of reform, and thus the program's chances of success. For example, it seems reasonable to suppose that the longer distorting policies have been in place, and the more distorting they are, the harder it will be for reform to succeed. The study indeed bears this out.

Strong programs of trade liberalization have a significantly better chance of enduring than do weak or hesitant programs. This is likely to be all the more true for countries that have a long history of severe trade restrictions, and for those that have made earlier, unsuccessful attempts at reform.

TABLE 2.4   Attributes of Episodes with Major Relaxation of QRs

Episode	Sustainability	Intensity	Change in Tariff Levels	Change in Real Exchange Rate
Chile 2	Sustained	Strong	Lowered	Depreciation
Greece 1	Sustained	Strong	Lowered	Depreciation
Indonesia 2	Sustained	Strong	No change	Depreciation
Israel 1	Sustained	Strong	No change	Depreciation
Israel 2	Sustained	Strong	Raised	Depreciation
Philippines 1	Partially	Strong	Raised	Depreciation
Singapore	Sustained	Strong	Raised	No change
Spain 1	Partially	Strong	Raised	Appreciation
Sri Lanka 2	Sustained	Strong	Raised	Depreciation
Turkey 2	Sustained	Strong	No change	Depreciation
Uruquay	Sustained	Strong	Lowered	Depreciation

Source: Compiled by the authors.

Quantitative Restrictions

Almost always, highly illiberal trade regimes involve the extensive use of quantitative restrictions. Relaxing these restrictions has been the main content—and sometimes the sole content—of many liberalization programs. Strong liberalizations, especially, have often included bold steps to reduce QRs. (Indeed, a radical reform of QRs is usually enough by itself to qualify a liberalization program as strong.) The evidence suggests a particularly powerful link between a bold relaxation of QRs and the longer-term success of the liberalization effort. This is one of the clearest results to emerge from the entire study.

Eleven of the liberalization episodes in the study included a major reform of QRs (see Table 2.4). No fewer than nine of the 11 were sustained, and the other two (Philippines 1 and Spain) were partially sustained. Perhaps the most radical of these episodes were Chile 2 and Greece 1, where a highly distorting array of QRs were virtually eliminated within a short span of time—one year for Chile and overnight in Greece. But all ten of the episodes are classified as strong, since in every case QRs had been the principal form of trade protection. All but two of these episodes (Israel 2 and Uruguay) were also fast liberalizations, with the reforms implemented over periods ranging from overnight (as in Greece 1) to within two years. Israel 2 is the only case of a trade liberalization that almost completely removed QRs over a long period and according to a pre-announced schedule.

The significance of QR reforms can be most clearly seen by comparing these eleven episodes with reforms that were bold in other respects, but did not include changes in QRs. Of all the strong programs, eight failed to reform QRs. Five of these collapsed, one was fully sustained, and two were partially sustained.

So the contrast is striking. About half of all strong liberalizations included a major reform of QRs. The success rate of these programs was nine out of eleven. The success rate for the strong programs that did *not* include a major reform of QRs was one out of eight. The superiority of strong programs is thus largely explained by the success of the episodes that included a major reform of QRs. In short, liberalization is likely to succeed if the overall reform program is strong and begins with a bold relaxation of QRs; otherwise it is likely to fail.

The problems facing governments that wish to liberalize their QRs may often be formidable. But the evidence from this study is that the gains from doing so should override their reservations in every case. Radical reform of QRs seems to be an all but necessary condition for the success of trade reform.

Real Exchange Rates

A real depreciation is, in effect, an increase in the price of tradeables relative to the price of non-tradeables. This relative price change should spur the production of tradeables, thus helping to boost exports. At the same time, trade liberalizations usually entail less protection for import-competing activities. Without a real depreciation, this might cause (at least in the short term) a deterioration in the balance of payments. On both counts, a real depreciation is likely to reduce pressure for trade reforms to be reversed.

To examine this more carefully, the study looked at the behavior of each reform's exchange rate at the outset of the program (the impact change in the exchange rate), during the program as a whole (the trend change), and in the closing stages of the episode (the closing change). The link between real depreciation and sustained reform seems strong in every case.

First, consider the *initial change* in the exchange rate. Most of the episodes that were fully sustained followed a real depreciation; in not a single case did a fully successful reform follow a currency appreciation. Most of the partially sustained programs also began with a depreciation. The failed episodes are roughly evenly divided between those with a rise or fall in the real exchange rate (see Table 2.5).

The association is only a little less clear for the *trend change* in the real exchange rate. Most of the sustained or partly sustained episodes saw the currency continue to depreciate in real terms during the course of the episode, or else stay roughly stable. In more than half of the failed episodes the currency appreciated over time, and of the remaining failures all but one were episodes with no trend change.

TABLE 2.5   **Relationship between the Impact of the Change in the Real Exchange Rate and the Sustainability of Liberalizations**

Long-term Outcome of Liberalization	EXCHANGE RATE CHANGE		
	Depreciated	*Stable*	*Appreciated*
Sustained			
	Chile 2	Colombia 1	
	Greece 1	Greece 2	
	Indonesia 2	Israel 3	
	Israel 1	Korea 1	
	Israel 2	New Zealand 2	
	Korea 2	New Zealand 3	
	Sri Lanka 2	Singapore	
	Turkey 2		
	Uruguay		
Partially Sustained			
	Colombia 2		Spain 1
	Pakistan 2		Spain 2
	Philippines 1		Spain 3
	Philippines 2		
	Portugal 2		
Collapsed			
	Brazil		Argentina 1
	Chile 1		Argentina 2
	Turkey 1		Peru
	Yugoslavia		Portugal 1
			Sri Lanka 1

Source: Compiled by the authors.

The *closing change* tells a similar story. A depreciation toward the end of a liberalization episode is a sign of likely survival, an appreciation a sign of likely collapse. Often the appreciation of the currency toward the end of the episode was the most important single cause of the program's collapse.

Strong episodes of reform are generally accompanied by a real depreciation at the outset, but less commonly thereafter. This is suggestive. A depreciation that happens at the beginning of a program makes that program, in a sense, all the more powerful in its effects on relative prices. The association between early depreciation and the strength of reform therefore helps to explain why strong reforms (as the study defines them) have proved more successful than the others.

But this raises a question. The real exchange rate is not an instrument of policy like tariffs, tax rates, or public spending. So how does a government achieve the real depreciation that seems to be virtually a requirement for success? A nominal devaluation of the currency provides a real depreciation at least for a time, but if the inflation rate of the country concerned is higher than that of its trading partners, the real devaluation will gradually be eroded. After a while, the country's currency may even appreciate in real terms. So anti-inflationary monetary and fiscal policies are needed to ensure that an initial depreciation is not reversed. The next section looks at macroeconomic policy in greater detail. However, as noted above, the initial change in the real exchange rate shows the closest association with the success or failure of reform. For an initial real depreciation, a nominal devaluation is practically a necessary condition.

Fiscal and Monetary Policies

Macroeconomic policy's most useful role in liberalization is to keep inflation low and thus support a real depreciation of the currency. Is there more to be said? One striking fact is that only a single episode of reform (Israel 2) was fully sustained after being introduced alongside an expansionary fiscal policy. But the stance of fiscal policy at the *beginning* of the reform does not discriminate between the partially sustained programs on the one hand and outright failures on the other (Table 2.6). Much the same is true for the stance of monetary policy at the outset of reform.

The stance of macroeconomic policy at the *end* of the reform episodes seems to have a bigger say in the success or failure of reform. Sustained reform was usually accompanied by either a restrictive or neutral fiscal policy; the same is true for monetary policy. Where fiscal policy was expansionary and monetary policy accommodating at the end, the programs were, as a rule, only partially sustained or else collapsed altogether. The study indicates that expansionary fiscal and monetary policies are the single most important cause of a reversal of trade reforms. Altogether, then, restrictive monetary and fiscal policies significantly improve the chances that trade reform will prove a success.

The Importance of Initial Conditions

Countries have embarked on trade liberalization in a wide variety of circumstances. What effect did these different starting points have on the outcome? At the risk of over-simplifying, initial conditions might be grouped under three broad headings: distress, stability, and intermediate cases. The study indicates that programs begun under great economic strain tended to be strong and fast, and therefore relatively durable. The programs undertaken in placid circumstances, and especially those that followed earlier

TABLE 2.6   Direction of Fiscal Policy and Sustainability of Liberalizations

	DIRECTION OF FISCAL POLICY		
Long-term Outcome of Liberalization	*Restrictive*	*Neutral*	*Expansionary*
Sustained			
	Chile 2	Korea 1	Israel 2
	Greece 1	Korea 2	
	Indonesia 2	New Zealand 2	
	Israel 1	New Zealand 3	
	Israel 3	Singapore	
	Sri Lanka 2		
	Turkey 2		
Partially Sustained			
	Colombia 2		Pakistan 2
	Pakistan 1		Portugal 2
	Philippines 1		Spain 2
	Philippines 2		Spain 3
	Spain 1		
Collapsed			
	Argentina 1		Peru
	Argentina 2		Sri Lanka 1
	Brazil		Turkey 1
	Chile 1		

Source: Compiled by the authors.

successful episodes of reform, also fared quite well. The in-between cases—reforms begun amid signs of economic deterioration, but falling short of a full-blown crisis—were the least likely to succeed.

Initial conditions, it seems, promote success to the extent that they promote bold reforms and the monetary, fiscal, and exchange-rate policies needed to back them up. Economic distress has this effect. On the other hand, a relatively stable economic background means that reform has a smaller task. Even weak programs stand a good chance under such circumstances. When the economic background is unstable, but not so unstable that strong measures are deemed necessary, the reforms that tend to be adopted are rarely up to the task.

The Short-Term Effect of Liberalization

An obvious danger when barriers to imports are first lowered is that the balance of payments might deteriorate. Another is that unemployment might rise if workers displaced from inefficient jobs are not quickly re-employed. For similar reasons, output might also be lower during the transition. In addition, the changes could have an adverse effect on the distribution of income. In principle, if these short-term costs are large, the long-term gains (suitably discounted) may not be enough to make reform worthwhile. But even if the long-term gains are substantial (as the study assumes), the short-term pain may make liberalization politically infeasible.

The difficulties of reform are not to be underestimated. However, the study found that fears concerning the effects of liberalization on the balance of payments, output and employment, and the distribution of income are all misplaced. To a surprising extent, the signs are that the costs of adjustments are very small, even in the short term.

The Balance of Payments

Trade liberalization, by definition, erodes the protection enjoyed by certain domestic producers, generally with the deliberate aim of opening the economy to a greater volume of imports. So it is natural to fear at least a short-term deterioration in the balance of payments. In fact, the study found that this was rare.

In the great majority of liberalization episodes, countries added to their foreign-exchange reserves in the months immediately following the start of their program. Reserves declined in just two cases (Korea 2 and Israel 3), whereas in a few others there was little change in either direction. In most cases, liberalization rescued the country from a worsening balance-of-payments position and falling reserves. Indeed, a rapidly worsening external position was quite often the reason why the reforms had been implemented in the first place.

In about half of the reform episodes, imports did tend to increase in the months after liberalization began. In most of the other episodes they showed no trend, either upward or downward. Imports actually fell in only four episodes. Many of the programs that included a major relaxation of QRs saw particularly big increases in imports. Of the eleven such episodes, suitable data were available for eight; imports increased sharply in six of them. This is not surprising. The countries that had relied on highly restrictive QRs were the ones most likely to be suffering from the greatest pent-up demand.

Because imports, by and large, either showed no trend or increased, the overall improvement in balance-of-payments positions must have been due to rising exports. And so it was. In every case but one, countries that imported more exported more as well. (The exception was New Zealand 3, where exports remained steady). In the sample as a whole, roughly two-thirds of the episodes saw a clearly rising trend of exports in the months immediately after the launch of the reforms. Usually this represented an improvement over the pre-reform position. Taking an average of the 31 episodes for which good trade data were available, the growth rate of exports rose from 4.9 percent in the year preceding the reforms to 11.3 percent in the year of liberalization (see Table 2.7).

Clearly, then, export performance improves markedly after the introduction of trade reforms—which is perhaps to be expected. What may be more surprising is that the improvement is both quick enough and large enough to bring about, as a rule, an immediate improvement in the balance of payments.

Employment and Growth

The separate country studies used a variety of methods to estimate the effects of liberalization on employment. What matters in judging the overall change in welfare is the *net* effect of trade reform on jobs—that is, the extent to which jobs lost in contracting industries were offset by gains in employment elsewhere. To trace this in detail is difficult. It would require a great deal of information at the level of individual economic sectors and industries, and preferably individual firms. The data were not usually available.

Moreover, the pattern of employment after liberalization should ideally be compared not with the recent past but with the pattern that would have occurred in the absence of liberalization. For a few countries, simulation studies were used to attach numbers to these hypothetical outcomes. But of course it is difficult to separate the effects of liberalization from changes caused by other factors, except approximately.

Altogether the evidence suggests that the effects of trade liberalization on unemployment have been small. In most countries, employment was not lowered even in broad individual sectors of the economy, such as manufacturing. This implies that the reallocation of labor was achieved largely within sectors, causing less disruption than might have been feared.

Chile shows how important it is to distinguish between the effects of trade liberalization and the effects of other factors. Its overall rate of unemployment rose from 4.8 percent in the last year before its reform episode began to an average of 12.3 percent during the course of the program. Yet simulation studies suggest that the net impact of trade reform on jobs was positive. The rise in unemployment was due to stabilization policies, or sometimes to the exchange-rate policy. The implication is that if not for trade reforms those policies would have caused an even sharper rise in unemployment.

In any case, Chile is unusual. Its second liberalization program was the only one that reduced employment in a broad sector of the economy. The number of jobs in the electrical and non-electrical machinery sectors fell by nearly half, and in manufacturing as a whole employment fell by about 10 percent. (These losses were then more than offset by gains in farming and in other sectors.) In most of the other countries studied, trade liberalization

TABLE 2.7 Trade Liberalization and Export Performance

Typology of Episodes	Year before Liberalization			Annual Rate for Period	Year of Liberalization and After				Annual Rate for Period[b]	Annual Rate for Period[c]
	1	2	3		1[a]	2	3	4		
All episodes	1.2	6.6	4.9	4.2	11.3	18.1	9.7	10.2	11.1	11.0
Number of episodes				(31)					(31)	(31)
Strong	-1.1	9.0	3.9	3.9	12.4	17.3	10.8	8.6	12.3	12.3
Number of episodes				(17)					(17)	(17)
Weak	4.0	5.3	6.1	4.6	9.9	8.1	8.3	12.2	9.6	9.8
Number of episodes				(14)					(14)	(14)
Sustained[d]	0.8	8.6	9.6	6.2	12.0	18.3	15.8	10.8	14.1	14.8
Number of episodes				(16)					(16)	(16)
Collapsed[d]	2.0	4.6	-0.1	2.1	10.5	7.6	3.1	10.3	7.9	7.0
Number of episodes				(15)					(15)	(15)

[a]Year of liberalization.
[b]Post-liberalization average annual real export growth rate, which includes the year of liberalization.
[c]Annual average real export growth rate after liberalization, which excludes the year of trade liberalization.
[d]All partially sustained episodes have been grouped here with "collapsed," except for all of Spain's, which are classified here as "sustained."
Source: Compiled by the authors.

TABLE 2.8   Employment in Manufacturing during Periods of Liberalization

| | EMPLOYMENT (thousands) | | |
| | Year before | | Year after |
Episodes	Liberalization	Average*	Liberalization
Argentina 1 (1967-70)	1,836	1,847	1,914
Argentina 2 (1976-80)	1,863	2,099	2,132
Brazil (1965-73)	1,780	2,182	3,397
Chile 2 (1974-81)	515	487	351
Korea 2 (1978-79)	2,000	2,196	2,099
Peru (1979-80)	675	717	736
Philippines 1 (1960-65)	1,456	1,647	1,825
Philippines 2 (1970-74)	2,056	2,313	2,596
Singapore (1968-73)	61	139	210
Sri Lanka 1 (1968-70)	74	108	97
Sri Lanka 2 (1977-79)	112	134	155
Turkey 1 (1970-73)	485	551	651
Turkey 2 (1980-84)	799	829	---

*Average for the liberalization period.
Source: Compiled by the authors.

merely reduced the rate of growth of jobs in manufacturing and other previously protected sectors; it did not reduce the absolute number of jobs (Table 2.8). In such cases, employment gains in the sectors that had previously been discriminated against became net gains for the economy.

As we know, this low transitional unemployment cost cannot be explained by supposing that all the liberalization programs were weak and gradual. Many were strong and fast—Chile 2 especially so. By and large, the unemployment cost of trade reforms in countries with strong and fast programs was as low as in the others.

In line with these results, the study also found that liberalization has not meant lower output or lower economic growth, even in the short term. If anything, trade reform—especially strong and fast reform—is associated with higher growth from the beginning. If not for the findings on trade liberalization and employment, this result would have been rather surprising (see Table 2.9).

In most cases, the pre-reform trade regimes had discriminated against agriculture. As soon as this policy was reversed, agricultural output began to grow faster and the sector began to increase its share of the national income. This experience contradicts the popular view that farmers react slowly to changed incentives. Meanwhile, the growth of output in the countries' manufacturing sectors (the most heavily protected part of these

TABLE 2.9   Trade Liberalization and Economic Performance

Typology of episodes	PtL	1[a]	2	3	4	Annual Rate for Period[b]	Annual Rate for Period[c]
Summary of GDP Performance (real, annual rate of growth)							
All episodes	4.4	4.7	5.4	5.3	6.0	5.6	5.3
(number of episodes)						(31)	(31)
Strong	3.5	4.9	4.9	5.2	6.2	5.4	5.3
(number of episodes)						(17)	(17)
Weak	5.6	4.4	6.2	5.4	6.7	5.7	5.4
(number of episodes)						(14)	(14)
Sustained[d]	4.7	6.1	5.4	5.6	6.6	6.0	6.0
(number of episodes)						(16)	(18)
Collapsed[d]	4.1	3.2	6.6	4.6	5.2	5.1	4.6
(number of episodes)						(15)	(15)
Summary of Agricultural Sector Performance (real, annual rate of growth)							
All episodes	2.8	2.9	5.5	2.6	3.9	4.1	3.8
(number of episodes)						(29)	(29)
Strong	2.7	4.7	5.3	5.1	3.9	4.6	4.6
(number of episodes)						(17)	(17)
Weak	2.9	0.4	5.7	-0.4	4.1	3.1	2.4
(number of episodes)						(12)	(12)
Sustained[d]	2.8	3.4	8.4	2.5	6.3	5.7	5.2
(number of episodes)						(15)	(15)
Collapsed[d]	2.8	2.3	2.4	3.2	1.4	2.3	2.4
(number of episodes)						(14)	(14)
Summary of Manufacturing Sector Performance (real, annual rate of growth)							
All episodes	6.7	5.3	6.9	6.9	5.0	7.3	6.5
(number of episodes)						(29)	(29)
Strong	5.6	3.5	6.0	5.3	5.5	6.2	5.5
(number of episodes)						(17)	(17)
Weak	5.4	7.8	8.2	8.4	9.9	8.8	5.6
(number of episodes)						(12)	(12)
Sustained[d]	7.0	7.7	6.6	7.7	9.3	7.9	7.8
(number of episodes)						(15)	(15)
Collapsed[d]	6.5	2.7	7.2	6.1	5.5	6.6	5.6
(number of episodes)						(14)	(14)

[a]Year of liberalization.
[b]Post-liberalization average annual real export growth rate, including year of liberalization.
[c]Annual average real export growth rate after liberalizaion, excluding year of liberalization.
[d]All partially sustained episodes have been grouped here with "collapsed," except for those which are classified as "sustained."
Source: Compiled by the authors.

economies) was slow, as a rule, in the first year of reform. But the slowdown was temporary and quickly recouped. Even in the first year of liberalization, manufacturing output did not fall below earlier levels.

The Distribution of Income

In addition to worrying about the effects of trade reform on aggregate income, governments may fear that the short-term costs of liberalization, such as they are, will fall disproportionately on the poor. This risk would be great if the short-term costs in lost output and unemployment were large. An increase in unemployment would be almost sure to have an adverse effect on the distribution of income. In fact, as we have seen, these aggregate short-term costs are small. Does this mean that fears of a worsening of the income distribution are entirely misguided?

In principle the answer is no, because trade reform will cause other changes that may have an impact on income shares. For instance, by relaxing and perhaps eliminating the anti-export bias of most pre-reform trade regimes, reform will tend to increase the share of exports in national income, and reduce the share of import substitutes. The effect this has on income distribution will then depend on labor intensity in these two parts of the economy.

Evidence from previous studies has strongly suggested that in developing countries the exports sector is relatively labor-intensive whereas import substitutes tend to be capital intensive. If so, liberalization will increase the demand for labor, and increase the share of wages in national income. In developing countries, this improvement in the income distribution should be reinforced by the fact that the sector to expand most rapidly after liberalization will usually be agriculture, where wages are low. The sector most likely to contract (at least in relative terms) will usually be manufacturing, where wages are higher.

Similarly, a depreciation of the currency (which has generally accompanied successful trade reform) promotes the production of tradeable goods relative to services. So if incomes are higher in services than in manufacturing and primary production taken together (which they often are), there should be an improvement in the distribution of income.

The distributional implications of relaxing QRs, as opposed to reducing tariffs, are a bit more complicated. Relaxing QRs makes consumers, on average, better off, and the previous owners of the quota rents worse off. This should improve the income distribution. If the QRs are replaced by equivalent tariffs, then taxpayers (rather than direct consumers) gain a big slice of the benefit, again at the expense of the rent-holders. In this case too, the income distribution should be improved. However, the removal of QRs often happens alongside the relaxation of price controls and rationing. This ought to bring considerable aggregate benefits, but the end of rationing in itself could worsen the income distribution if it were to deny the poor preferential access to goods.

These are all *a priori* arguments. What does the evidence show? Unfortunately, it is mixed and fragmentary. In some cases (for example, Argentina 1 and 2, Israel 1, Philippines 1 and perhaps 2), the income distribution worsened during the course of liberalization. In roughly as many others (Colombia 2, Greece 2, Indonesia 2, Pakistan 1 and 2, Spain 1, 2, and 3), the reforms improved the income distribution. But in most cases it is hard to be sure. Often liberalization appeared to have no clear effect (Korea 1 and 2, Brazil, Chile 2, and more); sometimes it seemed to worsen the income distribution at first, then later improve it (Sri Lanka 2).

The empirical evidence leaves the issue open. There is no proof that low-income groups gain particular benefits from liberalization (beyond sharing in the aggregate benefits). Equally, there is no support for the popular view that reform is bound to make the poor worse off.

Conclusions: Some Basic Rules

Trade reform can work anywhere, regardless of initially unfavorable circumstances, and without serious short-term drawbacks. Governments with highly distorted trade regimes need not fear the consequences of a well-designed liberalization program.

What does a well-designed program look like? Many aspects of policy will influence the outcome over the longer term. Non-inflationary macroeconomic policy plays a very important role. So does the proper sequencing of reform. Credible pre-announcement of further measures can help. Other factors with a say in whether the program will succeed or fail may be partly or entirely beyond the government's control: external events, for instance, and domestic political stability.

But for reform to succeed, a smaller group of factors—each entirely within the government's control—appears to be what really counts. The program should be bold and it should start with a bang. If quantitative restrictions are in place, they should be rapidly dismantled. Where appropriate, the program should begin with a substantial depreciation of the currency. And a stable macroeconomic environment is a *sine qua non*. Almost every program that has followed these four simple rules has succeeded.

Notes

1. Demetris Papageorgiou, Armeane M. Choksi, and Michael Michaely, *Liberalizing Foreign Trade* (Oxford: Basil Blackwell, forthcoming), in seven volumes: Vol. 1, *The Experience of Argentina, Chile, and Uruguay;* Vol. 2, *The Experience of Korea, the Philippines, and Singapore;* Vol. 3, *The Experience of Israel and Yugoslavia;* Vol. 4, *The*

Experience of Brazil, Colombia, and Peru; Vol. 5, *The Experience of Indonesia, Pakistan, and Sri Lanka;* Vol. 6, *The Experience of New Zealand, Spain, and Turkey;* and Vol. 8, *Lessons of Experience in the Developing World.*

2. Table 2.2, however, lists only those liberalization episodes with major relaxation of QRs.

3

Liberalization Attempts and Outcomes

Rolf J. Langhammer

The main thrust of this essay will consist of sketching some principles of liberalization strategies, exposing the crucial importance of political vested interests in promoting or blocking liberalization attempts, underlining the necessity of consistency and continuity in successful liberalizations, and considering the external prerequisites of liberalization, such as access to absorptive export markets and private risk capital from abroad. Within this framework, seven major issues will be laid out. First, the historical conditions at the beginning of liberalization attempts will be given due attention. Second, objectives of liberalization strategies are analyzed. Third, the consistency requirement will be discussed. Fourth, the timing and sequencing debate, which recently gained much interest, is recalled. Fifth, differences in the elements of policy reforms between specific groups of countries are exposed. Sixth, politically rooted resistance and vested interests are dealt with. And finally, external constraints are investigated. The last section concludes with some results.

Liberalization Attempts in a Historical Setting

With the exception of Hong Kong and partly Singapore, all developing countries and the newly industrialized countries (NICs) have begun to open their economies to the world market in a period in which their governments more or less actively interfered in the private sector. But this is the only element they have in common. Broadly speaking, there are at least two different patterns at the beginning of liberalization: one of liberalizing in a state of crisis, and one under favorable external and internal conditions.

Most countries began to liberalize in a state of crisis. In many cases, crises were creeping, in the sense that over a long period governments were responsible for setting policy signals toward delinking domestic prices from world market prices. Such government conduct was accompanied by an explicit discrimination between inward- and outward-oriented sectors and within sectors, to the detriment of the latter. Discrimination went even further if firm size was a relevant determinant of privileges and if subsidies were biased toward large firms. The most frequently analyzed examples of this sort of crisis were excessive import substitution policies with high rates of effective protection of manufactures, large discrepancies in protection rates between industries, an increasing reliance on quantitative restrictions instead of pricing interventions, overvalued exchange rates, and a waste instead of generation of foreign savings.[1]

Alternatively, crises broke out after external shocks, with domestic policies unable to cope with them. Such shocks have been particularly relevant for primary commodity export-dependent countries facing temporary price hikes in international markets. They led to the so-called Dutch disease problems of rising prices for non-tradeables relative to tradeables (real appreciation) and to a diminishing competitiveness of non-primary sectors if the exchange rate policy was inflexible.[2] This happened because governments failed to sterilize the sudden surge of foreign exchange earnings through debt repayment or payment of compensation to a fund;[3] instead, they launched large investments in the public sector.[4] Such investments often turned out to be non-performing; and favored a crowding out of private investors and a sizeable decrease of capital productivity.

Other crises spurred by external shocks had their origin in domestic policy decisions that turned out to be fatal in a suddenly changing external environment. The best-known case in point is the Chilean decision of 1979 to fix the exchange rate to the dollar just when the dollar began to appreciate strongly in real terms and to maintain rigidities in the labor market (wage indexation). The result was a substantial decline in international competitiveness for Chilean exportables.[5]

Apart from creeping and sudden crises, structural deficiencies in an economy can lead to a permanent malaise that impedes private capital formation and makes the country even more vulnerable to external shocks. In this case, it is a climate of political instability, rent-seeking, and excessive dominance of para-statals—often run by combatants of political leaders—rather than the escalation of specific interventionist policies that leads the country into an impasse. This case can often be found in those Sub-Saharan African countries where the tax base shrank dramatically and where the "property" rights of privileged groups to receive fringe benefits irrespective of the tax base continued to exist. The most pronounced result of crises in the "structural case" is the emergence of a flourishing shadow economy in goods as well as factor markets.[6]

Liberalization under favorable external and internal conditions has mainly remained the privilege of some East and Southeast Asian countries. They started to introduce policy measures toward a more neutral incentive system between production for domestic market and exports rather early.

Apart from favorable external conditions, such as persistent high growth at the end of the 1960s and lacking shock elements, the countries enjoyed some other internal assets.[7] First, their governments were dedicated to growth and provided a minimum of public goods efficiently. In short, governments were administratively competent, politically well-organized, and found compatriots for growth coalitions in the urban middle-income classes. When policy mistakes were made, such as in South Korea at the end of the 1970s and Singapore during the early 1980s, governments were able to correct them rapidly. Second, the monetary environment was characterized by stability and thus foreseeability. Central banks were not degraded to rubber stamps for financing budget deficits but were allowed to run a conservative monetary policy regardless of changes in the governments. Third, domestic savings rates were relatively high. They could be absorbed by well-functioning domestic capital markets that were gradually integrated into international markets. Fourth, wage resistance—in the sense of workers organizing themselves to impose costs on those groups whose actions threaten their income shares—were lower in East Asia than anywhere else in developing countries.[8] As a result, degrees of unionization, strikes, collective bargaining, and other institutional elements of wage resistance were rather weak. Fifth, there is evidence to argue that East Asian workers place material wealth higher on their scale of values than do workers in, say, Latin America.[9] Such attitudes would make incentive systems on the micro (firm) level very effective.

Compared to "unforced" liberalization as a deliberate policy choice, "forced" liberalization in a situation of crisis has been the rule rather than the exception in developing countries. It may have been this situation of not being free to choose that contributed to inconsistencies, failures, and aborted liberalization programs.

Motives of Liberalization

Viewed from a *normative* angle of politicians' conduct, liberalization in a crisis aims at restoring the international creditworthiness of a debtor country. Binding the policy internationally—i.e., under the GATT, the IMF, or other institutional frameworks—can be an appropriate way to restore the credibility of economic reforms in international capital markets and also to diffuse domestic political opposition against reforms. This normative view, however, misses the economic rationale of political decision making. Under a *positive* theory of politicians' conduct, liberalization is instrumental in regaining control over a state in which the official economy shrinks and the unofficial one flourishes as a result of a growing "transfer" state.[10] In this view, liberalization is intended to turn the tide and to encourage a revival of the official economy in order to expand the tax base with public expenditures remaining unchanged. This one-sided approach confined to the revenue part of public budgets led many developing countries to implement partial "minimum" liberalization programs, which soon proved to be ill-fated because they lacked credibility. For instance, the ad hoc removal of import licensing requirements and other controls on imports in order to secure access to necessary intermediates and capital goods aggravated balance-of-payments problems. This happened because private agents anticipated that this measure would soon be reversed because it remained unaccompanied by other liberalization measures. Such anticipation induced them to hoard imported goods, which led to a rapid deterioration of the balance of payments and ultimately to the abortion of the liberalization measure itself. Many examples of such stop-and-go policies in developing countries can be reported that inherited their basic weakness from the motive to achieve fiscal equilibrium solely by more growth and hence more government revenues. Fundamental disequilibria remained untackled, and once the official economy recovered slightly, adjustment efforts slowed. The delicate task to reduce "entitlements" for subsidies paid to the political clientele was not fulfilled in many countries as governments with a very short time horizon preferred to choose the "minimum" approach of regaining control over the economy.

The Consistency Requirement

The experience of many aborted liberalization attempts suggests that governments that were unwilling to change the structure and volume of subsidies paid to the clientele failed to meet the consistency requirement of liberalization. Liberalizing one market and leaving the others regulated can result in fully different effects than those expected. In other words, in a disequilibrium the removal of one distortion does not necessarily bring the economy nearer to the optimum.

In many cases, for instance, the missing link between liberalized imports and still-regulated domestic capital markets appeared as a major stumbling block to success. With increased competition from abroad after liberalization of imports, parts of the installed capacity in import substitution industries became obsolete while expansion into new profitable activities, such as non-traditional exports, created new demand for credit to finance the necessary investment. The ease and the speed of the liberalization process thus heavily depended on whether this demand could be met. Therefore, in order to channel domestic savings into the domestic financial sector and to attract external savings, it became imperative to deregulate the banking sector, not only by allowing for a positive real rate of interest but also by removing privileges in sectoral credit allocation. A relaxation of banking regulations, on the other hand, required adopting anti-inflationary policies, lowering the government's dependence to collect an inflation tax for financing budget deficits. Such policies, however, were threatened by delayed single-step devaluations of the exchange rate, as the experience of resource-rich countries (i.e., Indonesia between 1974 and 1986) suggests. In many cases such exchange rate adjustments fueled inflation because they were not accompanied by liberalizing imports or other measures in order to expand total supply on domestic goods markets.

Timing and Sequencing of Liberalization

The questions of whether markets should be liberalized abruptly or gradually (timing) and, if gradualism is preferred, which markets should be liberalized first (sequencing) have stimulated intensive debates in literature as well as in economic policy advice.

As far as timing is concerned, three major arguments have been raised in favor of a shock approach. First, no resource misallocation during the transition period would impede the adjustment process. Second, instantaneous adjustment would prevent political opposition to the reform programs from diluting them. Third, uncertainty about the credibility of the reform package would be reduced. Because costs of economic liberalization tend to increase with the level of expectations of private agents that the reforms will fail—again, this may be a function of the extent of policy distortions—this third argument is an important one. However, except for Bolivia, whose recent reform came close to the shock approach, developing countries have relied on gradualism probably because the level of adjustment costs and hence the level of distortions was assessed as too high, given short-run immobilities of capital and rigidities in wages.

Without going into the technical details of the sequencing debate,[11] the discussion on the order of liberalization has basically led to a distinction between two views. One is the so-called "technocratic" view, which says that the capital account of the foreign exchange should be liberalized last, whereas the removal of domestic distortions in the goods and asset markets should be given priority. In addition, restrictions on capital flows should only be lifted after imports of goods are liberalized.[12] The main thrust of this view is that after an early opening of the capital account, a massive capital inflow would occur because of rapidly rising real interest rates in domestic capital markets. Under fixed as well as floating exchange rates, such capital inflows would lead to a real appreciation of the domestic currency, and this short-run movement of the exchange rate would jeopardize all efforts to increase the export volume and to diversify exports. South Korea in mid-1966, as well as Chile from 1977 onward, are often-cited examples for this effect.

This "technocratic" view has been challenged by those who highlight the utmost importance of expectations of private agents and the activities of pressure groups in the liberalization process (the so-called "political economy view"). They emphasize the budget disequilibrium of fixed "entitlement"-based expenditures and the shrinking tax base and thus argue in favor of a priority given to the reduction of the fiscal deficit. This policy should be accompanied by a removal of domestic capital distortions. In the second stage, the transition to a free floating exchange rate, with exchange controls eliminated, should be managed; and only in the third stage should a pre-announced phased program of dismantling restrictions in goods markets be implemented.[13]

This view comes close to the advice to separate the stabilization phase from the trade liberalization phase.[14] During the stabilization phase the key measure would be to reduce the budget deficit to levels that can be financed in a non-inflationary way, combined with a large depreciation of the currency. Only if the budget can be financed without rising inflation will trade liberalization be achievable or sustainable. Experience in Latin America suggests, however, that any mechanistic textbook advice on the "right" order is threatened by failure. Overshooting in the real exchange rate may also occur if trade liberalization occurs first—for instance, if improved prospects for exports induce capital inflows. Central banks may succeed in managing the nominal exchange rate but not the real rate, especially if distortions in domestic goods and factor markets remain in place. The Southern Cone experiments support the view that it was the inconsistent mix of exchange rate policies and domestic economic policies that resulted in overshooting the exchange rate, rather than the first-order liberalization of the capital account. In particular, the attempt to use the exchange rate for breaking expectations of rising inflation while prices for non-tradeables were allowed to rise further has been responsible for real appreciations and for damaging effects with respect to the production of tradeables. In general, the risks associated with trying to peg the real exchange rate were by no means smaller than those stemming from destabilizing capital flows. Again, the importance of expectations must not be underrated. Expectations of the unsustainability of a policy of stabilized real exchange rates favor a persistent high level of interest rates when inflation rates begin to decelerate and consequently attract high capital inflows.

Perhaps more than strict policy recommendations on the "right" order of liberalization measures, some general guidelines deserve attention which, nevertheless, have to be operationalized in the light of specific conditions prevailing in the countries. Gradualism in the sense of step-wise managing tends to be self-defeating with respect to stabilization and exchange rate policies; import and capital markets may be better candidates for a step-wise removal of controls. Again, though, some qualifications have to be born in mind. For instance, at least a partial deregulation of the domestic capital market will have to be implemented soon in order to facilitate the mobilization of funds necessary to finance investments in the export sector after anti-export biases have been reduced. Even if risks of unwarranted short-run real appreciation should emerge, the liberalization of the capital account should not be postponed until the goods sector has fully adjusted. If monetary policies are believed to become stable and thus foreseeable, private agents can anticipate a later real depreciation and thus make their choice according to an intertemporal allocation of investable funds between the non-traded goods sector expanding first and the traded goods sector growing later. Nevertheless, if inflationary processes remain unbroken because the authorities do not succeed in reducing the fiscal deficits, any discussion on the "right" sequencing is futile.

Liberalization Requirements in Different Country Groups

Given the very different economic structures in developing countries and newly industrialized countries, any clustering of countries according to common issues of liberalization is debatable. Even within low-income Sub-Saharan African (SSA) countries, where common liberalization requirements can perhaps be more easily defined, differences arise. For instance, francophone countries, which peg their common currency to the French franc, do not have balance-of-payments problems as long as they trade within the franc zone; consequently, they cannot pursue an active exchange rate policy as anglophone countries can. Instead, they have a budgetary problem to mobilize domestic resources for debt service.[15]

Nevertheless, some stylized aggregation seems to be justified. To begin with, low-income countries of the African type are characterized by an overproportionately dominant role of the public sector, including para-statals, public wage leadership, managerial weaknesses, political partisanship, inadequate infrastructure, and highly segmented economic and political markets. Under such conditions of "institutional" and "structural" problems, liberalization takes more time to deliver results (supply responses are delayed) and is permanently threatened by political opposition. Because the transition period is extraordinarily long in this type of country, gradualism does not seem to be promising. Pressure groups do not face high costs of mobilization if success takes a long time to materialize. An important mortgage of low-income countries in SSA and elsewhere is their vulnerability to external shocks as a result of their commodity export dependence. Furthermore, manufactured exporters enjoy much more rapid progress in export volume growth than commodity exporters if anti-export biases are removed.[16]

Middle-income developing countries often fall into the group of "creeping crisis" economies. Over a longer period, import substitution becomes excessive when it is expanded to intermediates and capital goods so that reforms of trade policies and of the exchange rates become necessary to cure the misallocation. Yet because the industrial basis is relatively well-developed compared to low-income countries, and because the inflationary policies are often not as prominent as in highly indebted countries, credibility of reforms can more easily be regained than in the latter group.

Apart from their critical external financial situation, governments of highly indebted countries often rely heavily on the collection of an inflation tax to finance large fiscal deficits. Restoring an equilibrium on domestic financial markets is therefore of utmost importance. It requires a large amount of monetary discipline over a long period combined with cuts in budget deficits and more exchange rate flexibility to restore a new environment for private investments and to discourage private capital flight. Again, within this group, countries with a diversified manufacturing base respond faster to changing price incentives than more commodity-dependent countries.

In short, challenges to liberalization cover different policies in each of the country groups. Institutional reforms geared at more transparency in economic and political markets as well as reduced barriers to market entry are essentials in low-income countries, whereas trade policies and monetary reforms have become priority issues in middle-income and highly indebted countries, respectively. Of course, there are overlaps between the groups. Common to all groups seems to be that freeing prices has been subject to fewer controversies than dismantling non-price interference. This is not surprising; legal and quantitative restrictions are the most appropriate tools for bureaucrats and politicians to discriminate among sectors, industries, firms, and even individuals.

Politically Rooted Resistance and Vested Interests

Generally speaking, liberalization contributes to a larger number of options for both consumers and producers and thereby may help to reduce rent elements in prices. It may also erode the sovereignty of governments to redistribute income—an important instrument to influence the electorate or, in authoritarian regimes, the political clientele. Governments are thus one source of resistance against liberalization. Another is organized pressure groups. These groups negotiate with governments to obtain factor protection for their members, and they invest financial and other resources into such lobbying activities. This investment is profitable as long as marginal returns in terms of subsidies exceed marginal returns from non-lobbying activities, i.e., from so-called productive investment. It has been shown that the better the group can control free riders, and the smaller the group of beneficiaries is relative to the number of taxpayers or consumers, the greater is the efficiency of each group in producing political pressure. Excessive demand by pressure groups, however, stir resistance of those who have to carry the burden in the form of high tariffs or prices. Shifts in demand and/or tax avoidance, then, would limit the success of pressure groups.

Although the theoretical appeal of such hypotheses may be high, empirical evidence is extremely scarce and episodic. Analyses undertaken in the Kiel Institute are illustrative but by no means exhaustive. For instance, Amelung has tried to explain the rate of effective protection in Brazilian manufacturing industries in a cross-sectional analysis by introducing the following exogenous variables (the sign of the variable is in parentheses): concentration level approximated by the share of the ten biggest firms in total turnover of the industry (positive); the share of exports in total production (negative); the locational structure of the industry approximated by the share of value added concentrated in the industrial centers of Brazil in total value added of the industry (negative); the share of value added in gross output (negative); and finally, the concentration of sellers of intermediates and industrial purchasers of the industry (positive).[17] The results indicate that the Brazilian government has protected relatively well-organized, domestic-market-oriented industries, located in backward areas, with low local content, and a large number of suppliers of intermediates. Yet a high concentration of industrial clients has had little influence on the protection rate.

Another analysis made by Amelung on the temporal process of import substitution and trade liberalization in Turkey points to the dynamics of pressure groups and their changing interests in protection over time. He argues that the political feasibility of trade liberalization measures in Turkey by 1980 was a function of the sustainability of excessive import substitution policies in the 1970s. The sustainability depended on the availability of foreign exchange, which was necessary to meet the increasing import demand for intermediates and capital goods. The external crisis—that is, the shrinking availability of foreign exchange—proved to be the first precondition for trade liberalization. Parallel to the external crisis, internal tensions among interest groups culminated. This happened because the increasing segmentation of markets associated with excessive import substitution also led to a segmentation of political markets—that is, a fragmentation of interest groups (capital owners and labor unions). This splitting added to the weakness of the government, which revealed a high time preference rate and favored the status quo against trade liberalization. In 1980, the stalemate situation between the dominant interest groups under a weak government changed in favor of groups pro trade liberalization after the military coup. The military paved the way to trade liberalization by backing the leading pro group indirectly through "revealed preferences" rather than directly through a coalition. This pro group consisted of first-generation import substitution industrialists who:

- were heavily dependent on foreign exchange and imported inputs;
- faced the increasingly limited scope of the domestic market;
- disposed of financial resources sufficient to sustain short-run losses;
- secured protection for final products by recommending the liberalization of industrial inputs; and
- could discourage free-rider behavior—that is, non-payment of short-run costs while pocketing the long-run benefits—by confining the membership to a small group of companies and diversified conglomerates.

Unlike the former civilian government, the military took a firmer stance toward pressure groups, for both political and economic reasons. Politically, the military aimed at containing social unrest and could launch reforms over a longer time horizon without being forced to pay tribute to short-run interests of the electorate. This lower time preference rate met with the targets of the pressure group. Economically, it had vested interests in the well-being of the pressure group in order to secure access to funds flowing from this group to the military.

The Brazilian and Turkish episodes highlight the vital importance of vested interests and pressure groups in the closing and re-opening of markets. Further studies on ASEAN and East Asian countries have documented the large influence of growth coalitions between governments and interest groups on principal decisions to open the economy.

External Constraints to Liberalization Attempts

External constraints can be separated into two major groups. One group comprises price and volume fluctuations in world markets, especially commodity markets and private financial markets; the other comprises policy-induced constraints, such as delayed public assistance by donor countries, protectionism, and destabilizing macroeconomic policies in the OECD countries.

With respect to the first group, various compensatory facilities have been introduced by the IMF as well as individual donors (STABEX by the EC) in order to stabilize foreign exchange earnings. The problem is especially relevant for low-income commodity export-dependent countries, which see liberalization attempts threatened by a high vulnerability to such external shocks. However, empirical analyses show that the compensatory financing facility of the IMF and the STABEX system suffered from a number of shortcomings. In many cases these schemes did not sufficiently stabilize national export earnings as a consequence of time lags in compensatory payments and financial constraints. Furthermore, existing schemes are not pure stabilization schemes but, by offering grants or loans at non-market terms, contain implicit income transfers that are distributed independently of indicators of need. The efficiency of stabilization schemes for export earnings could probably be improved if advance-payments rules would be more applied than in the past and if stabilization and transfers would be strictly separated by reducing the implicit grant element. Instead, the funds could be enlarged and more budgetary support could be given in order to alleviate short-run budgetary bottlenecks that appear after an exchange rate adjustment because of a rising debt service in domestic currency.

The second major constraint—that is, policy-induced barriers to success caused by the OECD countries—is much more difficult to handle. As far as bilateral donor response to liberalization is concerned, recent studies show that the sustainability of policy reforms was seriously impeded by no response or delayed response. To bridge the gap, multilateral donors could act as stabilizers under a "compensatory aid allocation principle" if bilateral donors would fail to coordinate their aid policies by agreeing to common guidelines of reform support.

As far as protectionism is concerned, there is room for fear that the OECD countries' governments have not yet understood how counterproductive and psychologically damaging it is to recommend liberalization strategies in developing countries on one hand and then prevent them from becoming effective by impeding market access on the other. The political opposition in developing countries against liberalization can easily be fueled if competitiveness cannot be transformed into export performance. So can "fallacy of composition" arguments be nourished by saying that the success of the East Asian NICs is unique and cannot be repeated by other developing countries because absorptive capacity of OECD countries is lacking.

For example, agricultural policies of the OECD countries have lowered world prices and thereby distorted the shadow price of food production in developing countries. Additionally, the OECD countries have contributed significantly to the instability of world prices in agriculture by isolating their domestic markets from the world market, thus avoiding stabilizing adjustments of their producers, consumers, and traders to changing world market conditions. These policy-induced instabilities raise the market risk of developing countries in international food trade.

In the manufacturing sector, it is mainly the NICs group that is threatened by selective non-tariff barriers such as VERs, anti-dumping procedures, and countervailing actions as well as quotas and ceilings. No politician in the OECD countries denies the existence of protective measures against the NICs. But it is argued that such successful exporters should no longer behave like free-riders in the international trading system and should reciprocate by opening up their economies also. This view reflects a mercantilistic understanding of international trade and an ignorance of the long-term costs of protection for the OECD countries themselves in terms of income losses and resource waste.

For low-income countries, their claim for opening up the OECD markets seems redundant, it is often argued, given the far-reaching special and general preferences that the low-income countries have been granted (Lomé, Caribbean Basin Initiative, GSP). This view is misleading on several grounds. Protectionist instruments are subtle but by no means less effective. To begin with, preferential tariffs are bound to the requirements of minimum domestic valued added content and of "double-tariff-item jumps." Meeting such rules would often require not buying at the cheapest source available—that is, to violate the basic principle of liberalization. Second, there is a continuing threat that the OECD countries might apply quantitative restrictions. The U.K.'s barriers against Bangladesh's clothing exports are a case in point. Such measures add a large amount of uncertainty to investment and may contribute to widespread reluctance to invest.

Moreover, even after several multilateral trade negotiation rounds, the tariffs applied by the OECD countries still rise with increasing stages of fabrication. This so-called escalation effect shifts effective protection upwards and hinders developing countries from attracting export-oriented investments for processing. There is a sizable body of both theoretical and empirical research on the costs of protection. Yet domestic interest groups in many OECD countries that claim factor protection still dominate public discussion over those who argue for consumer protection. This is why effective international sanctions should be introduced and executed. Neither the GATT nor the OECD have effective sanctions at their disposal to discipline their members. A way out of this impasse may be a commitment by the OECD countries to compensate developing countries for refused liberalization via additional (contingent) aid payments.

A final aspect of external constraints refers to the macroeconomic policies of the OECD countries that have destabilizing effects on the world economy. It has often been recommended that macroeconomic policies should be coordinated through concerted actions of the major industrial countries.[18] A possible alternative to concerted actions would be a system of pre-announcement of national policies in order to increase their transparency and to weaken incentives toward beggar-my-neighbor policies. More competition among national policies rather than cartelized harmonization would also enlarge options for the developing countries to link to those OECD countries with which they have a macroeconomic target mix in common.

Conclusions

Consistency and continuity are the two most badly needed requirements of successful liberalization in the developing countries and newly industrializing economies. Without consistency, ad hoc policy measures intended to liberalize a specific market often fail to impress investors, and lead to fully undesired results for the whole economy.

The lesson to be learned from such experiences points to a critical role of governmental management and monetary policies. What separates more from less successful liberalization experiments is mainly the capability of governments to correct inconsistencies of individual policies and policy mistakes. Permanent feedback and revision send strong signals to the actors in the economy to believe in the credibility of policy reform and not to postpone investment decisions. Yet it was not only superior political administration that gave the Asian countries a competitive edge in policy reforms over the Latin American countries; it was also the better institutional preconditions for fighting inflationary tendencies. Central banks, which were allowed to articulate and enforce their own preference system in favor of conservative monetary policies, helped to stabilize expectations. Monetary authorities thus earned a premium for the whole economy in terms of lower time preference rates and higher local savings spent for domestic capital formation. The positive effects on the tax base compensated the public agencies for refraining from collecting an inflation tax. Notwithstanding the controversies on timing and sequencing, consensus exists on the paramount importance of exchange rate policies, budgetary policies, and domestic capital market policies, as well as on the necessity to neutralize external shocks by combining different policies as shock absorbers.

Of course, the vast variety of developing countries in terms of resource endowment and points of departure for liberalization suggests that a standard detailed recipe cannot be offered. But to say this is fairly trivial. At any stage of development, relatively open markets have performed better than markets delinked from the world economy, and courageous liberalization attempts have impressed national and international private agents more than have a "muddling-through" approach intended to appease both established rent-seekers and forward-looking newcomers.

Notes

1. See, for example, Bela Balassa, "Export Incentives and Export Performance in Developing Countries: A Comparative Analysis," *Weltwirtschaftliches Archiv*, Vol. 114, No. 1 (1978), pp. 24-61; Juergen B. Donges, "A Comparative Survey of Industrialization Policies in Fifteen Semi-Industrial Countries," *Weltwirtschaftliches Archiv*, Vol. 112, No. 4 (1976), pp. 626-657; Anne O. Krueger, *Foreign Trade Regimes and Economic Development: Liberalization Attempts and Consequences* (Cambridge, Mass.: Ballinger, 1978); and, for a comprehensive overview, Sebastian Edwards, *Openness, Outward Orientation, Trade Liberalization and Economic Performance in Developing Countries*, NBER Working Paper, No. 2908 (Washington, D.C.: National Bureau of Economic Research, 1989).

2. Warner M. Corden, "Booming Sector and Dutch Disease Economics: Survey and Consolidation," *Oxford Economic Papers*, Vol. 36 (1981), pp. 359-380.

3. Bela Balassa, "Temporary Windfalls and Compensation Arrangements," *Weltwirtschaftliches Archiv*, Vol. 125, No. 1 (1989), pp. 97-113.

4. Shantayanan Devarajan and Jaime de Melo, "Adjustment with a Fixed Exchange Rate: Cameroon, Côte d'Ivoire and Senegal," *World Bank Economic Review*, Vol. 1 (1987), pp. 447-487; and David L. Bevan et al., *Trade Shocks in Controlled Economies: Theory and an Application to the East Africa Coffee Boom* (Oxford, 1988).

5. See Larry A. Sjaastad, "Failure of Economic Liberalism in the Case of Latin America," *The World Economy*, Vol. 6, No. 1 (1983), pp. 5-26.

6. Ernesto May, *Exchange Controls and Parallel Market Economies in Sub-Saharan Africa: Focus on Ghana*, World Bank Staff Working Paper, No. 711 (Washington, D.C.: The World Bank, 1985).

7. James Riedel, "Economic Development in East Asia: Doing What Comes Naturally?" in Helen Hughes, ed., *Achieving Industrialization in East Asia* (Cambridge, Mass.: CUP, 1988), pp. 1-38.

8. Taric Banuri and Edward J. Amadeo, *The Importance of Institutions and History in Development Policy: A Comparison of Macroeconomic Experience in Asia and Latin America* (Helsinki: Wider, 1987).

9. David Morawetz, *Why the Emperor's New Clothes Are Not Made in Colombia* (New York: Oxford University Press, 1981), Part II, p. 7.

10. Deepak Lal, "The Political Economy of Economic Liberalization," *The World Bank Economic Review*, Vol. 1, No. 2 (1987), pp. 273-299.

11. See, for example, Sebastian Edwards, *The Order of Liberalization of the External Sector in Developing Countries: Essays in International Finance*, No. 156 (Princeton, N.J.: December 1984).

12. See, for example, Ronald I. McKinnon, "The Order of Economic Liberalization: Lessons from Chile and Argentina," in Karl Brunner and Allan Meltzer, eds., *Economic Policy in a World of Change*, Carnegie-Rochester Conference Series on Public Policy, Vol. 17 (Amsterdam: North-Holland, 1982).

13. Lal, *op. cit.*, p. 288.

14. Martin Wolf, "Timing and Sequencing of Trade Liberalization in Developing Countries," *Asian Development Review*, Vol. 4, No. 2 (1986), pp. 1-24.

15. Peter Dittus, "The Budgetary Dimension of the Debt Crisis in Low-Income Sub-Saharan Countries," *Journal of Institutional and Theoretical Economics*, Vol. 145 (1989), pp. 358-366.

16. The World Bank, *Adjustment Lending. An Evaluation of Ten Years of Experience*, Country Economics Department, Policy and Research Series, No. 1 (Washington, D.C.: 1989).

17. Torsten Amelung, "Zum Einfluss von Interessengruppen auf die Wirtschaftspolitik in Entwicklungslaendern," *Die Weltwirtschaft*, H. 1 (1987), pp. 158-171.

18. John Williamson, "The 'Bluepoint' Proposals for International Monetary Reform," paper prepared for the *Third Annual of the Lloyds Bank Review* (1989), mimeo.

4

Policy Choices in the Newly Industrializing Countries

Bela Balassa

This chapter will compare the policies and economic performance of newly industrializing countries (NICs) in the Far East and Latin America. The two groups of countries are comprised of Hong Kong, Korea, Singapore and Taiwan, and Argentina, Brazil, Chile and Mexico, respectively. The essay tries to show what factors, besides foreign economic policies, are of critical importance in explaining differences in economic performance. Thus, it provides the context in which different foreign economic strategies have an impact on economic performance.

Information will be provided on economic growth, domestic savings ratios, the efficiency of investment, and export performance. Next, the results will be explained in terms of the policies applied. The chapter covers the 1963-87 period.

Growth Performance

The Far Eastern NICs had relatively low income levels in 1963. In terms of income per head, even Hong Kong and Singapore were behind Argentina, Chile, and Mexico (see Table 4.1). The situation changed dramatically in the following 24 years. By 1987, all four of the Far Eastern NICs increased four-and-a-half to six times. Among the Latin American NICs, per capita incomes increased two-and-a-half times in Brazil, one-and-a-half times in Mexico, and by less than one-quarter in Argentina and Chile.

Further interest attaches to inter-country differences in increases in per capita incomes over time. Table 4.1 provides data for the benchmark years

The author is indebted to Shigeru Akiyama and Peter Uimonen for research assistance. The author alone is responsible for the contents of this essay. His views should not be interpreted as reflecting the views of the World Bank.

TABLE 4.1   Gross Domestic Product per Capita (U.S. dollars)

	At Purchasing Power Parities in 1980 prices					At Exchange Rates
	1963	1973	1981	1987	1963-1987	1987
Hong Kong	2,247	4,552	7,751	11,193	4.98	8,249
Korea	747	1,553	2,457	3,707	4.96	2,849
Singapore	1,777	3,838	6,308	10,680	6.01	7,623
Taiwan	980	1,976	3,029	4,265	4.35	4,804
Argentina	2,949	4,157	3,935	3,622	1.23	2,563
Brazil	1,400	2,338	3,252	3,499	2.50	2,305
Chile	3,231	3,502	4,443	3,751	1.16	1,492
Mexico	2,312	3,403	4,576	3,754	1.62	1,749

Sources: 1963-81 figures from R. Summers and A. Heston, "A New Set of International Comparisons of Real Product and Price Levels Estimates for 130 Countries," *Review of Income and Wealth,* March 1988. The 1987 estimates represent 1985 figures updated by utilizing national data on economic growth rates.

of the 1963-73 period of world economic boom, the 1973-81 period of two oil shocks, and the 1981-87 period of the debt crisis.

It appears that the Far Eastern NICs started gaining on the Latin American NICs already in the 1963-73 period; per capita incomes doubled in the Far Eastern NICs, far surpassing the performance of any of the Latin American countries. The Far Eastern NICs increased their lead during the period of the oil crises, notwithstanding their reliance on imported petroleum, while Argentina suffered declines in per capita incomes.

Differences in economic performance increased further in the period of the debt crisis. The Far Eastern NICs experienced increases in per capita incomes by one-third to one-half. In turn, apart from small gains in Brazil, incomes per head fell in the Latin American NICs. In this connection, reference may be made to differences in the foreign debt situation. There is a contrast between the high degree of foreign indebtedness of Latin American countries and the low external debt of the Far Eastern NICs (discussed later).

Domestic Savings and the Efficiency of Investment

Various factors may explain differences in growth performance. They include differences in domestic saving ratios and investment efficiency, as well as the changing relative importance of exports. A comparison of the Far Eastern and Latin American NICs does not show overall differences in domestic saving ratios in the 1963-73 period while there were considerable

TABLE 4.2   GDP Growth Rates, Domestic Savings Ratios, and Incremental Capital-Output Ratios (ICORs)

	1963-73			1973-81			1981-87		
Country	GDP Growth Rate	Domestic Saving Ratio	ICOR	GDP Growth Rate	Domestic Saving Ratio	ICOR	GDP Growth Rate	Domestic Saving Ratio	ICOR
Hong Kong	8.9	24.3	3.6	9.1	29.0	3.4	7.2	28.3	4.0
Korea	9.3	13.0	2.1	7.8	23.6	4.2	8.9	29.8	3.5
Singapore	10.3	16.5	3.1	7.8	32.8	5.0	5.3	42.0	8.4
Taiwan	11.1	24.4	1.9	8.0	32.8	3.7	7.6	33.7	2.9
Argentina	5.0	20.5	4.2	1.1	24.2	20.2	0.4	16.0	31.4
Brazil	8.2	26.3	2.2	5.8	21.2	4.4	3.8	20.5	4.4
Chile	2.8	14.3	7.5	3.7	14.2	4.5	0.6	14.5	24.8
Mexico	7.4	19.2	2.7	6.7	22.1	3.4	-0.2	25.5	-81.9

Source: World Bank Data Base.

differences within each group. The superior growth performance of the Far Eastern NICs during this period is thus explained by their higher investment efficiency, measured, however imperfectly, by incremental capital-output ratios (ICOR). Among Latin American NICs, Brazil and Mexico had relatively low incremental capital-output ratios (Table 4.2).

The situation changed in the 1973-81 period. All Far Eastern NICs increased their domestic saving ratios to a substantial extent, while in the Latin American NICs the increases were smaller, or domestic saving ratios declined. At the same time, the Far Eastern NICs maintained higher levels of investment efficiency than their Latin American counterparts. An apparent exception is Mexico, where newly found oil raised GDP growth rates, thereby reducing incremental capital-output ratios.

In the 1981-87 period, negative GDP growth rates in Mexico and very low growth rates in Argentina and Chile do not permit deriving meaningful estimates of incremental capital-output ratios. Negative growth in Mexico occurred despite the rise in domestic saving ratios while growth rates in Brazil continued to fall behind those of the Far Eastern NICs.

The Role of Exports

In the far Eastern NICs, high rates of economic growth were associated with high export-GDP ratios (Table 4.3). These differences cannot be explained by disparities in country size. Thus, while Brazil and Mexico have large economies, Korea's population and GDP are greater than Argentina's, and Taiwan's population and GDP are greater than Chile's.

TABLE 4.3   Export and Import Shares

	Export-GDP Ratio				Import-GDP Ratio			
	1963	1973	1981	1987	1963	1973	1981	1987
Hong Kong	NA	66.7	73.9	104.1	NA	74.4	83.9	104.1
Korea	2.3	24.2	30.8	39.0	14.6	31.2	37.9	33.8
Singapore	124.5	88.0	151.0	143.7	153.4	123.5	198.5	163.3
Taiwan	15.3	42.1	47.6	56.6	16.7	35.6	44.7	76.5
Argentina	10.1	8.4	7.3	18.5	7.2	5.7	7.6	17.0
Brazil	5.7	12.8	8.2	8.2	5.2	14.5	8.5	5.1
Chile	10.4	11.4	12.1	25.0	11.2	10.2	19.5	18.6[1]
Mexico	6.2	4.1	8.1	13.2	8.0	6.9	9.2	19.0[1]

[1]Latest figures are for 1986.
Sources: GDP and exchange rate data are from IMF, *International Financial Statistics*, various issues. Merchandise import and export figures are from IMF, *Direction of Trade Statistics*, various issues. All data for Taiwan from Council for Economic Planning and Development, Republic of China, *Taiwan Statistical Data Book*, 1988. All data for Hong Kong from DRI, ASIA data base.

In Korea and Taiwan, the export-GDP ratio increased greatly between 1963 and 1987, indicating the leading role of exports in the growth process. This was the case, to a lesser extent, in Hong Kong and Singapore that already had high export-GDP ratios at the beginning of the period. At any rate, the figures for these countries are greatly affected by entrepôt trade. The results are further affected by the importation of inputs for processing to export that raised the ratio for Singapore above 100 percent. (In any case, export values and value added as measured by GDP are not strictly comparable.)

Export-GDP ratios increased much less in the Latin American NICs than in Korea and Taiwan. They declined in Brazil. In Mexico's case, the oil finds raised the export-GDP ratio; in Chile, an even larger increase occurred as economic policy shifted after 1973 in an outward-oriented direction.

Export expansion in the Far Eastern NICs involved an increasing shift towards manufactured goods. In Korea, the share of manufactured goods in total exports rose from 45 percent in 1963 to 92 percent in 1987; in Taiwan, the corresponding figures were 38 and 92 percent.[1] Smaller changes occurred in Hong Kong, which already had a 92 percent manufactured export share in 1963, and in Singapore, where entrepôt trade in primary products is of importance.

The share of manufactured exports increased also in the Latin American NICS, but it remained much lower than in the Far Eastern NICs. The

TABLE 4.4   Per Capita Exports of Manufactured Goods (US$)

	1963	*1973*	*1981*	*1987*
Hong Kong	179.6	866.9	2,664.7	4,273.1
Korea	1.5	79.2	492.8	1,035.3
Singapore	175.0	730.0	4,139.0	7,243.0
Taiwan	10.8	237.7	1,110.8	2,456.8
Argentina	3.7	29.4	62.6	63.8
Brazil	0.5	12.2	73.4	86.6
Chile	2.6	4.7	25.5	31.6[1]
Mexico	3.7	19.6	28.5	120.4

[1]Data refer to 1986.
Source: United Nations, COMTRADE data base.

relevant shares for 1963 and 1987 (1986 for Chile) are: Argentina, 6 and 32 percent; Brazil, 3 and 47 percent; Chile, 4 and 8 percent; and Mexico, 17 and 46 percent.

Data on the share of manufactured exports are affected by the availability of natural resources, in particular, copper in Chile. At the same time, interest attaches to per capita manufactured exports that provide an indication of a country's success in these export products.

Table 4.4 shows the rapid expansion of manufactured exports in the Far Eastern NICs. These exports were negligible in Korea and Taiwan in 1963, but reached $1,035 per head in the first case and $2,456 per head in 1987. The rate of expansion was slower in Hong Kong and Singapore that started with a higher base (nearly $180 per head in both cases in 1963). But the absolute figures are much higher ($4,273 in Hong Kong and $7,243 in Singapore in 1987), although a portion of the total represents re-exports.

The per capita manufactured exports of the Latin American NICs are dwarfed by those of the East Asian NICs. In 1987, these exports hardly surpassed $120 per head in Mexico, $80 per head in Brazil, and $60 per head in Argentina; they were $32 per head in Chile in 1986.

The Policies Applied

The data show that, for the 1963-87 period as a whole, superior growth performance in the Far Eastern newly industrializing countries was associated with high domestic saving ratios and high levels of investment efficiency. At the same time, exports played an important role in the growth process, contributing to the efficient use of investment funds.

Apart from Hong Kong, all developing countries passed through the first stage of import substitution, involving the replacement by domestic production of the imports of nondurable consumer goods and their inputs. The manufacture of these products, including clothing and textiles, shoes and leather, and furniture and wood, conform to the production possibilities of the developing countries. They utilize in large part unskilled labor, involve the use of simple production processes, are not subject to important scale economies, and do not require the existence of a sophisticated industrial structure.

Once the first stage of import substitution has been completed, the rate of growth of industrial production cannot continue to exceed that of consumption without policy changes. Countries face two choices: embarking on the exportation of nondurable consumer goods and their inputs, or moving to the second stage of import substitution, replacing by domestic production the imports of producer and consumer durables and intermediate products.

Among present-day newly industrializing countries, the choice was made in the early 1960s for the first alternative in Korea, Singapore, and Taiwan. These countries also carried out financial reforms that permitted raising domestic saving ratios.

Negative real interest rates (nominal interest rates exceeded by the rate of inflation) led to financial repression in the Latin American NICs that was not conducive to increasing domestic saving and to their efficient allocation. Moreover, these countries shifted to the second stage of import substitution that proved costly to them because the commodities in question did not conform to the production possibilities of the countries concerned.

The manufacture of producer and consumer durables requires the existence of a sophisticated industrial structure to provide parts, components, and accessories made to precision. Also, such vertical specialization, as well as a horizontal or product specialization, need a large domestic market for manufactured goods.

Large domestic markets are also necessary for the production of intermediate goods, where traditional economies of scale obtain. Furthermore, the manufacture of producer and consumer durables relies to a considerable extent on skilled and technical labor, whereas intermediate products are highly capital intensive. At the same time, the margin of value added by the transformation of basic into intermediate products is often small and can be squandered through the poor organization of production.

The resulting high domestic costs reduced the efficiency of investment in countries pursuing a strategy of continued import substitution. In order to compensate for the higher costs, these countries also increased import protection, thereby discriminating against exports.

As the costs of continued import substitution became apparent, leading to declines in export expansion and economic growth, the three large Latin American NICs undertook reforms aimed at providing improved incentives to exports in the mid-1960s. The most far-reaching reforms were carried out in Brazil. Mexico's favorable balance-of-payments position, due to workers' remittances, tourism, and border industries, hampered the reform effort. In Argentina, the opposition of urban interests obstructed the course of economic reforms.

The reforms undertaken in the mid-1960s permitted reducing the bias of the incentive system against exports in Brazil, to a lesser extent in Mexico, and even less in Argentina. But not even Brazil had provided equal incentives to exports and import substitution, as was the case in the Far Eastern NICs. Finally, after initial efforts, reforms were jettisoned by the Allende government in Chile in the early 1970s.

Policies changed again following the oil crisis of 1973-74. The quadrupling of oil prices, together with the ensuing world recession, imposed a considerable cost on the economies of the newly industrializing countries. The cost of external shocks is measured as (1) the balance-of-payments effects of the deterioration of the terms of trade, and as (2) the export shortfall resulting from the slowdown of the world economy. The costs were largest in the East Asian NICs that were most exposed to foreign trade, as shown in Table 4.5.

Table 4.5 further shows the balance-of-payments effects of the policies applied in response to external shocks, including additional net external financing, export promotion, import substitution, and deflationary policies. Additional net external financing has been derived as the difference between actual financing and that estimated on the assumption that past trends in exports and imports would continue. The effects of export promotion have been calculated in terms of changes in export market shares. Import substitution has been defined as savings in imports associated with a decrease in the income elasticity of import demand compared with the preceding period. Finally, the effects on imports of changes in GNP growth rates in response to the macroeconomic policies followed have been estimated on the assumption of unchanged income elasticities of import demand.

The Far Eastern NICs accepted an initial decline in the growth rate of GNP in order to limit reliance on external financing. Subsequently, economic growth accelerated as the countries in question maintained their outward-oriented policies. At the same time, adopting realistic exchange rates helped not only exports but also import substitution. The chapter by Park in this volume provides a wealth of details about the policies pursued by Korea and Taiwan.

Among the Latin American NICs, Chile shifted to outward-oriented policies in response to the external shocks it suffered. These policies led to considerable gains in export market shares while reliance on external financing was reduced. In turn, Brazil and Mexico relied to a considerable

TABLE 4.5   External Shocks and Policy Responses to External Shocks

	External Shocks (% of GDP)	Additional Net External Financing	Export Promotion (% of External Shocks)	Import Substitution	Deflationary Policies
1974-78					
Hong Kong	NA	NA	NA	NA	NA
Korea	10.5	-88	90	128	-30
Singapore	20.9	42	11	-24	70
Taiwan	7.2	-92	14	96	82
Argentina	0.5	-168	-13	146	136
Brazil	3.3	30	15	66	-11
Chile	6.0	-48	71	18	60
Mexico	1.2	123	-70	33	14
1979-81					
Hong Kong	NA	NA	NA	NA	NA
Korea	9.4	-18	-7	8	116
Singapore	30.4	39	89	-59	31
Taiwan	13.1	-40	27	91	22
Argentina	1.2	423	-109	-281	67
Brazil	2.5	-33	38	49	47
Chile	3.9	257	50	-133	-74
Mexico	-0.5	309	412	-756	-64

Source: Author's computations, based on World Bank data.

extent on external borrowing in order to finance the adverse balance-of-payments effects of external shocks while, self-sufficient in petroleum, Argentina experienced practically no external shocks.

The three large Latin American NICs also increased the extent of inward-orientation of their incentive systems, thereby promoting the replacement of imports by domestic production. Only Brazil, which continued with the export subsidies introduced in the preceding period, made some modest gains in exports; Argentina and Mexico lost export market shares.

The effects of the policies followed in regard to foreign borrowing are presented in Table 4.6. It shows considerable increases in the external indebtedness of Brazil and Mexico between 1973 and 1978. By contrast, Korea and Singapore experienced a decline and Taiwan's external debt remained small.

Having found oil that led to rapid export expansion, the ratio of external debt to exports declined in Mexico after 1978. Brazil also reduced reliance

TABLE 4.6 External Debt Ratios (Gross)

Country	External Debt/Exports				Debt Service/Exports			
	1973	1978	1981	1987	1973	1978	1981	1987
Hong Kong	–	–	–	–	–	–	–	–
Korea	122	101	107	66	15	16	24	26
Singapore	18	13	10	15	9	8	8	7
Taiwan	–	–	–	–	–	–	–	–
Argentina	197	134	249	852	23	51	61	76
Brazil	209	368	279	420	33	59	60	82
Chile	266	253	234	382	42	60	91	57
Mexico	398	517	271	489	40	85	57	59

Sources: World Bank, *World Debt Tables;* IMF, *International Financial Statistics;* and *Balance of Payments Statistics,* various issues.

on external borrowing and adopted a mixture of policies to increase exports and import substitution, and to slow the economy. In turn, Argentina and Chile experienced a considerable capital inflow as a result of the overvaluation of the exchange rate aimed at reducing inflation.

After 1978, the Far Eastern NICs again accepted a slowdown in economic growth in order to limit reliance on foreign borrowing while maintaining their outward-oriented policies that led to the subsequent acceleration of economic growth. Only Korea engaged in foreign borrowing but its debt-export ratio hardly changed. The results of alternative policies are apparent in the debt situations of the NICs on the eve of the debt crisis. While in Korea the debt-export ratio was 1.1 in 1981, this ratio reached 3.3 in Chile, 2.8 in Brazil, 2.7 in Mexico, and 2.5 in Argentina. Also, debt service ratios ranged between 90 percent (Chile) and 56 percent (Mexico) in the Latin American NICs, compared with 24 percent in Korea. These high ratios necessitated corrective action on the part of the Latin American NICS, leading to a decline in their per capita incomes after 1981. By contrast, growth continued in the Far Eastern NICs, where Singapore and Taiwan accumulated a net asset position abroad.

Conclusions

This essay has reviewed economic developments in the Far Eastern and Latin American newly industrializing countries. The results show that in the 1963-87 period, the Far Eastern NICs attained much larger increases in per capita incomes than their Latin American counterparts.

Differences in economic growth rates find their origin in differences in savings ratios and investment efficiency. While savings ratios differed little between the two groups of countries between 1963-73, in subsequent years these ratios increased substantially in the Far Eastern NICs as they employed measures encouraging savings.

Investment efficiency was higher in the Far Eastern NICs than in the Latin American NICs throughout the period. The Far Eastern NICs achieved high levels of investment efficiency in the framework of an export-oriented economy, with high and rising ratios of exports to the gross domestic product. Export expansion involved an increasing shift towards manufactured goods. Exports in the Far Eastern NICs were promoted by the system of incentives that entailed no discrimination, or limited discrimination, against exports (as detailed in several subsequent chapters). Countries also relied to a considerable extent on export promotion in response to external shocks and did not engage in excessive foreign borrowing.

The favorable external-debt situations of the Far Eastern NICs also augur well for their future economic growth. Korea's external debt ratio declined to 0.7 in 1987 and it had a large trade surplus in 1988 when Taiwan and Singapore also increased their surpluses. In turn, the external debt ratio reached 8.5 in Argentina, 4.9 in Mexico, 4.2 in Brazil, and 3.8 in Chile in 1987.

The experience of the Far Eastern and Latin American NICs provides important lessons to other developing countries. It indicates the superiority of outward-oriented policies that provide similar incentives to exports and import substitution. It also shows that the continuation of outward-oriented policies permits overcoming the effects of external shocks, whereas reliance on external borrowing reinforces their adverse effects. That some of the Latin American countries are beginning to take this lesson to heart is suggested, for example, by the policy changes that Mexico began in recent years, the details of which can be found in Chapter 11 by Rhodes.

Countries that have accumulated large external debts should adopt outward-oriented policies that provide impetus to economic growth through increased exports while improving the balance of payments. Such policies involve the simultaneous promotion of exports and liberalization of imports.

These conclusions have important implications for Hungary and for the other Central and East European economies in transition. They call for the reform of the incentive system, increasing incentives to exports and reducing incentives to import substitution. They also suggest the promotion of savings and investment. But all these countries will have to take additional measures to transform their economic systems. They need to privatize public enterprises and to liberalize existing regulations. Of particular importance is the need to liberalize prices, imports, and foreign exchange. In this way, Hungary and the other countries can transform themselves into market economies characterized by outward orientation.

Notes

1. Computed on the basis of UN, *Commodity Trade Statistics*, various issues.

5

Foreign Trade Strategies of Nations: A New Interpretation

Neng Liang, Paul Marer, and Joseph Battat

Conventional Classification of Trade Strategies and Its Limitations

In the literature on trade strategies, export promotion (EP) and import substitution (IS) are usually depicted as polar opposites. Yet the two are not necessarily mutually exclusive. EP and IS can, and indeed have been found to coexist.[1] Some of the export-oriented East Asian countries, namely South Korea and Taiwan, are well-known for employing selective IS measures in their development.[2] However, previous research on alternative trade strategies has paid insufficient attention to the nature of such coexistence. The success stories of the mentioned East Asian countries are often interpreted almost exclusively in terms of the merits of their EP strategies.

The reason for this is that, conventionally, trade strategy has been defined in a bipolar spectrum, with inward-orientation at one end and outward-orientation at the other end. The ratio of "incentives to exports" to that of "incentives to import substitution" is conventionally used as a basis for classifying a country's trade strategy as outward oriented or inward oriented, respectively.[3] If more incentives are provided for import substitution, the strategy is IS, or inward oriented; otherwise, the strategy is EP, or outward oriented. This bipolar classification is based on a common view that incentives for the exportable-goods and importable-goods sectors are negatively correlated. That is, import protection leads to a anti-export bias and export promotion requires a liberal import policy.

Though useful in isolating the polar cases of "pure" EP and IS, the bipolar classification of trade strategies has several limitations. The most important is its inability to distinguish, in terms of conceptualizations as well as measurement, between strategies that are neither pure EP nor pure IS. This and other limitations of the conventional classification have recently come to the attention of researchers.[4]

The emerging theory of "strategic trade policy" has provided supporting arguments why a country may employ IS and EP strategies simultaneously.[5] But, to our knowledge, no alternative classification cum empirical verification has yet been proposed. To do this is the purpose of this chapter.

Proposed New Typology of Trade Strategies

Underlying the bipolar classification of trade strategies is the standard two-sector trade model, in which one sector produces exportable goods, the other importables. Bhagwati used such a model to define alternative trade strategies.[6] In such a two-sector model, EP and IS are necessarily mutually exclusive. If importable-goods production increases, exportable-goods production will have to decrease, and vice versa.

To accommodate those cases where EP and IS are both present or absent, we extend the Bhagwati model into a three-sector one: the importable, the exportable, and the non-tradeable sectors. By varying the amount of non-tradeable goods production, a country can shift its tradeable-goods production into or away from both exportable and importable goods. This simple extension leads to the logical conclusion that protection of the importable-goods sector and promotion of the exportable-goods sector are not mutually exclusive. A trade strategy may provide a high level of protection for the importable sector and strong incentives for export promotion, at the expense of the nontradeable-goods sector. Further, it is also possible to place disincentives on both exports and import substitutes, and thereby favor the nontradeable-goods sector.

The relationship between EP-IS (dis)incentives and trade strategies in our proposed new typology is illustrated in Figure 5.1. The horizontal axis represents the policy incentives (+) or disincentives (-) for IS activities. The vertical axis represents the incentives (+) and disincentives (-) to exports. At the center point "E," the two incentives are neither positive nor negative. The new typology is thus bi-dimensional.

Each quadrant, plus their intersection point at "E", represents a distinct combination of IS-EP incentives/disincentives and corresponding trade strategies. A "pure" EP strategy is represented by quadrant 1. The protection for export activities is positive while the protection for IS activities is negative (that is, there is a bias against the domestic production of import substitutes). Exports are promoted and imports are favored over the domestic production of importable goods. This represents a combination of positive export incentives and a liberal import policy. A "pure" IS strategy is represented by quadrant 4. Import substitution receives a positive incentive while exports face a disincentive. A "free trade" strategy is represented by the center point "E," where neither export nor import substitution activities receive any incentives or disincentives.

The proposed classification scheme allows the introduction of two

FIGURE 5.1   Relationship Between Trade Incentives and Trade Strategies

IS Activities

		Disincentives (-)	Incentives (+)
EP Activities	Incentives (+)	**1** Export Promotion (EP)	**2** Protected Export Promotion (PEP)
	Disincentives (-)	**3** De Facto Import Promotion (DIP)	**4** Import Substitution (IS)

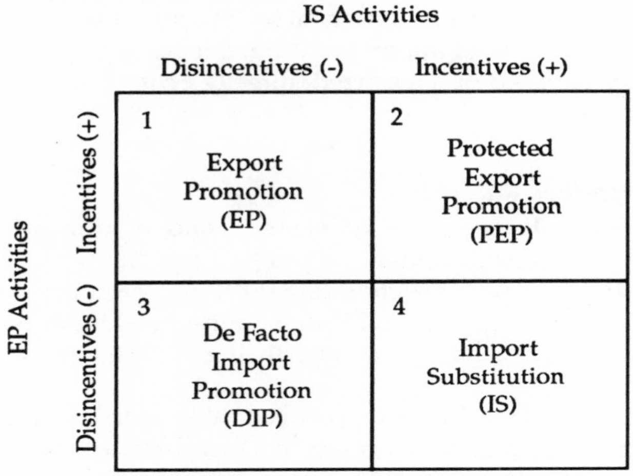

additional situations that are important in real life but are generally not recognized in the literature. One such situation is depicted in quadrant 2. It shows the co-existence of incentives for both import substitution as well as export promotion. We call this a "protected export promotion" (PEP) trade strategy. PEP is an outward-oriented strategy, based on the "infant-exporter" type argument. Its essence is promoting import substitution for the sake of developing new exports. The other such situation is that shown in quadrant 3. It depicts a bias against EP as well as a bias against IS, generating pressures for soaring imports while constraining exports. We call this a "de facto import promotion" (DIP) strategy.

DIP is a domestic-market-expansion-led strategy of growth. It minimizes exports and maximizes imports, intentionally or unintentionally, in order to provide the needed resources and incentives for domestic investment and consumption. We term this a "de facto" strategy because most DIP regimes come into existence not as purposeful trade strategies but as the unintended outcomes of other economic policies. Examples of countries pursuing each of these strategies will be given later, after a discussion of the measurement of incentives, disincentives and trade strategies.

Measuring Trade Incentives and Disincentives

Measurement of Incentives and Disincentives

A trade strategy is implemented primarily through various incentives and disincentives that affect resource allocation among sectors and economic activities. Incentives include protection measures (tariff and nontariff measures), credits, and tax preferences. Imports are affected by tariff-type measures, such as ad valorem tariffs, specific duties, import taxes and subsidies; advance deposit requirement for imports; as well as quantitative restrictions in the form of import licensing, quotas, or import prohibition. Exports may be taxed or subsidized, directly or indirectly, via multiple exchange rates.

Effective Protection Rate (EPR)

To be quantifiable, the various incentives/disincentives must be expressed in terms of their effect on the domestic prices of inputs as well as output. The concept of the effective protection rate (EPR) has been developed in the literature to capture the joint incidence of output and input protection on processing activities and to examine their effects on the allocation of resources.[7]

EPR is defined as the difference between value added in domestic prices (VAD) after the application of protective measures, and value added in world prices (VAW), expressed as a percentage of the latter. Value added is the difference between the price of a product and the cost of its intermediate inputs.

$$\text{EPR \%} = \frac{\text{VAD - VAW}}{\text{VAW}} \times 100$$

EPR_m is the effective protection rate on import-substitution activities. It indicates the extent an import-substituting producer is protected from import competition.[8] EPR_x is the effective protection rate on export activities. It indicates to what extent an exporter is subsidized or taxed.

Effective Subsidy Rate (ESR)

Effective Subsidy Rate (ESR) is an extended version of EPR. It is defined as the percentage excess of domestic value added, adjusted for credit and tax preferences, over world market value added. It thus quantifies not only the effect of protective measures, but also credit and tax preferences.

Net Effective Subsidy Rate (NESR)

The above calculation of EPRs and ESRs is conducted in local currency. To bring such calculation to a common denominator, world prices are converted to local currency at the prevailing exchange rate. Thus, if the exchange rate is significantly over- or under-valued, that will have an impact on the measured EPRs and ESRs. NEPR (NESR) is calculated by adjusting the EPR (ESR) for the extent of currency over- or under-valuation.[9]

NESR above (below) zero will then indicate that an activity is favored (disfavored) by both the trade protective and credit and tax measures relative to the free-trade situation.[10] The above concepts and incentive measures have been well developed and are commonly used in the literature.[11]

Conventional Measurement of Trade Strategy

Trade strategy is conventionally measured by a country's "orientation ratio."[12] It is defined as the ratio of average EPR_m to average EPR_x.

$$\text{Orientation ratio} = \frac{\text{Incentives to IS activities}}{\text{Incentives to EP activities}} = \frac{1 + \text{Average EPR}_m}{1 + \text{Average EPR}_x}$$

A ratio equal to one suggests that the incentive to sell on the domestic market is the same as the incentive to export. Trade orientation is thus "neutral," and the strategy is said to be one of EP, and thus outward oriented.[13] If the ratio is greater than 1, so the incentive to sell on the domestic market is greater than the incentive to export, then the strategy is "inward-oriented," or biased toward IS.

The following examples reveal the shortcomings of this "orientation ratio" measurement of trade strategy. If a country subsidizes its export activities (say, $EPR_x = 30\%$) while protecting its IS activities (say, $EPR_m = 30\%$), its orientation ratio will be:

$$\frac{1 + 30\%}{1 + 30\%} = \frac{1.3}{1.3} = 1$$

Conversely, if a country discourages export activities (say, $EPR_x = -30\%$), and encourages imports ($EPR_m = -30\%$), the orientation ratio will again show it to have a "neutral" policy:

$$\frac{1 + (-30\%)}{1 + (-30\%)} = \frac{0.7}{0.7} = 1$$

Although neither of the above cases truly fits the definition of an EP strategy, both will appear as EP, according to the conventional measurement, together with situations that are truly close to that of free trade.

Proposed Measurement of Strategies for the New Typology

The measurement of the new typology is depicted in Figure 5.2. The horizontal axis indicates the net effective subsidy rate for IS activities; the vertical axis, the net effective subsidy rate for export activities. Each quadrant, together with the center point E depicting "free trade," thus defines an

FIGURE 5.2   Two-Dimensional Measures of Trade Strategies

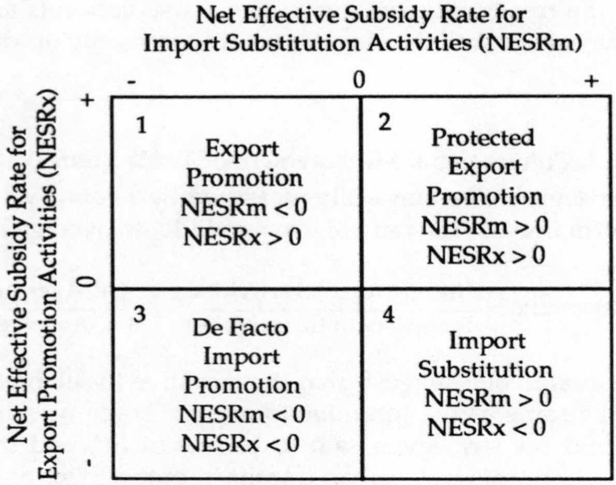

Net Effective Subsidy Rate for
Import Substitution Activities (NESRm)

	-	0	+
+	**1** Export Promotion $NESRm < 0$ $NESRx > 0$	**2** Protected Export Promotion $NESRm > 0$ $NESRx > 0$	
0			
-	**3** De Facto Import Promotion $NESRm < 0$ $NESRx < 0$	**4** Import Substitution $NESRm > 0$ $NESRx < 0$	

Net Effective Subsidy Rate for
Export Promotion Activities (NESRx)

incentive/disincentive combination for a corresponding trade strategy as specified by the label in the quadrant. For example, if a country's incentives for both IS and EP activities are positive and therefore fall into quadrant two, the country is considered as following a PEP strategy.

The Sample and Data

The Sample

Over the last four decades, numerous country studies have been undertaken. Among the major ones are the World Bank and Inter-American Development Bank project,[14] covering Brazil, Chile, Mexico, West Malaysia, Pakistan, Philippines, and Norway; the NBER project,[15] covering Brazil, Chile, Colombia, Egypt, Ghana, India, Israel, Philippines, South Korea, and Turkey; and the World Bank project,[16] covering Argentina, Colombia, Israel, Singapore, South Korea, and Taiwan. From among these studies, the countries sample in the World Bank project is chosen for our research, because this sample includes three of the four famous "strongly outward oriented" East Asian NICs (Singapore, South Korea and Taiwan), and one of the best-known "strongly inward-oriented" case—Argentina. This sample also includes two in-between cases: Colombia and Israel. Therefore, this small group of countries provides a relatively complete coverage of each trade-orientation category.

Further reason to choose this sample is that in the Balassa project where the "orientation ratio" measurement of trade strategy was proposed and applied, the same countries were covered, and the measurement results were later used in the *World Development Report 1987*, in which the East Asian countries' strategy was given the controversial "neutrality" assessment.

The Data

The empirical data of incentives and disincentives for the six countries (EPR$_m$ and EPR$_x$ for the conventional system; NESR$_m$, NESR$_x$ for the proposed system, at both national and sectoral level) are taken from the World Bank study. The data were collected by a research team led by Balassa in 1969.[17] For South Korea only a follow-up study was undertaken using the same Balassa measurement in 1978.[18] Therefore, except for South Korea, this study will not allow drawing any dynamic inference. The data collected by the Balassa team and subsequently by Nam are used in several World Bank studies, including the World Bank's *World Development Report 1987*.

Our essay relies on the existing country studies for empirical data of nations' incentive structures, not only because of resource constraints, but also because of methodological considerations. To validate the new typology and juxtapose the results with those obtained under the conventional classification, it is desirable to use the same data set to eliminate the error possibility that may arise from using a different data set. With the same data set being applied to two alternative frameworks, whatever difference that may be revealed is attributable to the difference between the two typologies.

Empirical Findings

Results Based on the Conventional Classification

Figure 5.3 depicts the trade strategies of Argentina, Colombia, Israel, Singapore, South Korea and Taiwan, using the conventional "orientation ratio" measurement. The "orientation ratios" of South Korea (1968 and 1978), Taiwan (1969), and Singapore (1968) all have the same value of 1.1. These results suggest that the three countries had followed identical or at least very similar strategies. Yet it is well documented that their trade strategies had differed significantly. South Korea was well known for its highly restrictive import policies;[19] Taiwan was moving toward a free trade position faster than South Korea,[20] and Singapore reportedly followed a free trade strategy.[21]

Furthermore, it is well documented that, from 1968 to 1978, South Korea was returning to a "second stage IS" strategy, and increased its protectionist measures substantially.[22] But its orientation ratio had remained the same

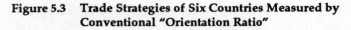

Figure 5.3   Trade Strategies of Six Countries Measured by
              Conventional "Orientation Ratio"

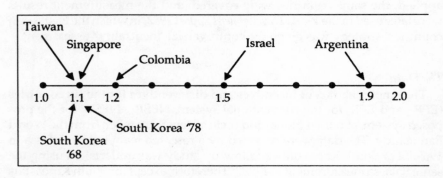

(1.1), implying that no major policy change had taken place. Colombia in 1968, on the other hand, was turning "outward" and made major policy changes to liberalize its trade.[23] Its import policy was actually much less protectionist than that of South Korea (as will be revealed by our result), but the orientation ratio gives Colombia a more "inward-oriented" rating (1.2) than South Korea (1.1).

Thus, the conventional classification and measurement do not capture important differences among the trade strategies pursued by the different countries.

Results Based on the New Classification: Overall Strategies

Figure 5.4 presents the empirical results for the six countries based on the proposed typology. The horizontal axis measures incentives/disincentives for IS activities, using $NESR_m$; the vertical axis, incentives/disincentives for EP activities, using $NESR_x$. A "PEP" strategy is indicated, when a country's measured NESRs for EP and IS activities fall within the upper right quadrant. South Korea in 1978 is a case in point. It had a NESR of 18% for EP activities and 30% for IS activities, placing it into this category.

If the coordinates place a country into the lower left quadrant, with negative incentives for both EP and IS, that represents a "DIP" strategy. Colombia places into this category, with a -23% NESR for EP activities (disincentive to export) and -14% NESR for IS activities (incentives to import).

Contrary to the result based on the conventional measurement, which gives Colombia (1969), Singapore (1967) and South Korea (1978) almost identical orientation ratios, the proposed new classification captures the

FIGURE 5.4   Overall Strategies of Six Countries (Based on the New Typology)

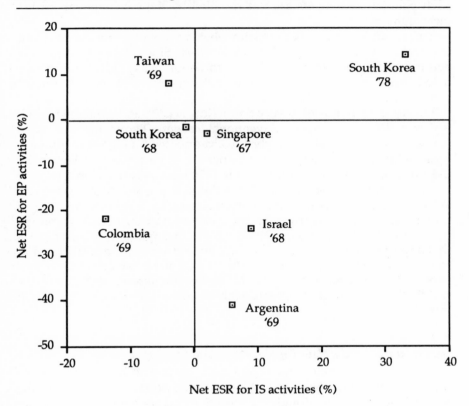

significant policy differences among the three countries, and indicates that they had pursued quite different strategies (DIP, FT, and PEP respectively).[24] South Korea (1978) ranked highest on both IS and EP incentives. We are thus able to show empirically its "dual policy," which others have noted simply by verbal statements, namely, that it simultaneously pursued EP and IS strategies.[25] For Colombia in 1969 the results show that while trade liberalization had reduced IS incentives to a negative level, it could not bring up EP incentives to a positive level. Hence, the country is identified with a DIP strategy. Singapore, just off the center point, is very close to a free trade regime, corresponding to a fact that many observers have noted.

We note, further, that the policy shift of South Korea between 1968 and 1978 is captured by our classification while it is missed by the conventional one, which shows the same orientation ratio of 1.1 for both periods. The new typology and its measurement, on the other hand, indicate a significant movement toward IS, combined with a sizable increase of EP incentives. Such parallel movements are not revealed by the conventional "ratio" measurement.

This result is more consistent with what is generally understood about the evolution of South Korea's trade strategy. Since the early 1970s, the South Korean government has been promoting heavy industries, designated them as so-called strategic industries, giving them both import protection and export incentives.[26]

Finally, the difference between South Korea (1978) and Argentina (1968) is noteworthy. Based on the conventional measure (Figure 5.3), Argentina was a country labeled "strongly inward-oriented," and South Korea a country labeled "strongly outward-oriented."[27] Our result in Figure 5.4 indicates, however, that South Korea in 1978 is actually more protectionist than Argentina in 1968 (NESR$_m$ 32% in South Korea vs. 6% in Argentina). What distinguishes South Korea from Argentina is not the absence of import substitution incentives, but the presence of strong export promotion measures (NESR$_x$ 14% in South Korea vs. -41% in Argentina). This indicates that import protection does not necessarily lead to an anti-export bias, and import liberalization may not be "the most direct means" to promote export, as was suggested by the *World Development Report 1987*.[28] Rather, the real challenge facing governments might be how to provide effective export incentives.

Results Based on the New Typology: Sectoral Strategies

The preceding section measured trade strategies based on average incentives at the national level. This section extends the analysis to the sectoral level (Figures 5.5 and 5.6). Incentive data for ten major sectors are employed to identify sectoral strategies. Each data point in Figures 5.5 and 5.6 in this section represents the IS/EP incentives for a particular sector. Sectors are numbered as follows:

1. Agriculture
2. Processed Food
3. Beverages and Tobacco
4. Mining
5. Construction Materials
6a. Intermediate Products 1
6b. Intermediate Products 2
7. Nondurable Consumer Goods
8. Durable Consumer Goods
9. Machinery
10. Transport Equipment

Contrasting South Korea 1968 and 1978

Panels A and B in Figure 5.5 represent South Korea's sectoral strategies in 1968 and 1978, respectively. In 1968, there was no sector following a PEP strategy. In 1978, however, seven out of eleven sectors moved into the PEP quadrant. At the same time, the number of sectors in the EP quadrant increased from three to four.

A notable change of the two periods happened in sectors 8 and 10, consumer durable goods and transport equipment, respectively. Both sectors were in the IS quadrant in 1968, and enjoyed the highest rate of protection among all sectors. In 1978, import protection in both sectors increased sharply: from $NESR_m$ 20% to 134% for the consumer durable goods sector, and from 119% to 139% for the transport equipment sector.

Contrary to the effect of import protection in many other countries, import protection did not seem to prevent these sectors from developing international competitiveness. South Korea is ranked among the top ten most competitive countries in both sectors in an United Nations Industrial Development Organization study (UNIDO 1986), with all major industrial countries included. Part of the reason for the two sectors' success might be that while they were given the highest import protection in that period, the incentives for them to export also increased significantly. From 1968 to 1978, export incentives ($NESR_x$) increased from -95% to 26% for transport equipment, and from -10% to 38% for the consumer durable goods sector. One plausible explanation for their success is that when sectors are oriented toward the international market, as are indicated by the positive export incentives, import protection actually helps these sectors to achieve international competitiveness.

Contrasting South Korea (1978) and Argentina

Panels A and B in Figure 5.6 depict the sectoral strategies of South Korea (1978) and Argentina (1969). Seven out of eleven sectors in Argentina fall in the IS quadrant, with strong import protection and substantial disincentives to export; the rest of the four sectors fall in the DIP quadrant. The striking feature of Argentina's sectoral strategy portfolio is that, protected from imports or not, every sector in Argentina faced an anti-export bias (disincentives to export). The South Korean portfolio is just the opposite. Most of its sectors enjoyed no less, or even more, protection than their counterparts in Argentina, but none of them suffered from disincentives to export. Every sector in South Korea (1978) had positive export incentives, irrespective of whether or not it had import protection.

This simple comparison of sectoral strategies between South Korea and Argentina suggests that what distinguishes the "outward-oriented" strat-

FIGURE 5.5   Sectoral Strategies: South Korea, 1968 and 1978

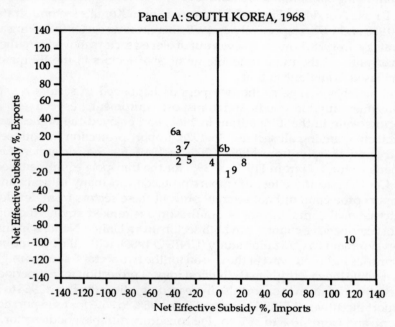

Panel A: SOUTH KOREA, 1968

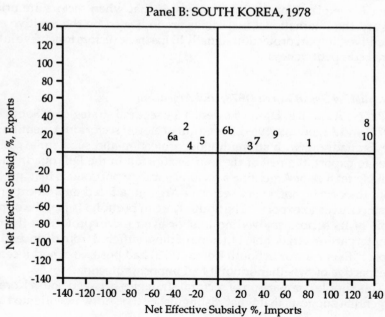

Panel B: SOUTH KOREA, 1978

FIGURE 5.6   Sectoral Strategies: South Korea (1978) and Argentina (1969)

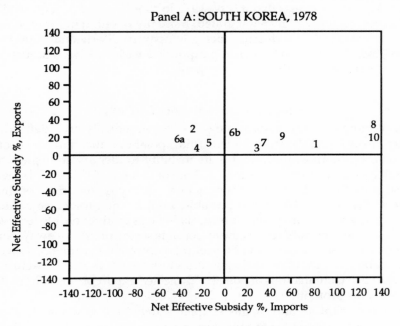

Panel A: SOUTH KOREA, 1978

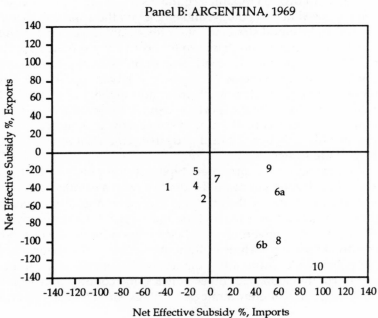

Panel B: ARGENTINA, 1969

egy of South Korea from the "inward-oriented" strategy of Argentina is not the *absence* of import protection but the *presence* of export incentives. The South Korea case attests that it is possible to coordinate import protection and export incentives in an integrated, mutually re-enforcing way so that the selected strategic industries facing temporary disadvantage are protected, but exports from the existing export industries are not discouraged and the gains from trade are not foregone.

Summary and Relevance for CPEs

A country's foreign trade strategy has conventionally been defined as either inward- or outward-oriented. This bipolar classification has several limitations; the most important is its inability to identify strategies that represent a combination of IS and EP. The coexistence of IS and EP is made possible by the fact that the economy of a country is comprised of three sectors: the importable, the exportable, and the non-tradeable sectors. Therefore, a country may shift its tradeable-goods production into (or away from) *just* the exportable or *just* the importable sector, or into (or away from) *both* of them simultaneously. Hence, the protection (promotion) of the importable- and the exportable-goods sectors are not mutually exclusive. We call such combinations of policies "protected export promotion" or "de facto import promotion."

The empirical section of this chapter showed the kinds of data and computations needed to pinpoint a country's trade strategy in accordance with the proposed new typology, and employed the approach to identify the national and sectoral strategies of six important developing countries. Some of the East Asian countries are found to have pursued an "infant exporter"-based, "protected export promotion" strategy rather than, as commonly perceived, a static "comparative advantage"-based "export promotion" strategy. Their import protection measures are found to be integrated elements of their export strategy, not just isolated exceptions. These empirical results are plausible because they are consistent with the findings of other, though more descriptive, empirical studies of those countries' trade strategies.

An implication of the proposed typology for policy is that it calls attention to the fact that to correctly identify what a country is doing, one needs to consider not only the impact of incentives and disincentives that apply directly to its tradeable sectors, but to also take into account the overall impact of all government policies that—advertently or inadvertently—affect all sectors, including the nontradeable goods sector. Focusing only on policies *intended* to affect the tradeable-goods sector can be misleading; in combination with other policies, the country may *de facto* be pursuing altogether different strategies on its exportables and importables.

We believe that the (-,-) incentives structure of DIP characterizes the trade incentives of the traditional as well as reformed CPEs, which have an insatiable "import hunger" and systemic bias against exports, as elaborated in the contributions in this volume by Gács as well as Obláth. This is, among other reasons, because firms have a "soft" budget constraint, an ever-present "expansion drive," and face chronic shortages on their home markets.[29]

In the case of CPEs, or even reformed socialist countries like Hungary, however, their trade strategies cannot be measured empirically via the method we recommend in this chapter because their administrative incentives and disincentives to trade are generally not reflected and cannot be readily converted into price effects.

As more and more countries learn that extreme protection harms more than helps the economy in the long run, but remain convinced that there are indeed "strategic sectors" in the economy that a country should protect and promote, the search is intensifying for national strategies that will enable a nation to enjoy the gains from trade as well as to enable it to secure a fair share in the important "strategic sectors" of the world economy. The conceptual framework and approach to measurement proposed in this paper should be helpful in this endeavour.

Notes

1. Anne O. Krueger, "Export-Led Growth Reconsidered," in Wontack Hong and Lawrence B. Krause, eds., *Trade and Growth of the Advanced Developing Countries in the Pacific Basin* (Seoul: Korea Development Institute, 1981).

2. Howard Pack and Larry E. Westphal, "Industrial Strategy and Technological Change," *Journal of Development Economics*, Vol. 22, 1986.

3. Bela Balassa and Associates, *Development Strategies in Semi-Industrial Economies* (World Bank, 1982); World Bank, *World Development Report 1987* (Oxford University Press, 1987).

4. George N. Yannopoulos, "Trade Policy Options in the Design of Development Strategies," *Discussion Papers in Economics*, Series A, No. 181, University of Reading, England, November 1986; Ronald Findlay, "Comment" (on Haberle's 'Liberal and Illiberal Development Policy'), in Gerald M. Meier, ed., *Pioneers in Development*, Second Series (Oxford University Press, 1987); Paul Marer, "Comparing the Foreign Economic Strategies of Market and Centrally Planned Economies," in Christopher T. Saunders, ed., *Macroeconomic Management and Enterprise in East and West* (London: Macmillan Press, 1988); and Neng Liang, "Beyond Import Substitution and Export Promotion: A New Typology of Trade Strategies with Empirical Verification and Policy Analysis," unpublished Ph.D dissertation, Indiana University, Bloomington, Indiana, 1990.

5. Paul R. Krugman, "Import Protection as Export Promotion," in H. Kierzkowski, ed., *Monopolistic Competition and International Trade* (Oxford: Oxford University Press, 1984).

6. Jagdish N. Bhagwati, "Export-Promoting Trade Strategy: Issues and Evidence," *The World Bank Research Observer*, January 1988.

7. Balassa and Associates, *op. cit.*

8. To illustrate, assume that automobile components cost $5,000 per unit at world prices and are levied a tariff at 20%, with a total cost of $6,000 per unit for the domestic producer. Assume, further, that a finished automobile sells for $8,000 on the world market and can be imported with a 50% tariff, so that the domestic price is $12,000.

For this manufacturer, value added in domestic prices is:

($8,000 x 150%) - ($5,000 x 120%) = $12,000 - $6,000 = $ 6,000.

Value added at world prices is:

$8,000 - $5,000 = $ 3,000

In this case, the effective protection rate for this auto maker is:

EPR_m = [($ 6,000 - $ 3,000) / $ 3,000] x 100% = 100%

9. The Balassa study used a balance of payments concept to estimate the hypothetical free-trade exchange rate, which involves two steps. The first step is the estimation of the decrease of exports and increase of imports that would result from the elimination of protection and subsidies; the second step is to estimate the extent of devaluation that would then be necessary to eliminate the deficit in the balance of payments. The resulting free-trade exchange rate is then used to derive NEPR. (For the equation systems used in the calculation, see Balassa and Associates, *op. cit.*, p. 354.)

10. *Ibid.*, p. 16.

11. See, for example, World Bank, *op. cit.*; Balassa and Associates, *op. cit.*; and W. M. Corden, "The Structure of a Tariff System and the Effective Protection Rate," *Journal of Political Economy*, Vol. 74, June 1966.

12. Balassa and Associates, *op. cit.*, p. 38.

13. A ratio less than one is also considered "outward-oriented" and is termed an "ultra-EP" strategy by Bhagwati, *op. cit.*

14. Bela Balassa, et al., *The Structure of Protection in Developing Countries* (Johns Hopkins University Press, 1971).

15. Bhagwati, *op. cit.*; Krueger, *op. cit.*

16. Balassa and Associates, *op. cit.*

17. For some countries, the data are for 1968 or 1967. For the details of data collection procedure and the calculations of EPRs and NESR, see Balassa and Associates, *op. cit.*, Chapter 1.

18. Chong Hyun Nam, "Trade, Industrial Policies, and the Structure of Protection in Korea," in Hong and Krause, *op. cit.*

19. Pack and Westphal, *op. cit.*

20. Kuo-Shu Liang and Ching-ing Hou Liang, "Trade Strategy and Exchange Rate Policies in Taiwan," in Hong and Krause, *op. cit.*

21. Lawrence B. Krause, "Summary," in Hong and Krause, *op. cit.*

22. Nam, *op. cit.*

23. Thomas L. Hutcheson and Daniel M. Schydlowsky, "Colombia," in Balassa and Associates, *op. cit.*

24. They all had an orientation ratio of 1.1 if NESRs were used. When EPRs were used, Colombia showed a orientation ratio of 1.2 while the ratio for South Korea

(1978) and Singapore (1967) remained unchanged at 1.1. See Appendix B for the ratios.

25. Pack and Westphal, *op. cit.*

26. Nam *op. cit.*; Pack and Westphal, *op. cit.*

27. World Bank, *op. cit.*

28. World Bank, *op. cit.*, p. 80.

29. János Kornai, *Contradictions and Dilemmas: Studies on the Socialist Economy and Society* (Cambridge, Mass.: MIT Press, 1986).

6

Liberalization and Foreign Direct Investment

András Inotai

In the last decade, an increasing number of medium- and less-developed countries became significant exporters of manufactured goods (including skill- and technology-intensive goods), improved the overall efficiency of their economies, enhanced growth and investment and acquired modern technology and management. In large measure, these achievements were closely related to the substantial and rapidly increasing inflow of foreign direct investment (FDI). Many countries, including the reform-minded East-Central European economies and the Soviet Union, also began to attract FDI in order to enhance export earnings and improve their balance of trade and payments. Competition on commodity markets has been complemented by competition to attract FDI. In some countries, liberalization of FDI rules was accompanied by far-reaching trade and factor-market liberalization; in others, more generous treatment of FDI and the opening of other fields of the economy were not pursued simultaneously.

This survey is divided into five sections. The first section summarizes the main trends in the relationship between commodity exports by and FDI in host countries. The second section deals with foreign trade regulations affecting the behavior of FDI. The third section elaborates aims and the implications of the general economic policies of host countries on the patterns of FDI. The fourth section points to the role of economic diplomacy in enhancing the efficiency of FDI activities in host economies. The final section formulates some concluding remarks and draws lessons for the East-Central European countries.

This essay should not be interpreted as necessarily reflecting the views of the World Bank.

Impact of FDI on Export Performance

Several surveys indicate a positive correlation between the inflow of FDI and the export performance of the host countries. A study based on the experiences of 23 developing countries concludes that, on the average, every dollar of FDI resulted in two dollars of additional exports. The more open the general economic policy of a host country, the higher is the contribution of FDI to exports.[1] In Singapore, 84 percent of total commodity exports are due to FDI. The amount of exports directly connected to FDI in Taiwan or the Republic of Korea is 18 to 25 percent; in Ireland, about 32 percent; in Portugal, about 40 percent. The rapidly increasing commodity exports (basically of non-traditional goods) of many other medium- and less-developed economies during the last decade are also connected with FDI. In most cases, FDI contributed to increased exports to a larger extent than did other factors. This is clearly indicated in the growing share of FDI-related exports in the total exports of the developing and OECD countries.

The above average dynamism of exports connected with FDI is based on FDI's key role in manufactured goods exports. For countries at a medium level of development, sectors such as mining, agriculture or raw material and unskilled-labor-intensive manufacturing require much less foreign investment per unit of output in order to become competitive on international markets than does technology- and skill-intensive production and exports to oligopolistic markets. [2] In the 1980s, this linkage became even stronger. Machinery, electronic equipment, optical, measuring and scientific instruments, pharmaceutical products, computers, and most of the sophisticated components and spare parts can become competitive and thus marketable in international trade in most cases only if special production and marketing conditions are observed. The requirements generally cannot be met without the active contribution of FDI. The experience of successful exporters indicates that the more sophisticated and technology-intensive a product, the higher is the share of foreign direct capital in total exports of the given product. In the Republic of Korea during the 1970s, FDI generated 31 percent of total manufacturing exports, 57 percent of chemical, 89 percent of electrical machinery, and 93 percent of non-electrical machinery exports, but only 12 percent to total textile exports and 9 percent to total processed-food exports.[3] In Mexico, national companies overwhelmingly exported non-durable consumer goods and labor-intensive products, while foreign companies concentrated on the exports of durable consumer goods and machinery. Labor-intensive goods accounted for 40 percent and machinery products for only 14 percent of total manufacturing exports of national companies. By contrast, manufacturing exports of foreign-owned companies were dominated by machinery products (56 percent), with labor-intensive goods lagging substantially behind (11 percent). [4]

The industrial pattern of FDI is greatly influenced by the development level of the host economy. In less-developed countries and at an early stage of industrial development, where traditional activities dominate, even the export of raw materials and low-skill-intensive products is hardly possible without the active contribution of FDI.

The export-orientedness of FDI correlates positively with ownership. The production of technology-intensive goods generally requires a higher, in most cases predominant or exclusive, participation of foreign direct capital. Countries that, for different reasons, imposed substantial limitations on the share of FDI in joint ventures either did not attract foreign capital, or foreign investments became directed predominantly to the domestic market. In the open or opening economies, the wholly- or majority-owned foreign companies sold most of their production on the international market, while minority ventures usually gave preference to the domestic market.[5] A survey of the behavior of West German companies in Southeast Asia shows that wholly- or majority-owned West German companies planned to export 50 to 100 percent of their local production of electronic goods and machinery, while minority-owned companies producing cars were overwhelmingly (77 percent) domestic-market-oriented. In Singapore, already in the 1970s, wholly-owned foreign companies exported more than two-thirds of their annual production, while the corresponding figure for the majority-owned companies was 16 percent, for minority-owned companies, only 9 percent.[6]

In the past, most capital-importing developing countries supported the establishment of new companies with the participation of foreign capital. Partial or total buy-out of existing companies by foreign capital was not encouraged or was strictly forbidden. Recent evidence, however, shows that the export inclination of newly found ventures is generally lower than that of companies purchased by foreign capital. Three factors may explain the different behavior: (a) new ventures need considerable time to start production, whereas existing companies can start right up; (b) new ventures often represent experimental cases and serve market research or public relations objectives, whereas a company bought outright immediately becomes an integral part of the parent firm's global strategy; and (c) new ventures are often not allowed to penetrate the traditional markets of the foreign partner, whereas companies overtaken are more likely to become integrated into the marketing network of the foreign investor.

Foreign Trade Regulations and FDI

Companies producing for export in the host countries are frequently exempt from ownership restrictions. In Thailand, companies producing exclusively for exports and in Trinidad and Tobago companies selling at least 75 percent of production in external markets, can be wholly foreign-owned firms. The same kind of FDI in the Philippines can start with 100 percent ownership if 60 percent of the shares will be transferred to local shareholders in 30 years. In Malaysia, companies producing for the domestic market are allowed to obtain a 30 percent foreign-equity share; in firms producing for exports, the share varied between 51 and 70 percent in the early 1980s but is up to 100 percent today. Indonesia increased the maximum share of foreign capital in the initial stage of the venture from 80 to 95 percent. In Mexico, small and medium-sized majority-owned foreign companies can be established without previous authorization if the company meets two major external economic qualifications: a 35 percent export share of production and balanced convertible currency transactions.

In most host countries, production for exports is tax-free or enjoys preferential tax treatment. Malta offers a 10-year tax holiday if the foreign company exports 95 percent of its local production. Five to eight years of tax exemption is common in many medium-developed and manufactured-goods-exporting countries, with the possibility of extending the tax-free status or applying reduced taxes afterwards. According to the recent Polish law, convertible-currency exports by joint ventures enjoy a 60 percent tax reduction: while profits are generally taxed at a 50 percent rate, profits connected with export activities (as measured by the share of exports in total production) are taxed at a rate of 40 percent of the original tax (i. e. 20 percent of total profits from exports). If the entire production is exported, the profit tax is at the level of 10 percent.[7]

Higher exports involve preferential terms of profit repatriation. The transfer limit is often determined as a percent of the registered capital. In Ecuador, foreign-equity ventures are authorized to repatriate their profits up to 30 percent of their registered capital. However, this limit is 40 percent for the export sector, and there is no limitation if at least 80 percent of the production is exported to countries outside the Andean Group.

In the Far Eastern economies, generous, usually free trade status is granted to all activities that generate export value added.[8] Access to local credits is easier and some countries provide special interest rate for financing export-oriented projects.

In countries with non-convertible currencies, various instruments serve to enhance the interest of joint and foreign-owned ventures for giving priorities to exports. Many Latin American countries apply preferential exchange rates for export earnings in convertible currency and/or allow a certain or larger share of the export earnings to be retained by the exporter in foreign currency. In Poland, only 15 percent of the foreign exchange earned by joint ventures must be sold to the Central Bank. In Czechoslovakia, the new foreign capital law exempts the foreign producer that exports from having to surrender his foreign-currency earnings. Chile and Venezuela went even further: companies with convertible currency earnings are allowed to deposit their export income in foreign banks. This is a fundamental advantage especially in countries that have severe foreign-exchange controls and other annoying bureaucratic practices.

Higher export commitments generally imply preferential customs procedures and sometimes even access to otherwise forbidden or limited imports. Machinery, installations and technology exported by the investor as his contribution to the joint venture are generally duty-free. Additional materials required for continuous production may enjoy temporary customs-free status. For example, the Republic of Korea offers duty-free imports for six months; Turkey for three months. Taiwan provides a five-year deferred duty payment for companies producing only for export. In Brazil and certain other countries, second-hand machinery can be imported duty-free. The Republic of Korea does not impose import duties on products produced by Korean firms outside the country. In export processing zones, imports used in the production of exports are in most cases duty-free.

Preferential import regulation may be quite important. For instance, the time necessary for duty formalities is a not negligible competition factor. In Indonesia, as recently as the early 1980s, duty procedures usually took 45 days, while in neighboring countries they took just three days. In order to ensure continuous production, companies had to accumulate a high inventory of raw materials, spare parts and intermediate products, leading to higher production costs and lower competitiveness. Another important factor is the detrimental impact of the sometimes rather complicated and controversial import-licensing mechanisms. While allegedly prompted by balance-of-payments considerations, in reality they protect old and create new import monopolies. Recent experience shows that the radical abolition of monopolies which regulate imports and preserve an uncompetitive import pattern is a key positive measure for improved international competitiveness and increased attraction for FDI.

Spectacular modifications have occurred in two main foreign trade-related fields that used to restrict FDI. During much of the 1950s through 1970s period, export requirements and local content prescriptions were key elements of FDI regulation. In the 1970s especially, very much in consensus with the import-oriented development strategy that many countries pursued, emphasis was laid on the high (and often even rising) local content of production. But in the 1980s, the growing pressure to export and changing economic policy priorities had tended to weaken such previously strict rules. For example, one of the main reasons why India did not become an attractive place for FDI was that at least 30 percent of production—based on very high compulsory domestic input content—had to be exported. This share reached 75 percent in technologically less sophisticated sectors, e. g. in the textile and clothing industry. Joint companies that were unable to meet their export targets were severely punished after three to five years: they had to pay in convertible currency the difference between the planned and actual exports and special penalty fees were also imposed on them.

In recent years, several countries eased substantially both local content and export requirements and are turning from a stick to a carrot approach. "Export-oriented status", including special benefits, is granted to companies exporting 65 percent instead of 85 percent of production in Indonesia, and 50 percent instead of 80 percent in Thailand. Even India made exceptions to its strict rules by lowering the export requirement from 75 to 33 percent in the case of the Bata-Adidas venture in sport shoes and from 30 percent to 10 percent in the case of Digital Equipment's joint venture in computers. Canada went even further: in order to enjoy the beneficial effects of free trade with the United States, it had to abolish all export requirements and local content rules.

Venezuela offers five-year exemption of profit taxes if 50 percent of the production of foreign-owned companies consists of local products. In Malaysia, the foreign firm is encouraged only to find a "suitable" local partner. This means foreign-owned companies are not obliged to buy the products of any local partner, even if the government can identify such a producer, if the foreign firm can present plausible objections (e. g. loss of competitiveness, disrupted technology, higher costs). To be sure, local content rules have been employed not only by developing countries. On several occasions, both the United States and the European Community (EC) have urged Japanese investors to use a higher share of domestic input in their production located in the U. S. and in Western Europe, respectively.[9]

In the past, strict export requirements and import controls were considered the main instruments for assuring that FDI will have a positive impact on the trade balance of the host country. In several countries, policymakers expected FDI to produce a net export surplus immediately. The evident failure of this policy has led many countries to abandon this practice or to make the requirements more realistic. For example, in Mexico, prospective foreign investors have to present a five-year convertible-currency plan. Investment requests are positively treated if the manufacturing activity of the FDI gradually increases exports and narrows the initial gap between imports and exports. At the beginning, 50 percent of imports should be covered by exports, which is expected to grow to 75 percent of imports in five years. India now would like to achieve balanced external trade of FDI activities in five years. Australia allows seven years for the FDI to cover 50 percent of imports by exports. In smaller, world-market-oriented economies, this "coverage ratio" is generally much higher. However, the favorable balance is brought about not by stricter rules but by a more liberal economic environment in which the FDI is functioning.

Economic Policy of Host Countries: The Key Factor
In several countries, more liberal, internationally competitive FDI regulations alone did not increase FDI substantially, while other countries, with

less liberal incentive systems have registered spectacular inflows of international capital. This development underlines the fact that the decisive impact on FDI comes from the general and, first of all, external economic strategy of the host country. In the last decade, far-reaching changes have taken place in a number of countries which have abandoned their import-substituting, autarchic economic policies and opted for a world market-oriented development strategy.

Up until the 1970s, national economies with large internal markets had attracted the lion's share of the FDI directed to developing countries. From the mid-1970s on, however, market considerations, always the cornerstone of FDI decisions, shifted from the domestic to the international area. Countries offering a liberal, world market-oriented economic environment were provided access to international markets, considerably widening their generally very small, and therefore in itself not attractive, domestic markets. The dynamic inflow of FDI into the Far Eastern economies, into certain semi-peripheral European countries (Ireland, Spain, Portugal) can to a large extent be explained by such a policy change. The share of FDI in the GDPs of the inward-looking economies has been declining in the last decade, while the share has grown in the world market-oriented economies.

Why is an inward-looking economic policy less able to attract FDI than a world-market-oriented policy? Mainly because the level of interest of foreign capital is determined by the size of the market. In the initial period of FDI, the domestic market may be attractive, especially in countries with several tens of millions of population which generally have a large consumer demand, even if the income level is low or income is very unevenly distributed. However, this market soon becomes more and more saturated. Even large profits, made possible by protected production, prove to be unable to change the trend of growing disinterest of undertaking new investments.

But this is not the only problem. More important is that the impact of FDI that considers the host market exclusively, tends to be detrimental to the longer-term development of the host economy. National economic losses caused by protectionist policies are in effect aggravated by FDI working in this environment. Artificial, substantially overvalued exchange rates make imports relatively cheap, shifting production factors toward capital-intensive investments.[10] These products, however, can only be sold on the domestic market and only as long as the high level of protection remains. Not only high-cost national companies but also high-cost international companies enjoy the "fruits" of protectionist policies, while impeding the entry of small and medium-scale firms, both local and foreign. In addition, since international firms are generally stronger (both in financial and organizational terms), they tend to "outcompete" their national rivals and thus increase their control over the host economy. Attracting foreign direct capital while maintaining protectionist trade policy thus ends up in a trap: FDI does not increase international competitiveness; it eliminates part of the national economy that, according to the very essence of the inward-looking economic policy, should have been protected; FDI strengthens the monopolistic structure of the economy. It may also give birth to strong alliances between foreign and national monopolies against trade liberalization attempts of the host government.

The foreign partner's long-term interests may be hurt also if, in a highly protected environment, its competitiveness and performance decline. There is an interesting contrast between the behavioral pattern of FDI in most Latin American countries or in Spain: foreign firms that have invested there during the era of import substitution are generally much less mobile, flexible and risk-taking than are foreign firms arrived during the more recent phase of liberal world market-oriented policies.[11]

The basic policy conclusion is this: host governments should concentrate on how to accelerate the learning process and make national entrepreneurs capable of cooperating with international companies, instead of prescribing detailed behavioral rules for foreign firms and/or offering them a special status with automatic discrimination against local business. A world-market-oriented policy leads to efficient import substitution, and, in several cases, to direct exports by the local companies that have been already supplying the foreign company in the host country. In the Republic of Korea, in 1977 FDI accounted for 18.7 percent of total exports and absorbed 28.7 percent of total imports. Ten years later, FDI's share in total exports increased to 29 percent, in imports it declined to 23.3 percent.[12] In Brazil, a less world-market-oriented economy, in 1974 electrical machinery production relied heavily on imports (34 per cent). By the late 1970s, this share declined to 15 percent and stabilized at this level in the 1980s, accompanied by a moderately growing share of exports (from 5 to 10 percent).[13]

The attractiveness of a host country can be additionally enhanced by liberalizing its banking sector and financial services. Large foreign companies often make decisions in favor of those host countries in which the banking sector is developed and/or in which liberal rules prevail. In a number of cases, international banks are preparing the way for FDI. For companies not well-acquainted with the host country environment, local offices of their traditional (domestic) banks generally are a confidence-building factor. But liberalization does not mean only opening up the country for foreign companies. At the same time, special attention should be paid to the weaker but dynamically growing local capital. National producers should be given the same treatment as foreign producers, and they should enjoy the same liberal environment as the one offered to foreign capital.

Economic Diplomacy,
Regional Integration, and FDI

Although a world-market-oriented economic strategy is certainly the key factor of attracting FDI producing for exports, the role of economic diplomacy cannot be underestimated. Since the key factor influencing FDI decisions is the size of the potential market, preferential treatment or membership granted to a prospective host country in larger economic groups (regional integrations) has proved to be a substantial additional factor of attracting FDI.

The broadest trade preferences are offered by the Generalized System of Preferences (GSP). This covers practically all developing countries. Various countries could use this for attracting international capital producing for markets which grant trade preferences. However, it must be emphasized that these preferences were an additional, complementary instrument for attracting FDI and orienting FDI production to exports. If production costs are high and the economic environment is considered to be unattractive, trade preferences usually do not offer adequate compensation. Relatively few developing countries belonging to the Lome Convention have been chosen by FDI just because they enjoy trade preferences offered by the EC. More US, Japanese and recently Western European attention has been paid to certain Caribbean islands that were granted various trade preferences simultaneously (Lome Convention for the EC market, the Caribbean Basin Initiative for the US market and Commonwealth membership). Nevertheless, FDI remained relatively more important in the world-market-oriented Far Eastern and certain Latin American economies, even though the trade preferences enjoyed by them had been less essential.

The most substantial trade policy impacts come from regional integrations, mainly from the EC. The dismantling of tariff walls, the free trade in industrial products between the EC and EFTA, and the progressive elimination of non-tariff barriers, with the liberalization of the movement of production factors by 1993, have been a key incentive for FDI decisions. Regional integrations among developing countries also attracted a growing number of foreign firms. However, the limited size of the regional market, the existence of major barriers to trade on the national level, and the prolonged import-substitution strategy on the regional level, seriously hindered the host economies in making use of the potential benefits expected from FDI.

The conclusion can be drawn that it is not integration in itself, but the large market which is a decisive factor. Countries oriented on neighboring (or not so near) large and dynamic markets could attract a considerable amount of international capital producing for this market. World-market-orientation and increasing cooperation with international companies in the rapidly growing Asian economies would hardly have been possible without the immense import capacity of the North American market. The spectacular rise of Mexican manufactured goods exports is also closely connected with the country's geographic position and its maquiladora industry enjoying special treatment in the United States.

Additional potential for attracting FDI can be developed by addressing the nationalities living in the main capital-importing and capital-exporting economies. Japanese and German immigrants in Brazil or in the United States have established important channels for attracting capital from their original countries. On the other hand, Korean, Chinese, Irish and Mexican nationalities living in the United States have played a not negligible role in growing US direct investments in their home country. As an interesting development in the 1980s, the majority of foreign ventures established in the People's Republic of China originated from Chinese businessmen in Singapore, Taiwan and, first of all, Hong Kong.

Concluding Remarks and
Lessons for Central and Eastern Europe

Reform-minded Central and East European economies and recently also the Soviet Union attach increasing importance to the role of FDI in improving their technological levels, enhancing exports to convertible currency areas and strengthening the economic performance and overall competitiveness of their economies. Despite more liberal and internationally mostly competitive legal and financial treatment of foreign capital, and repeatedly announced export priorities notwithstanding, so far foreign investors have made only limited commitments. Even after many of the old political and ideological obstacles and reflexes have been dismantled, confidence-building is still a time-consuming process. But perhaps the main problem is that the FDI already located in the region or currently being attracted has a basically domestic- and CMEA-market-orientation. The reason is that many of the conditions that are likely to influence foreign investors decisively toward the world market, are still absent. These ingredients are:

1. Liberalization of the treatment of FDI should be closely connected with ongoing trade liberalization. Better terms of FDI activities in Central and Eastern Europe are unable to compensate for trade policy rigidities and even less to replace genuine trade liberalization.

2. Depending on the extent to which a Copernican change from inward-looking to outward-looking economic strategy takes place, the basic objectives of foreign capital will be reshaped and world market orientation will become a priority in strategic decisions. FDI, by itself, is neither capable of nor is it its task to transform an autarchic, inward-looking economy into an outward-looking one.

3. It is not export-orientation but world-market-orientation which attracts higher amounts of capital investments and increases exports considerably. It is not specific sectors or enterprises that should be made export-oriented (which is an extension of the old autarchic central plan concept and behavior), but the ability of many firms to export and to improve their overall competitive positions.

4. Short-term and short-sighted balance-of-payments considerations do not contribute to the correctly set goal of attracting FDI for a longer term, export-led cooperation. On the contrary, they either dissuade international investors from entering into ventures or shift their interest towards small-volume, large-profit, once-and-for-all and domestic-market-oriented operations. Competitive production by FDI in the Central and East European economies, that have been isolated from the world economy for decades, usually requires substantial imported inputs which can be replaced only gradually by domestic production. During a transitional period—the length of which depends on the scope and speed of the reform process—FDI activities directed to convertible-currency-markets will require relatively high import content and may even generate temporary trade deficits. These should not necessarily be considered harmful, as has often been the case in the past. First, even in the worst possible case, this deficit would be a negligible portion of the deficit accumulated year-by-year by importing a wide range of products in order to maintain uncompetitive and highly subsidized production for the domestic and CMEA markets. Second, stopping or rescheduling production by FDI when a temporary import surplus appears, would impede the unfolding process of cementing export interests and linkages and lower the probability of getting a balanced trade or an export surplus in the foreseeable future. Third, the trade-balance impact of FDI generally cannot be restricted to the direct production of the foreign-owned or joint venture. The company may produce various goods efficiently for the domestic market that previously had been imported. At the same time, it can offer different inputs to other domestic enterprises, enabling them to become internationally competitive. Also, hardly quantifiable spill-over effects have to be considered (technological improvements, up-to-date management methods and organization, higher-skilled manpower, more and better information on international markets, identification of potential partners, etc.).

5. The most important condition for enlarging the small domestic market is the general liberalization of the economy and the introduction of rules of the game in conformity with world-market-requirements. This involves dismantling the obstacles to exports and imports, liberalization of the foreign exchange market, setting realistic exchange rates, and the elimination of institutional and bureaucratic bottlenecks, along the lines recommended in the introductory essay in this volume by Köves and Marer.

6. Domestic firms should be encouraged to enhance their participation in the international economy by creating ventures in other countries. Direct capital flows are always a two-way street, even though the small Central and East European countries should become or remain substantial net direct capital importers in the foreseeable future.

7. An additional but significant role should be played by an active economic diplomacy. The Central and East European countries should give special emphasis to institutionalized relations with the EC and the EFTA. Obtaining improved access or the same treatment as the Western European economies, on the large and dynamic markets in Western Europe, is one of the key elements of successfully attracting FDI.

8. Simultaneously, strong attempts should be made to exploit the vast potential of the Soviet market while, at the same time, avoiding likely traps and handicaps. Most prospective foreign investors have a keen interest in exporting to this market of 290 million consumers, by increasing the share of their potential production in the reforming Central and East European countries. Better possibilities for exporting to the Soviet Union seems to be one of the preconditions for a qualitatively larger inflow of foreign capital and the establishment of multinational regional headquarters in certain countries of the area. However, the mechanism of the CMEA and bilateral trade relations that were still in effect in 1990 have been completely inadequate to meet this goal, for the reasons elaborated in the chapter by Köves. To what an extent transition to current world market prices and payments in convertible currency by 1991 might encourage FDI and reshape the global and regional strategy of international investors, remains to be seen.

Notes

1. G. Nwanna, "The Contribution of Foreign Direct Investment to Exports: An Empirical Study of 23 LDCs," *Intereconomics*, November-December 1986.

2. A. Inotai, *A működőtőke a világgazdaságban* [*Direct Capital in the World Economy*] (Budapest: Kossuth, 1989).

3. Chung H. Lee, "United States and Japanese Direct Investment in Korea: A Comparative Study," *Hitotsubashi Journal of Economics*, February 1980.

4. K. Unger, "El comercio exterior de manufacturas modernas en México: El papel de las empresas extranjeras," *Comercio Exterior*, May 1985; and R. Jenkins: "Foreign Firms, Manufactured Exports, and Development Strategy: The Case of Mexico," *Boletín de Estudios Latinoamericanos y del Caribe*, December 1977.

5. J. Halbach, *Multinationale Unternehmen und Zulieferindustrien in der Dritten Welt* (Frankfurt, New York: Campus Verlag, 1985). p. 172.

6. Zhia Siow Yue, *Direct Foreign Investment in Manufacturing in Developing Countries: The Case of Singapore* (University of Singapore, 1979).

7. K. A. Lis and H. Sterniczuk, "Joint Ventures with Foreign Capital in the Polish Economy: From Ideology to Market System" (Warsaw, 1989. unpublished).

8. C. Frischtak, "Competition as a Tool of LDC Industrial Policy," *Finance and Development*, September 1989.

9. For some recent detailed analyses, see: G. de Jonquieres, "Coping with Local Sensitivities," *Financial Times*, October 13, 1989; "The New Kid on the Block," *Financial Times*, June 28, 1989; P. Montagnon, "Welcome Mats and Cold Shoulders," *Financial Times*, July 10, 1989.

10. According to a World Bank survey, autarchic economic policy may cause considerable loss compared with open economic policy. On the scale of social return, losses can reach 30 percent in chemicals, 50 percent in clothing and textiles, and 70 percent in automobile production. D. J. Encarnation and L. T. Wells, "Evaluating Foreign Investment, "Investing in Developing Countries," in Thomas Moran, ed. *Investing in Development: New Roles for Private Capital* (Washington, D.C.: Overseas Development Council, 1986).

11. A German survey stated that "old German capital" allocated in Catalonia preserved its exclusively host market orientation also after substantial liberalization of the Spanish economy took place, while the "new German capital" entered Spain with international market orientation. *Blick durch die Wirtschaft*, June 19, 1986.

12. *Far Eastern Economic Review*, February 18, 1988.

13. Ph.Pochet, "Les Investissements Étrangers au Brésil," *Université Libre de Bruxelles*, September 1986.

7

Economic Liberalization in Spain

Guillermo de la Dehesa

If we analyze, from an economic point of view, what democracy has meant for the Spanish economy, we can sum it up in two words: openness and liberalization. After almost three decades of economic autarky first and state intervention and regulation later, the new democratic governments elected after 1977 could only try, as a coherent policy, to open up the economy and to integrate it with Western Europe.

Although in some countries progressive economic policy has been related to greater intervention of the state to compensate for the imperfections of the market and to avoid monopolistic or oligopolistic positions, liberal democracy in Spain could only go one way: to try to free the economic potential from all the complex and inefficient interventionism of the past regime. To liberalize the regulated markets was much more urgently needed than any other measure. This is why, in spite of the traditional anticapitalist sentiments of the Spanish left, after the death of Franco and during the period of transition to the new democracy, both the definition of the Spanish economy in the new constitution as a "market economy" and the decision to join the more liberal economic market of the EEC were approved with the support of the socialist and communist parties. Spain decided to match the rest of Western Europe both politically and economically.

This does not mean that during Franco's rule the Spanish economy did not liberalize at all. Actually, there were two episodes of trade liberalization. One occurred in 1959 and was brought about by two factors: the need to overcome the serious deficit of the balance of payments and complete exhaustion of foreign currency reserves that were the result of autarky, and the desire to gain credibility by joining the IMF, the GATT, and the (then) OEEC. The main requirement imposed by those institutions was to start opening up to foreign trade and investment. The second attempt at liberalization, begun in 1970, was also forced, externally, by Franco's desire to join the EEC and to obtain European political recognition. But the attempt yielded a mere preferential trade agreement that increased trade with the EEC. Nevertheless, it made trade more open and, in the long run, was very positive for the Spanish economy.

But the two main episodes of economic liberalization have had their roots in Spain's move toward democracy. The first one was in 1978-1979, after the Mocloa Pacts and the approval of the constitution; the second occurred in 1986, with the accession to the EEC. Let's look at both aspects of Spain's economic liberalization: domestic markets and foreign trade and capital flows.

Domestic Markets

During the 1980s, price controls were greatly reduced. In 1990 they cover only 12 percent of the total consumer price index. Price controls remain for certain energy products (which represent 8 percent of the total CPI), tobacco, telephone, public transport, some basic foodstuffs, and certain pharmaceutical products. These products are controlled mainly because most of them are provided by natural monopolies or because the state is by far the biggest buyer (such as in pharmaceuticals). All prices for services are free, including housing rents. Shopping hours are also free seven days a week.

The labor market has also been liberalized. In 1984, new legislation reduced restrictions on hiring, introducing the possibility of temporary contracts that allow employers to hire workers for definite periods (six months, one year, or three years). At the end of those periods workers can be hired on a permanent basis or let go. Part-time contracts have been made possible, the work week has been reduced to 40 hours, and the maximum overtime to 80 hours a year.

The financial markets started their liberalization in 1978 when savings banks were allowed to act as full banks and foreign banks were allowed to establish themselves in Spain, with a limit as to the number of branches and domestic resources they could open or capture. In 1981 interest rates on assets and liabilities were liberalized for maturities of six months and longer. But the bulk of liberalization occurred during 1987-1989. In 1987 all interest rates were liberalized. During 1987-1988, a number of new regulations made most financial markets and institutions freer and more flexible. One law opened up banks to all types of financial activities that previously were restricted, e.g., to issue mortgage securities, engage in leasing and stock market trading. Another measure reformed the stock markets that were a monopoly of public notaries, and opened up the seats to all financial institutions. Complete transparency in their operations were introduced, unifying and computerizing the four existing markets that now work continuously, and creating a supervisory body comparable to the Securities and Exchange Commission (SEC) in the United States. Another law introduced a pension fund scheme with large fiscal incentives; still another made it compulsory for most companies to have external audits.

Financial liberalization has also reached the public sector. One law has introduced a fixed limit to the stock of public debt that the Central Bank can hold. A second law has created a new computerized market for government debt that has made trading in it fully competitive. A third, very important law has abolished the possibility of state-owned banks (e.g., industrial, agricultural, mortgage, and local banks) to receive treasury finance at preferential rates of interest; they must obtain their financial resources in the marketplace, in competition with private banks.

Finally, there has been a large program of privatization and reprivatization of state-owned companies. Some of the larger ones (Tabacalera, Banco Exterior, Endesa, and Repsol) have been partly privatized in the Spanish and foreign stock markets. Others have been sold fully or in a majority to foreign or Spanish buyers without any nationalistic discrimination. For instance, SEAT was sold to Volkswagen, and Secoinsa to Fujitsu. All the previously nationalized Rumasa holdings have been reprivatized as well. Today the remaining Spanish state-owned companies, taken as a whole, are not losing money.

Trade Liberalization

The new democratic government elected in July 1977 introduced tariff reductions that by the end of 1980 had decreased the average nominal protection by about 20 percent. Roughly 86 percent of all imports by value and 44 percent of all tariff items were subject to tariff rates below 10 percent. Many commodities subject to quotas were liberalized as well.

From 1980 to 1985, the second oil shock on the one hand and Spain's difficult negotiations with the EEC on the other had slowed the pace of liberalization. Nominal protection remained more or less unchanged, but effective protection was reduced further. But since the accession to the EEC on January 1, 1986, Spain has engaged in a program of trade liberalization over a period of seven years, ending in December 1991, that is more important in scope than all the previous liberalization attempts combined. It will result in the total absence of trade barriers with the rest of the EEC and EFTA and the adoption of a lower common external tariff for goods coming from the rest of the world.

Spain accepted liberalization measures as part of its Treaty of Accession to the EEC and took on additional obligations with the adoption by the EC of the Single Act and the Internal Market. Tariffs for industrial goods coming from the EEC and EFTA countries will be reduced to zero by the end of 1992. The same timetable applies for agricultural goods, with the exception of fruits and vegetables; tariffs on them will be reduced to zero by the end of 1995. Tariffs for goods coming from the rest of the world will be brought down to the common external tariff of the EC, with the same timetable. Quantitative restrictions for goods coming from the EEC were reduced to 16 industrial and 26 agricultural products, and will disappear by 1992. Quotas for goods from third countries differ, depending on whether they originate from GATT or non-GATT countries, state-trading countries, or Japan. But in general, by the end of 1992 quotas will cover only around 40 tariff items, compared to 1986, when 240 tariff items were affected.

Figure 7.1 depicts the trend in Spain's trade liberalization via an index that takes into account nominal tariff rates, border adjustment taxes, export tax rebates, quotas, state trading, and the real effective exchange rates. The index shows that in 1955 the Spanish economy was completely closed, with the index close to zero. Thirty years later, in 1986, Spain's economy was very open, the index having reached 18.5—close to full trade liberalization. Imports as a percentage of GDP increased from 7.9 in 1970 to 14.1 in 1986, and reached 18 percent in 1989.

Financial Liberalization

Democracy in Spain also brought speedy liberalization of capital flows. In 1979 FDI was liberalized, as was the cross-border flows of most invisibles (trade finance, commissions, interest payments, transport, freight insurance and reinsurance, travel, technical assistance, and so on). In 1985 there was a complete liberalization of foreign investment—direct, portfolio, and real estate. This was a prerequisite of joining the EEC. In 1987 foreign currency holdings by banks were liberalized, as was the spot market for the peseta. In 1988 the liberalization process was extended to Spanish portfolio and real estate investments abroad. Domestic foreign-currency accounts could also be opened if connected with foreign-trade operations. Finally, Spain signed the EEC directive for the liberalization of short-term capital flows with member countries that will come into force in December 1992.

Figures 7.2 and 7.3 show the process of financial openness of the Spanish economy; Figure 7.2 presents capital inflows (both short- and long-term) as a percentage of GDP; Figure 7.3 shows capital outflows, also as a percentage of GDP. In 1989, capital inflows and outflows represented 14 percent and 10 percent of GDP, respectively; the corresponding figures in 1979 were 8 percent and 6.5 percent, respectively.

Lessons from the Spanish Experience

I would like to call to the attention of the liberalizing Central and East European countries three lessons of economic liberalization in Spain.

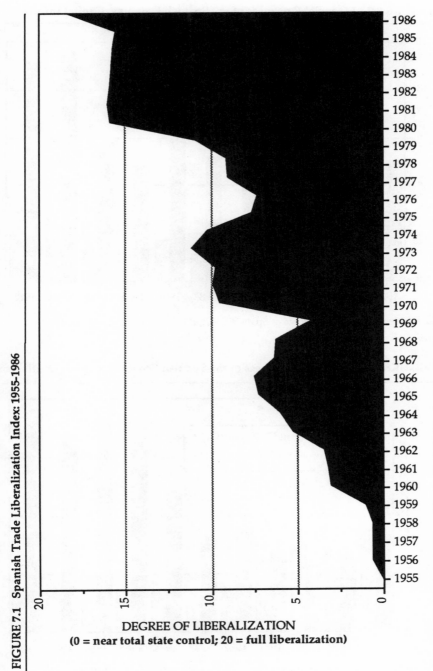

FIGURE 7.1 Spanish Trade Liberalization Index: 1955-1986

DEGREE OF LIBERALIZATION
(0 = near total state control; 20 = full liberalization)

Source: Central Statistical Office of Spain, *Statistical Yearbook* (various issues).

FIGURE 7.2   Financial Openness of the Spanish Economy: Capital Inflows

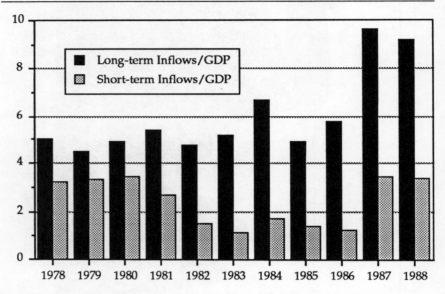

Source: Central Statistical Office of Spain, *Statistical Yearbook* (various issues).

FIGURE 7.3   Financial Openness of the Spanish Economy: Capital Outflows

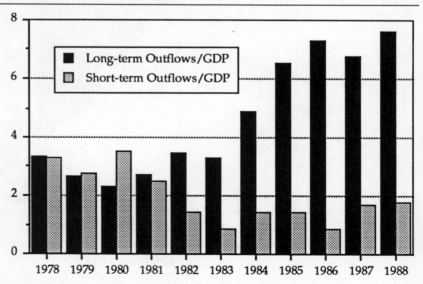

Source: Central Statistical Office of Spain, *Statistical Yearbook* (various issues).

International Agreements

A common feature of the Spanish liberalization episodes has been the agreements entered into with international or multilateral organizations that have imposed, reinforced, or sustained the liberalization measures adopted by the country's economic authorities, thereby giving them more credibility. In the first liberalization attempt (1959-1966), the OEEC and the IMF memoranda subscribed to by the Spanish economic authorities contained all the measures to be taken. Both agreements related to the reduction of trade protection, the liberalization of some domestic prices, and the gradual opening up to foreign investment. In the second episode (1970-1975), the preferential trade agreement with the EEC contained a timetable of trade liberalization. In the third liberalization episode (1977-1980), there was no guiding international agreement, but the expectations of an integration with the EEC and, above all, the choice taken by the Spanish people to follow the "European Model" influenced to a great extent the decision to liberalize. Finally, in the fourth episode (1986-1989), first the Spanish Treaty of Accession to the EEC and then the Single Act and the Internal Market agreement contained the most important liberalization measures ever taken by the economy. What is also important in these agreements is that they were ratified by the Spanish and EEC parliaments and there is no possibility of their reversal. Thus, the credibility of the process is complete.

Social and Political Consensus on the Liberal Economic Model

After a bloody civil war and twenty years of economic and political autarky and isolation, the Spanish people realized that this was not the right way to improve growth and welfare. The arrival in Spain of European tourists and businesspersons had convinced the people of Spain that life on the other side of the Pyrenees was much freer and more buoyant, and that Franco's political regime was an obstacle to such an achievement. "Spain is different" was a political motto of the Franco era that most Spaniards hated, because they wanted to be like the rest of the West Europeans.

All those years of "being different" convinced the new Spanish political and social democratic forces to have the same agreed target: to be part of Europe and to follow the West European economic and political model and way of life. This is why all the political parties, from communists to conservatives, voted unanimously in favor of joining the EEC and adopting a model for the economy based on market forces and the opening of existing domestic and foreign barriers.

The will to belong to Europe was so important that in 1984, in spite of the traditional international East-West neutrality preferred by Spain's political forces, the majority of Spaniards voted in favor of staying in NATO because they thought that by joining Western Europe they had a moral obligation to share its defense system. Those countries of Central and Eastern Europe that wish to join the rest of Europe must have a domestic consensus and then carry through the required political and economic liberalization.

The External Constraint

Another common feature of the economies of Spain and of Central and Eastern Europe is that they are not large economies, and hence the balance of payments situation and the level of external reserves are of crucial importance when making economic decisions. Spain's experience, which may or may not be generalizable, was that it could not synchronize perfectly economic restructuring and economic liberalization, even though they are interrelated. The experience can be summed up in the following way: only when the level of reserves is low enough and the balance of payments is in severe deficit are economic decisions taken to restructure the economy. The reverse holds true also: only when the level of reserves is high enough and the balance of payments is in surplus or equilibrium are economic liberalization decisions taken. It seems quite reasonable to liberalize when it is affordable, and to adjust and restructure when there is no choice.

In the case of Spain, other kinds of important disequilibria such as unemployment, large public-sector deficits, inflation, and so on have never been so important and decisive as to force decisions in one direction or the other. For Spain, the external constraint has always been the major one. Over the last thirty years, the liberalization restructuring sequence that has prevailed can be summarized as follows. First, the initial worsening of "economic conditions" ignites the economic adjustment process. "Bad economic conditions" usually mean a low level of reserves due to unsatisfactory performance of the balance of payments. Then, economic adjustment cum restructuring takes place. It usually consists of a strong devaluation, followed by fiscal and monetary tightening. Only after the balance of payments improves and the level of reserves recovers comes foreign economic liberalization, usually by means of partially removing trade protection and exchange controls. After a few years of economic liberalization, Spain experiences a worsening of the foreign balance and a deceleration or complete stop (never a clear reversal in the case of Spain) of the liberalization process. Then the sequence starts again.

At the beginning of 1990, Spain had a high foreign current account deficit (3 percent of GDP) but still enjoyed a high level of reserves ($46 billion). Nevertheless, there are already some preparatory measures for making a future adjustment. But the adjustment will in part be different from before, since a strong devaluation will be out of the question once the peseta has joined the EMS. Therefore, adjustments to gain competitiveness and to avoid the external constraint will have to be based on wage moderation, real interest rate adjustment, and fiscal restraint.

8

Trade Liberalization in Israel

Nadav Halevi

Historical and Economic Background

When Israel obtained its independence in 1948, it was the culmination of a long period of Zionist endeavor to reestablish a Jewish homeland in the historic area of ancient Israel. During the thirty years of the British Mandate for Palestine, a viable, fairly modern economy was developed in the Jewish sector, alongside but almost entirely unconnected to the less developed Arab sector. The growth of the Jewish sector was primarily the result of large-scale immigration and capital inflow.

Independence was gained after a protracted and costly war, at the end of which a small Jewish state was established in part of the territory of Palestine. Much of what was supposed to be an Arab state was annexed by Jordan, and a small enclave around the coastal town of Gaza was controlled by Egypt. As a result of the 1967 war, these areas came under Israeli control.

The new state was very small in territory—only some 20,000 square kilometers—and had a population of only 800,000. The first action of the new government was to open wide the gates for Jewish immigration, at first from the detention camps in Cyprus and for the remnants of European Jewry, and then from the Arab countries. Within a short period of time the population was swelled by mass immigration. This necessitated very rapid development, to which the Labor Party-controlled government was dedicated. It was confident of its ability to achieve rapid growth by implementing its labor-Zionist philosophy, which included very active government involvement in all aspects of the economy.

In addition to the problem of growth, the economy was plagued by three major problems: inflation, unemployment, and balance of payments deficits. Massive expenditures for the absorption of immigrants and for the war created demand pressures; these were repressed by price controls. Rationing was used to insure equitable allocation of scarce goods and foreign exchange, which was no longer freely available because the new state was excluded from the sterling area. The inflation of the early years was contained by the late 1950s, but inflation reappeared as a major problem after the Yom Kippur War of 1973 and the ensuing oil crises. The annual rate of price increases reached unusual proportions: first some 50 percent, then, after a temporary decline, an upsurge, in stages, with temporary rests at plateaus with rates of 100 and 130 percent. By 1985 the rate of inflation surpassed 400 percent and was threatening to reach hyper-inflation proportions. A drastic stabilization policy was adopted, which reduced the rate of inflation to under 20 percent.

Despite very high rates of investment, financed mainly by the public budgets, the massive immigration of the early years was not quickly absorbed, either in adequate housing or in productive employment. High unemployment led to the curtailment of mass immigration. Gradually, the previous immigration was absorbed and the slower pace of new immigration did not pose serious economic problems. Unemployment ceased to be a problem until the mid-1960s, when it rose briefly as a result of a policy-induced recession adopted to ease the balance of payments situation. Following the 1985 stabilization, unemployment reemerged as a more serious problem: in recent years it has been in the 6-8 percent range, extending beyond the upper limit in 1989. Such a high rate has social and political implications in Israel.

From 1954, Israel enjoyed an extended period of rapid growth, as measured by the annual increase in per capita income of between 5 and 6 percent. This growth rate disappeared in the early 1970s. Since then there has been virtual stagnation. In fact, Israel has not yet returned to the growth rates of the industrialized countries, let alone those of the more successful newly industrialized countries.

Israel has had a persistent balance of payments deficit, with an excess of imports over exports paid for by unilateral transfers and capital inflows. The main sources of foreign resources have been contributions from World Jewry, U.S. aid, and reparations and restitution payments from West Germany. This massive inflow of resources helped finance the high level of investments that contributed greatly to Israel's growth in the first two decades. Since the 1970s, U.S. aid has been the dominant source of funds, but most of this is for defense rather than investment. The import surplus fluctuated in the $250-350 million range in the 1950s, rose to higher levels in the 1960s, and by the early 1970s had reached the billion-dollar level. As a result of the 1973 war and its aftermath, the deficit surged to levels as high as $4-5 billion per annum.

Israel inherited from the British Mandate government a comprehensive system of exchange control. Over the years this system was eased, more with regard to trade restrictions than for capital movements. Other balance of payments policies were adopted and integrated with the exchange control system.

Whenever sources of foreign funds were readily available, Israel did not view the balance of payments problem as primarily important; but in years when the import surplus grew rapidly and foreign sources of finance were either not available in sufficient quantities or only at unacceptable cost, more drastic policy measures were adopted to reduce the import surplus: sometimes formal devaluation of the currency, and sometimes income restraint.

Until late 1977 Israel was on an adjustable peg exchange rate system. Until 1975 devaluations were infrequent, but between formal devaluations, subsidies and taxes on foreign trade were used to obtain effective devaluation.[1] From mid-1975 until late 1977, a crawling peg was used to prevent the rapid rate of domestic price increases from resulting in real appreciation of the currency. At the end of October 1977, Israel shifted to a fluctuating exchange rate system. This system is still officially in force; however, though market forces were given greater influence in determination of exchange rate changes for a relatively brief period, the Bank of Israel gradually tightened its control of the exchange rate, and since the 1985 stabilization policy a fixed exchange rate (with minor fluctuations and infrequent formal devaluations) has been announced as a cornerstone of stabilization.[2]

Trade Liberalization

The serious economic conditions prevailing at the time of independence—war, mass immigration, the need to create a civil service, and expulsion from the sterling area—necessitated drastic controls, not only on foreign exchange but on domestic prices and the distribution of commodities as well.[3] The trade regime consisted of a licensing system for all imports, and all export receipts had to be deposited with authorized foreign exchange dealers. Since the foreign exchange rate was pegged at an unrealistic level, and exchange rationing was very strict, domestic industries received virtually infinite protection, and the rationing system gradually was circumvented by growing black markets.

By late 1951 it was evident that drastic policy action would be necessary to deal with the suppressed inflation, and changes were needed in the exchange rate and in the foreign trade system to deal with the balance of payments problem and the distortions resulting from the existing system. The stage was set for the first phase of trade liberalization.

Trade Liberalization in the 1950s

The new policy was both anti-inflationary and for balance of payments improvement. In addition to restricting the growth of the money supply—which had been the major source of inflationary pressure and had originated primarily as a result of government deficit finance—the currency was devalued. Rather than changing the formal rate for all transactions, three formal rates were introduced, and products were gradually transferred from the lower rate (in terms of Israeli currency per dollar) to the higher rates. Thus, the price level was raised as a means of absorbing the purchasing power of the money balances created during the period of repressed inflation.

Can this type of policy be considered "trade liberalization"? If one requires liberalization to lead to an increase in imports, then the opposite occurred: the balance of payments deficit was reduced, mainly as a result of a decrease in imports. However, the new policy in effect meant that for many types of goods—raw materials, intermediates, and other goods not considered competitive with domestic production—the price mechanism was the major determinant of imports. Licensing was eased for these imports, often with custom duties added to the rate of exchange. In this sense this was an important first step in trade liberalization.

By late 1955 the shifting of products to higher rates of exchange was completed, and a new formal rate (IL1.80 per dollar) was established. This single formal rate was retained until 1962. Tariffs and other surcharges were placed on imports—thus raising the effective rate of exchange—and the gradual process of replacing quantitative restrictions by price instruments continued. This process did not apply to products produced domestically; for those, QR protection predominated. However, there was a gradual growth in the importance of economic considerations when protection was requested for new domestic production. Such protection was granted only when it was shown that the cost of foreign exchange saved was "reasonable."

Some raw materials and intermediates were still restricted by QRs. The licenses were granted to exporters, thus using quota profits in the domestic market as export subsidies. These, and direct export subsidies for foreign exchange value-added, helped reduce the divergence between the average effective exchange rate for imports and for exports. There remained very wide differences among products.

Thus, this period was one of continuing greater reliance on the price mechanism and greater outward orientation. However, the system created not only large inter-industry divergences but also wide divergences in rates for goods, services, and financial transactions.

The New Economic Policy of 1962

A major policy change was announced in February 1962. One of the purposes was to change the entire climate underlying industrial development. Specifically, it called for the gradual elimination of all protection of domestic industry. The goal was to attain competitiveness with Western Europe.

The first actual change was a devaluation to IL3 per dollar, a substantial (but far from complete) reduction of customs duties, and elimination of export subsidies. This substantially reduced the divergence among the exchange rates for goods, services, and financial transactions.

The reduction-of-protection part of the program ran into difficulties. Because of very strong opposition from industry, and from the minister in charge of industry, a much more gradual approach had to be adopted. First, committees studied commodities one at a time, and decisions were taken as to the replacement of QRs by protective tariffs. The tariffs imposed in this process were generally high enough to provide complete protection; rarely was some actual import allowed. Thus, the first stage of the reform was essentially a change in the form of protection, rather than any substantial lowering of protection levels. This stage was not completed until 1968.

Although some reduction in tariff protection levels was done in the five years following the 1962 reform announcement, the meaningful stage of reducing protection actually began in 1968, and has been carried out continuously since then.

Changes in Effective Rates of Protection, 1962-1977

Estimates of effective rates of protection for import-substitutes and exports have been made in Israel for the years 1965, 1968, 1972, and 1977.[4] In 1965 there was high bias in favor of import substitutes: the effective rate of protection was, on average, about 50 percent higher for them than for export value-added. The import penetration ratio—that is, the ratio of imports to total domestic purchases—was less than 10 percent. In 1968, the protection ratios had not changed much, though there was some increase in the import penetration ratio. Thus, the liberalization that had taken place was essentially that of changing the form, rather than the level, of protection.

From 1968 to 1977, much greater progress was made. The average rate of protection for industrial import substitutes fell from 96 percent to about 25 percent. The import penetration ratio rose to close to 30 percent. The dispersion among industries was greatly reduced. Of no less significance was the reduction in anti-export bias: the ratio of the effective rate of protection for exports to that for import substitutes was 93 percent. Thus, substantial—though of course far from complete—liberalization was achieved by the end of 1977.

Developments after 1977

In mid-1977 there was a major change in Israel's political regime: for the first time, the Labor Party, with its "socialist" ideology, was not the dominant political force. It was replaced by the Likud, a more rightist coalition of two parties, one of which (the Liberal Party) had a market-oriented economic philosophy. In late October a new economic policy was announced. This included three major elements: another large devaluation, elimination of export subsidies (which once again had gradually grown in importance between devaluations), and some tariff reduction. The devaluation and the concomitant reduction in the non-formal components of the effective exchange rate had a "liberalization" element in that they reduced inter-commodity exchange-rate disparity.

A second major element was the announcement of the abolition of exchange controls. The extent of this reform as regards capital movements is discussed in the next section; as regards current-account transactions, the reform was of limited importance. Most goods were already practically free of QR restrictions, and most transactions in services had also been previously liberalized. One important exception is Israeli tourism abroad: a very liberal foreign exchange allocation was now permitted.

The third component was the shift to a market-set floating exchange rate. For a time the exchange rate did fluctuate more than in the past, with somewhat greater play being given to market forces. However, conflicts between monetary and exchange rate goals brought about tight control of the exchange rate by the Bank of Israel. In any event, the trade liberalization aspects of the floating rate were insignificant.

Reduction of protection levels continued, and was really unaffected by the new economic policy. Beginning in 1970, Israel negotiated a series of preferential agreements with the EC. In 1975, a free-trade area agreement (on industrial goods) was signed. Though Israel quickly gained concessions for its exports, its own tariff concessions were more gradual. Final reductions of tariffs were made on January 1, 1989, thus effectively exposing Israel's industry to foreign competition. Israel's tariff reductions, even when officially required by this contractual agreement, were in keeping with a long-standing plan for gradual reduction in protection. It can be said that the EC agreement was more of a guarantee that Israel would not regress from the implementation of the philosophy announced back in 1962.

In 1985, Israel and the United States signed a free-trade area agreement. As regards industrial goods, this agreement has led to the extension to the U.S. of the tariff reductions Israel made to the EC countries. However, a differential tariff exists as regards other countries. Thus, Israeli industry is no longer subject to protection in principle, but can still be protected from competition from the Third World and Japan. No effective protection studies have as yet been carried out for the post-1977 period. Clearly, the free-trade agreements must have resulted in a reduced level of effective tariff protection. There are indications of some backsliding in QRs, at least with regard to non-agreement countries. There have also been some assertions that Israel has been making substantial use of an import revaluation system (for the application of ostensibly non-discriminatory sales taxes) to give hidden protection to its industrial production, thus circumventing the agreements. However, though the system can be used for such a purpose, it was originally designed for ease of fiscal administration rather than for protection, and no evidence has so far been provided to show that it has been intentionally misused.

Capital Account Liberalization and Regression

Until late 1977, capital flows were tightly controlled. Israel was interested in receiving foreign capital; in fact, very large sums were mobilized, mainly as loans to the government. Private investment was encouraged, but though there was considerable success in this area, the sums raised were much smaller than the public capital. Most private foreign borrowing could not be done without guarantee of foreign exchange for repayment. The government was reluctant to permit massive short-term private borrowing for fear that this would undercut domestic monetary policy. Domestic credit rationing not only made it possible to restrict the growth of the money supply, but also allowed the government to influence the direction of resource allocation by subsidizing credit to favored activities, such as exports and agriculture.

Outflows of capital were more rigidly restricted. Political and economic uncertainty would have led many to try to keep large sums abroad. In fact, it is believed that many people were able to get around the controls and hold foreign assets. Over the years significant concessions were made in controls to ease investment in both directions, but officially Israelis were prohibited from transferring sums abroad unless authorized.

Capital Liberalization

The economic policy reforms of October 1977 included major changes in regulations related to capital flows. Although the actual changes were far short of the publicly heralded "abolition of exchange control" (the legal framework was retained), the new regulations were far-reaching. However, the major changes were adopted without any substantial reorganization of the highly repressed, government-dominated domestic capital and money markets. They were imposed upon an existing structure, marked by wide differentials and variance in interest rates in favor of certain activities.

As regards capital outflows, the proclamations were cautious: controls would be retained to prevent injurious speculative flows. The main regulations were as follows:

1. Israelis going abroad were permitted to take $3,000 each;
2. Israeli residents could hold as much as $3,000 in foreign exchange (only $500 in cash);

3. Israelis could hold $3,000 in savings accounts abroad;

4. They could buy any amount of foreign exchange to pay for authorized current account transactions;

5. They could purchase unlimited amounts of foreign exchange with which to buy foreign securities (on recognized securities markets), provided these securities were held at domestic banks;

6. As a means of holding dollar-linked assets, Israelis could purchase unlimited amounts of "foreign exchange" to be deposited in Israeli banks; these could not be used for payments abroad.

The sum of these regulations was that Israelis were now given very extensive possibilities for risk-spreading in terms of investments and exchange linkage, and some means of security against drastic curtailment of future tourist privileges. But they were not legally given permission to hold unlimited assets abroad, with protection against major domestic political or economic upheavals. It was, however, much easier now for the average person to use loopholes in the legal regulations to build up illegal assets abroad—which the more affluent and business-wise investors had been able to do all along.

The reforms were more far-reaching as regards capital inflows. In the previous period, the government had to weigh the advantages of foreign exchange receipts against their monetary implications; consequently, neither private firms nor banks were permitted to borrow short-term funds freely. Now individuals and banks were permitted to borrow abroad at will. The result was a massive inflow of capital, and a substantial narrowing of interest differentials between foreign and domestic credit.

Reversals

The extensive liberalization of capital inflows did not last long. Although there was never an official announcement of a return to the previous control regime, there was a gradual reversal in various aspects of control.

The different aspects of the 1977 reforms worked in contradictory fashion as far as policy objectives were concerned. Failure to support the reforms with restrictive fiscal policy (particularly in the latter half of 1978) placed a high burden on restrictive monetary policy. However, curbs on domestic credit were circumvented by access to foreign borrowing. Moreover, such capital inflows tended to revalue the exchange rate when the Bank of Israel allowed market forces more influence in rate determination. An overvalued currency—in terms of purchasing power parity—discouraged exports and encouraged imports, defeating a major objective of the reforms.[5] The more the exchange rate lagged compared to domestic prices—and at this time the inflationary pressure increased very much—the more competitive were short-term inflows compared to domestic credit. A self-reinforcing cycle was thus created.

These developments led the Bank of Israel to start backtracking. Toward the end of 1978 the cost of foreign borrowing was raised by requiring that 20 percent of all direct private borrowing be deposited without interest. In March 1979 the Bank of Israel convinced the public that there would be more active intervention in the setting of exchange rates; in fact, there was a de facto return to a crawling peg system.

In 1979, controls were placed on borrowing abroad, with some switching in forms of controls and types of funds affected. Interest surcharges were alternated with quantitative restrictions. In general, the policy was to restrict short-term credit and limit long-term credit to loans and reasonable rates of interest. Sometimes controls were on private borrowing, at other times restrictions applied to bank borrowing. However, the public showed considerable ingenuity in switching to less controlled sources and types. Finally, the extent of controls was increased, effectively reducing foreign borrowing by non-government sources to a much lower level. The negation of this liberalization is attested to by the restoration of differentials in interest rates.

The reversals of the less far-reaching liberalization as regards capital outflows came later. In 1984, Israeli tourists were permitted to take only $2,000; this allocation was later further reduced, and then restored, but with a 15 percent surcharge. Permission to buy foreign securities was rescinded (except for those sold on the Tel Aviv Stock Exchange). From 1985, holding foreign-currency-denominated domestic deposits was restricted. Thus, by 1985 little remained of the 1977 capital and exchange rate reforms.

Some Inferences from the Israeli Experience

Capital vs. Trade Liberalization

There is a dispute among economists on the proper order of liberalization. Should trade liberalization precede capital liberalization, should it be the reverse, or should they come together? In Israel there was a consensus that trade liberalization should come first. In fact, liberalization of capital flows was attempted much later, and failed. Regardless of the reasons for the failure—be they inadequate accompanying policies or perhaps a basic inability to pursue an independent liberalization of the foreign capital flows without internal capital liberalization—this failure has not undermined the trade liberalization.

The Proper Sequencing of Trade Liberalization

The Israeli experience followed and supports the idea of gradualism. First came substitution of the price mechanism for QRs on non-competitive imports. This was followed by changing the form of protection from QRs to tariffs. The last stage has been a gradual reduction in levels of protection and in their dispersion. This sequence reduced the possible shocks to employment, which, in a country like Israel, where unemployment is considered a very serious social ill, weakened potential pressures for reversal. It may be argued that Israel was more cautious and slow in its liberalization process than was absolutely necessary.

Accompanying Policy

The most important policy relevant to liberalization is exchange rate determination. In fact, it could be argued that this is not a separate issue. Clearly, exchange rate changes can support or negate liberalization efforts. In Israel, devaluation has been an essential part of the early stages of liberalization, when the price mechanism was substituted for QRs.

A major cause for hesitation in trade liberalization, in addition to the fear of temporary unemployment, has been the possibility that liberalization will result in at least a temporary worsening of the balance of payments. If imports increase at once, whereas the efficiency attained as a result of liberalization will manifest itself in increased exports only at a later stage, the current account may indeed worsen. The early stages of Israel's trade liberalization did not lead to increased imports; devaluation and surcharges prevented this result. There was no separate stage of export promotion. Despite being given high priorities in the government's development programs, exports were discriminated against in effective protection rates. In the 1970s much of the anti-export bias was removed. Though it is true that the later stage of liberalization did lead to increasing import penetration, the gradualism of the process allowed favorable developments in export industries and more efficient import substitutes to compensate for this. Israel's current account has worsened over the years, but this cannot be attributed to the trade liberalization process. The availability of unilateral and long-term capital transfers, as well as substantial foreign exchange reserves, have prevented balance of payments considerations from leading to reversals in trade liberalization. Perhaps surprisingly, even in mid-1985, when the balance of payments situation (and inflation) was at its worst, there was no serious consideration of going back to QRs. It was felt that the stabilization policy, especially the reduction of the government deficit and devaluation, would be sufficient to contain the balance of payments.

Notes

1. For a discussion of the concepts of effective exchange rates and estimates of different rates for Israel, see M. Michaely, *Israel's Foreign Exchange Rate System* (Jerusalem: Falk Institute for Economic Research in Israel, 1971).

2. Israel's economic problems and policies in the first two decades are surveyed in N. Halevi and R. Klinov-Malul, *The Economic Development of Israel* (Jerusalem and New York: Bank of Israel and Praeger, 1968), and developments since the late 1960s in Y. Ben-Porath, ed., *The Economy of Israel: Maturing Through Crises* (Cambridge, Mass.: Harvard University Press, 1986).

3. This section draws heavily on N. Halevi and J. Baruh, "Liberalizing Foreign Trade: The Experience of Israel," in D. Papageorgiou et al., eds., *Liberalizing Foreign Trade*, Vol. 3 (Oxford: Basil Blackwell, 1989).

4. See J. Baruh, *The Structure of Protection in Israel, 1965 and 1968* (Jerusalem: Bank of Israel Research Department, 1976); J. Baruh, "Protection Levels in Israel, 1968 and 1972-1974," *Bank of Israel Economic Review*, No. 45-46 (1979); and M. Bar-Nathan and J. Baruh, *Protection in Israel, 1965-1977* (Jerusalem: Bank of Israel Research Department, unpublished, 1986).

5. For a discussion and analysis of exchange rate policy in this period see M. Michaely, "The Floating Exchange Rate in Israel: 1977-1980," in D. Bigman and T. Taya, eds., *Exchange Rate and Trade Instability: Causes, Consequences and Remedies* (Cambridge, Mass.: Ballinger, 1983).

9

Micro and Macro Foundations of Japan's Economic Success

Masaru Yoshitomi

Setting the Issues

Since World War II, Japan has very quickly gone through different stages of economic development, particularly in terms of the balance of payments constraints and the composition of industrial output and exports. Different stages determined correspondingly different sets of regulations and liberalizations at micro- and macroeconomic policy levels.

Until the mid-1960s, the basic constraint on economic expansion was the shortage of foreign reserves. Whenever domestic demand became strong together with strong import demand, larger deficits on the current account and the consequent decline in external reserves forced the authorities to tighten domestic demand management policies. This type of adjustment was repeated several times under the fixed exchange rate of the yen, which was established at ¥360 per U.S. dollar in 1949. Under such circumstances, the officially stated economic policy goal was to achieve economic independence—that is, to build an economy free of foreign-exchange constraints. Policies actually adopted were strict restrictions on imports and foreign direct investment, while pursuing growth-oriented policies such as accelerated depreciation and low interest rates.

However, the chronic as well as cyclical constraints of external reserves did not impose undue hindrance on the long-run rapid growth of the Japanese economy. In fact, after overcoming high rates of inflation of about 85 percent per year during 1946-1951, the economy enjoyed high growth of real GNP at 8 percent per year in 1951-1956 and steadily stepped up its growth rate to 12 percent in 1965-1970. Throughout the whole period after the Korean War, the wholesale price index (WPI) grew by less than 0.5 percent per annum (except in 1965-1970, when it grew by 2.5 percent), although the consumer price index (CPI) and the GNP deflator did rise by around 5 percent per annum. The latter higher inflation rates were attributable to differentials in productivity improvements between manufacturing (which dominates the WPI) on the one hand and non-manufacturing (which dominates the CPI) on the other.

During 1965-1970, Japan began to register external surpluses. In the 1970s and 1980s, the economy's growth rate slowed to 4-5 percent per year under various new shocks, such as excess-liquidity inflation at the extreme end of the fixed exchange rate period (the early 1970s), OPEC I (1973-1974), and OPEC II (1979-1980), and the abrupt (nearly 100 percent) appreciation of the yen against the U.S. dollar (1985-1988).

Two main features of Japan's economy in the 1970s and 1980s may be highlighted. One is the liberalization of restrictive external policies on imports and direct investment, accompanied by the gradual removal of growth-stimulating domestic policies. The other is the emergence of Japan as a chronic capital exporter, coupled with the long-run trend of the appreciation of the yen.

Having sketched these rather well-known features of Japan's development leads us to ask: What is the secret of Japan's economic success? No one knows the "true" answer. At one end of the wide spectrum of attempted answers, it is argued that the key to Japan's success is a targeting industrial policy by the state: infant industry protection, subsidization, credit allocation, preferential taxation, relaxation of anti-trust, and public procurements. By using industrial policy measures, the argument goes, the Japanese government has promoted technological innovation and gained competitive advantage over countries that have taken a more laissez-faire approach.

At the opposite end of the spectrum is another argument that Japan's economic development is the product of competitive factors within the private sector. According to this argument, levels of market concentration are relatively low, barriers to new entry are few, entrepreneurs are risk-taking, and the labor market is quite flexible in adapting to constantly changing technological developments.

In order to get closer to the balanced view in answering the question, it is useful to divide microeconomic developmental factors into actually implemented industrial policies on the one hand and private market mechanisms at work on the other. At the same time, macroeconomic development factors also have to be taken into account, since high rates of growth and rapid industrial development are made possible only by high investment and saving rates as well as by appropriate fiscal, monetary, and exchange rate policies. At the macroeconomic level, too, there is a distinction between policy-induced factors and essentially autonomous ones.

Thus, in the proposed framework we have a 2 x 2 matrix of economic factors responsible for Japan's economic performance (i.e., policy-induced versus autonomous factors at both micro- and macroeconomic levels). I will discuss each of them briefly.

Microeconomic Policy Measures

Microeconomic policy measures are composed of both external (trade and direct investment) and domestic (credit and fiscal policies) ones.

External Microeconomic Policies

In the 1950s, the initial import control measures consisted of foreign exchange allocations and quantitative import quotas. Meager foreign reserves were allocated to targeted heavy (e.g., iron and steel and ship-building) and petrochemical industries by allowing them easier access to imports of raw materials, capital goods, and advanced technologies. At the same time, foreign products that directly competed with products of targeted industries were under strict import controls through limiting the allocation of foreign exchange as well as imposing import quotas. In the early 1960s, 87 industrial and 68 agricultural products were under import quotas.

During the 1960s, gradual liberalization of QRs became more important as an industrial policy than the directed allocation of foreign exchange. In 1964, Japan accepted Article VIII of the IMF (and also joined the OECD), which required Japan to decontrol foreign exchange allocation and ease restrictions on foreign direct investment. During the early 1960s, imports of radios, motorcycles, iron and steel, and buses and trucks were liberalized, followed by color TVs in 1964, passenger cars in 1965, color film in 1971, auto engines in 1972, high-quality calculators and integrated circuits in 1974, and computers and related products in 1975. Thus, by 1972 the number of industrial products under import quotas declined to nine, and by 1975 to five (mostly leather goods), while QRs on agricultural products went down to 22 by 1975. In the 1960s effective tariff rates on manufacturing also declined, from a high of 32.3 percent in 1963 to 14.4 percent in 1973, generally reflecting strong development of heavy and chemical industries. The effective tariff rate on a product was cut, as the export/production ratio of the product steadily increased. Effective tariff rates remained relatively high for labor-intensive goods, such as textiles and wood and lumber products.

Throughout the 1950s and 1960s, total exports (in dollars) expanded by 16 percent per annum, coupled with continued upgrading of the export composition along the line of dynamic changes in comparative advantage. In the 1950s, exports of textiles, processed foods, and miscellaneous manufactured goods accounted for two-thirds of total exports. In 1960, the share of those labor-intensive products declined to less than half, while exports of medium-knowledge-intensive products, including ships and less sophisticated consumer durable goods such as radio sets and motorcycles, increased their combined share to more than 10 percent. It was not until the 1960s that exports of capital-intensive goods, such as machinery (in particular, electrical and precision) and iron and steel and chemical products expanded rapidly, accounting for two-thirds of total exports by the end of the decade.

Regulations on foreign direct investment into Japan were also restrictive to protect domestic industries from being dominated by foreign companies. This concern was even strengthened when in the 1960s certain key industries in Europe became dominated by monopolistic American corporations. Even after Japan joined the OECD in 1964 and accepted the code of free foreign direct investment, the liberalization process moved very slowly. There was only a gradual increase in the number of industries to receive automatic authorization for foreign direct investment. Regulations remained as to the rules associated with majority or minority foreign ownership of new enterprises and the proportions of foreign stock holdings of existing enterprises. Foreign direct investment into the automobile industry was liberalized only in 1971. It was not until 1973 that 100 percent liberalization in principle was adopted for foreign direct investment in general. Even so, liberalization of foreign direct investment into new strategic industries, such as integrated circuits, pharmaceuticals, electronic precision instruments for medical and electrical measurements, computers, information processing, and photosensitive materials was implemented only in 1974-1976.

In sum, infant industries in heavy and chemical manufacturing areas were insulated from external competition by strict import controls during the 1950s and 1960s. The basic aim of industrial policy was to establish an economy free of foreign exchange constraints through export promotion policies, such as the preferential treatment of imports of industrial inputs (including technologies) for protected heavy and chemical industries and, as will be explained later, priority financing of exports.

In the 1960s, import liberalization of both import quotas and tariffs gradually took place, increasingly exposing protected infant industries to external competition. This decade registered the rapid change in Japan's comparative advantage in export composition from labor-intensive (e.g., textiles) to medium-knowledge-intensive (e.g., simple consumer durable goods) to capital-intensive products (e.g., iron and steel and chemicals). In the 1970s and 1980s, knowledge-intensive, or R&D-intensive, products such as automobiles, consumer microelectronics, robots, numerically controlled machine tools, and office machines became the most important. This story, however, would not be complete without analyzing "domestic" microeconomic policies.

Domestic Microeconomic Policies

The bulk (80-90 percent) of total fiscal subsidies, which in the aggregate has accounted for about 2 percent of GNP, has gone to agriculture and forestry throughout the entire postwar period—and is still the case today. The remainder was shared by small- and medium-scale enterprises and textile industries (8-9 percent of the total since the mid-1960s). A relatively large proportion (around 10 percent) went to coal mining from 1960 to the early 1970s, and to marine transportation in the second half of the 1960s. Most of the subsidies represented "defensive" policy measures aimed at, first, near permanently protecting certain low-productivity sectors such as agriculture, and second, temporarily supporting declining industries such as textiles, coal mining, and marine transportation in order to smooth their phasing-out process.

In general, Japan's defensive industrial policies (except agriculture) are characterized by the OECD as "positive adjustment" to changing circumstances, as against the case of many European industrial policies, characterized as "negative adjustment"—i.e., protecting declining industries too long with increasingly larger subsidies.

More aggressive policy measures were adopted until the early 1970s. Targeted industries were iron and steel, coal mining, marine transport, electric power, and chemical fertilizers. As time passed, greater emphasis was placed on machinery components and petrochemicals. The main policy instruments were preferential tax treatments and priority allocation of credits through government financial institutions under the Fiscal Investment and Loan Program.

The year 1949 was the benchmark for overcoming postwar inflation by putting Japan's fiscal and monetary house in order, as well as for abolishing or substantially reducing quantity and price controls, compensatory subsidies for price differentials, and multiple exchange rates. Tax reforms made income taxes (corporate and personal) the major source of government revenue. Corporate income tax rates, including both central and local governments, were set at 50-55 percent.

In the early 1950s, special depreciation measures were introduced for specified machinery installed in targeted industries. However, these measures soon became too complex and detailed, proliferating in terms of specifications of the kind of machinery qualified for accelerated depreciation. In the early 1960s, these special measures were integrated into a uniformly shortened statutory depreciation period of an average of less than seven years, with accelerated depreciation of the rates. The industries that particularly benefited from these measures were iron and steel and automobiles from the mid-1950s to the mid-1960s, and ship-building and general machinery from the mid-1960s to the mid-1970s. The extra profits generated by the shortened depreciation period accounted for about 1 percent of total business investment in manufacturing, but in the aforementioned industries the percentage was above this average.

The Fiscal Investment and Loan Program (FLIP), which is sometimes called the second national budget but is not subject to Diet discussions, is funded largely by postal savings. FLIP extends loans through special governmental financial organizations to infrastructure investment (such as railways, roads, and telephones) and to priority industries. The Japan Development Bank (established in 1951), the Export-Import Bank (1951), the Small and Medium Firm Finance Corporation (1953), and the Housing Finance Corporation (1953) played key roles in allocating the financial resources with low interest rates. In the 1950s, infrastructural investment and basic industries, such as electricity, marine transport, coal mining, and iron and steel, received 40-50 percent of the total loans and investment extended by FLIP. In the 1960s, however, the share of loans extended to these basic industries declined quickly, replaced by increasingly larger allocations for improvements in the quality of life, such as housing, education, and social welfare. Throughout the 1950s and 1960s, infrastructure investment and small and medium-sized firms received around 25 and 15 percent of total resource allocations of FLIP, respectively.

The main purpose of the Export-Import Bank (EXIM) was to provide long-term finance to exports of large machinery, including ships. Between 1955 and 1965, around half of EXIM's total resources were allocated to shipbuilding. Such long-term finance could not be covered by the Bank of Japan, which discounted export bills at preferential rates (1-2 percent below the market rate). Such export bills discounted by the Bank of Japan accounted for about half of total export loans extended by commercial banks.

In the 1950s and 1960s, the prevailing "effective" market interest rates on industrial loans extended by commercial banks were around 10 percent. Lower interest rates on FLIP loans reduced the interest payments burden, particularly for marine transport (where the reduction of interest payments accounted for 20-35 percent of its business investment), and ship-building, electric power, and coal mining (between 5 and 10 percent).

All in all, the combined effects of the special depreciation measures and FLIP reduced the cost of production in the affected sectors by an amount equivalent to about 2 percent of total business investment in manufacturing in the 1960s. Each policy measure made a nearly equal contribution.

Microeconomic "Autonomous" Factors for Industrial and Export Development

In spite of all these microeconomic policy measures aimed at developing targeted infant industries through import protection policies and special depreciation and preferential allocation of FLIP financial resources, the subsidies given to manufacturing industries in the form of reduced taxes and interest payments were not extremely large in the 1950s and 1960s. Furthermore, a large number of new industries were created and exhibited excellent export performance without much help from the government. In the 1950s, such industries included sewing machines, bicycles, pianos, zippers, and transistor radios; in the 1960s, they included TVs, tape record-ers, magnetic recording tapes, video sets, fishing instruments, watches, table calculators, electric wires and cables, and so on. Fundamentally, autonomous microeconomic factors must have been at work, favoring rapid industrial and export expansion.

This suggests that the speedy transformation of Japan's export and industrial structure essentially reflects a rapid pace of improvement in internally generated efficiency and active innovations in the private sector in manufacturing. The key question here is how this high pace of efficiency improvement and dynamic innovation in the private sector was sustained under the shelter provided by the aforementioned protectionist import policies. In many other countries, protectionist measures reduced their industries' dynamic adjustment capabilities by cutting off foreign compe-tition. However, this was not the case in Japan. How were protectionist measures and private efficiency and innovation made compatible in Japan? An important answer lies in the fierce competition among private firms on the sheltered domestic market.

Japanese firms have generally pursued a policy of increasing market shares, particularly at the initial stage of the product life cycle, rather than maximizing short-term profits. This market-share-expansion strategy was partly motivated by the private firms' implicit commitment to the job security of their employees under the lifetime employment custom. This strategy and the associated longer-term investment approach are supported by long-term business relationships between enterprises and their banks as well as their customers, and also by substantial cross-holdings of stocks of production companies by the banks. A major consequence of competition for market shares is falling product prices as profit per unit of product is kept low. In doing so, firms both reduce costs of production through larger scale of output and improve product quality through the experiences accumulated in production. The effect of this cumulative experience is strongly at work in Japan's production system, owing partly to relatively low turnover ratios of production workers (the "lifetime" employment custom) and the seniority wage payment system, both of which enable senior workers to transfer their experiences and learned skills to junior workers and also encourage private companies to make educational and training investment in younger workers.

The lower price resulting from the market-share-expansion strategy by firms stimulates demand for the products, which in turn makes it possible for firms to recoup initial investment and development costs and to enjoy reasonable profits despite generally low rates of return on investment. The virtuous circle between falling prices and rising demand has clearly been demonstrated, particularly by the case of home electrical products as well as major intermediate industrial products.

The ability of Japanese firms to adapt rapidly to changing circumstances and external shocks is also noteworthy. This ability is attributable partly to certain well-functioning adjustment mechanisms, whereby firms can minimize adjustment cost associated with structural changes, such as shifting resources from unprofitable to profitable activities. Several features of such adjustment mechanisms stand out.

First, Japanese firms have commitments to employment security, but not to the specific jobs of individual workers. This system enables management to shift workers across different occupations but only through rather heavy retraining costs for employers and painful retraining for employees. The switching of occupations is made possible in relatively large firms or in a group of firms. Because major firms or firm groups typically contain several branches of an industry, and even industries, with a wide variety of occupations, production workers can be transferred. This intra-firm or intra-firm-group adjustment mechanism in the internal labor market is helped by a downward flexibility of wages and also by the relatively persistent rapid growth of domestic markets. These features, in turn, can be attributed to competitive private business investment aimed at greater market share as well as to the stable macroeconomic policies of the state.

Second, Japanese firms attempt to diversify production activities extending beyond their original fields whenever original activities become less promising. Such diversification of activities toward industries with better prospects for innovation and higher market growth has facilitated industrial adjustment. In contrast, American and European firms diversify their activities mainly through mergers and acquisitions (M&A). In Japan, firms transfer both labor and capital from their own declining branches or sectors to new activities, sometimes by establishing subsidiary firms, financed mainly by the parent company. This method can make access to funds for new risky investment relatively easy as compared with venture capital finance in the stock market. The diversification policy of private companies stimulates competition in new markets by introducing a handsome number of large firms into new production areas.

Third, low interest rates and the relatively easy availability of bank credit assisted by the high household saving rate have contributed to the relatively easier financing of adjustment, entry into new activities, and the creation of new business.

Fourth, government-sponsored "rationalization cartels" have, on occasion, attempted to ease the adjustment burden of declining industries when the decline suddenly accelerated for specific reasons. Unlike the experience in many other countries, these government actions have been rather quickly phased out and have not retarded much the adjustment process.

The market-share-expansion strategies and the distinctive adjustment mechanisms have contributed to maintaining and stimulating fierce competition even among large firms. This competitive oligopolistic behavior in business investment and technological innovation has facilitated the rapid but steady shift of production from items in which Japan has lost her comparative advantage to new items with newly gained comparative advantage, thanks to the steady accumulation of capital and skills in the face of scarce indigenous raw materials and land.

In sum, Japan's strong international competitiveness has its origin in severe competition among Japanese firms both on the sheltered domestic market and in world markets. In all dynamic industries, there were always several large firms, sometimes more than ten. Fierce competition among Japanese firms themselves has provided the key to continued improvement in efficiency and productivity in manufacturing, even in the absence of foreign competitors and under restrictive trade and foreign direct investment policies. Domestic competition has taken the place of foreign competition. At the same time, however, the announcement of timely import liberalization in advance forced Japanese firms to be prepared for the forthcoming exposure to foreign competitors and encouraged them to further speed up the improvement of their production system.

Macroeconomic Policies and Autonomous Factors

The overall effectiveness of the Japanese economic system has been due mainly to private enterprises' strong response to the signalled opportunities through distinctive adjustment and adaptation mechanisms. This strength has been reinforced by a favorable macroeconomic environment.

Bank Credit Rationing Paradigm

Near-zero inflation rates of the wholesale price index in the 1950s and 1960s should essentially be attributed to the stable domestic credit expansion by the Bank of Japan, although the concept of the money supply was not well known even among central bank economists until the end of the 1960s.

The Japanese financial system in the 1950s and 1960s can be characterized as the bank credit-control or rationing paradigm, in contrast to the market-determined open money market paradigm in the 1980s. The 1970s was the transitional period from the former to the latter. The bank credit-control paradigm refers to a financial system in which the non-bank public, mainly corporate, was provided with the necessary funds almost entirely by the banking system at regulated loan rates lower than would-be market rates. At lower-than-market rates, the demand for and supply of bank loans were equilibrated by credit rationing. The regulated loan rates were in turn linked to regulated deposit rates in both the banking sector and in the large postal saving system.

Therefore, the bank credit-control paradigm meant a "low interest rate" policy regime. In order for domestic savings to be bottled up for the high domestic investments that were encouraged by such low interest rates, foreign exchange controls were exercised to prevent possible capital out-flows.[1]

Regulated interest rates charged by commercial banks were 8-9 percent in the 1950s and 1960s and exhibited a gradually declining trend. Such rates were much lower than the underlying growth of nominal GNP at 13-15 percent. Effective interest rates were somewhat higher owing to the required compensation balances with lending banks by the borrowing enterprises.

Commercial banks collected deposits from households at artificially low interest rates of 5-6 percent per annum. At their relatively low income levels, consumers deposited most of their savings with commercial banks and post offices. Interest earnings of small savers were tax-exempt up to the outstanding financial assets of ¥9 million per person ($25,000 at ¥360/$). The saving rate of the household sector rose from 12 percent in the early 1950s to 23 percent by the mid-1970s.

Since issue rates on corporate bonds were also regulated at lower rates in the primary market than in the secondary market, new corporate bonds were rationed by a semi-official Bond Raising Board. As a result, the corporate bond market remained underdeveloped until the mid-1970s, when liberalization started. Long-term private credit banks (i.e., the Industrial Bank of Japan, the Long-term Credit Bank, and the Real Estate Bank) played an important role in providing long-term loans at low interest rates to capital-intensive and long-gestation projects, while commercial banks rolled over short-term loans. In many instances, long-term credit banks functioned as lead managers or co-managers in loan syndicates, whereby they effectively underwrote large industrial projects. These long-term credit banks (and a specialized foreign exchange bank, the Bank of Tokyo) alone were allowed to issue medium-term bank debentures, again at lower-than-market interest rates. The bulk of the new bank debentures were subscribed to by commercial banks, and so were the new corporate bonds.

At interest rates lower than market-clearing levels, commercial bank credits had to be rationed through window guidance by the Bank of Japan. The Bank of Japan thus exerted effective control over commercial banks' lending policies by manipulating inter-bank rates (e.g., call rates) and the discount rate, both of which affected the marginal costs of borrowing by the commercial banks.

This credit-rationing paradigm resulted in the rate of increase in the money supply at 16-17 percent per year—2 to 3 percentage points higher than the underlying growth of nominal GNP during the high growth period. Whenever excess domestic demand resulted in larger trade deficits, the Bank of Japan tightened monetary policy to prevent foreign exchange drains. This mechanism appeared to have prevented the money supply from being excessive and hence inflationary. Therefore, once the Japanese economy began to register current-account surpluses toward the end of the 1960s, and external reserves suddenly expanded due to the overall balance of payments surplus at the extreme end of the Bretton Woods period (1970-1972), the Bank of Japan lost control over the money supply (which increased by 20-25 percent per year), resulting in high inflation of 15-20 percent, which accelerated even further due to the oil price hikes in 1973-74.

It appears that at the exchange rate of ¥360 per U.S. dollar, the yen was initially overvalued. However, as productivity in manufacturing grew by more than 12 percent per year and there was near-zero inflation rate in the WPI, the fixed exchange rate gradually became "realistic" and then undervalued toward the end of the 1960s.

From Balanced Budget to Deficits

After having introduced an income-tax-based revenue system in 1949 and having overcome high price inflation, the buoyant economy combined with progressive income tax rates generated large surpluses on the government's "current account" (i.e., government savings), which in turn financed most of its own public works expenditures, with the remainder (i.e., government's capital account deficits) financed by issuing a small amount of the so-called "construction national bonds." Only in the 1970s, when OPEC I hit the economy and the growth rate slowed, did the central government begin to register large deficits, accounting for 5-6 percent of GNP toward the late 1970s and early 1980s. To finance the deficits on its current account, the government issued the so-called "deficit-financing national bonds," in addition to construction bonds.

As the outstanding stock of national bonds accumulated, amounting to nearly 50 percent relative to GNP by the early 1980s, market pressures mounted to force the government to, first, liberalize interest rates in the secondary market, and then issue rates in the primary market. Following such liberalization of interest rates in the security market and associated financial innovations, hitherto-regulated bank loan rates and deposit rates were gradually liberalized. Thus, the Japanese financial system has almost shifted to an open money market paradigm in which the Bank of Japan conducts open market operations in order to manage the money supply, leaving interest rates freely determined in the market.

At the same time, reflecting the underlying strong trend toward chronic surpluses on the external current account, regulations on capital movements were fully decontrolled at the end of 1980s. This has allowed all institutional investors to freely invest in foreign-currency-denominated bonds.

Thus, the key macroeconomic forces pushing the Japanese financial system toward liberalization both in the financial and foreign exchange markets were the large accumulation of national bonds and a chronic current-account surplus in the 1970s and 1980s. Importantly, both of these internal and external imbalances reflected the emergence of an excess of savings over investment in the private sector (including both households and corporations). This excess of private savings emerged because private business investment slowed down after OPEC I in response to the trans- formation of the Japanese economy from high to medium growth rates, whereas the household saving rate remained high, though declining gradually since the mid-1970s to about 15 percent in 1988.

Macroeconomic Autonomous Factors

It is difficult to distinguish, in the macroeconomic areas too, between policy effects and autonomous factors. It is still not fully known whether the low interest rate policy was really responsible for high business investment under the bank credit-rationing paradigm. The same question can also apply to the corporate income tax system coupled with special depreciation policy measures. This is partly because strong or statistically significant relationships have not been found between the growth of individual industries' business investment or value-added or productivity on the one hand and loanable funds allocated at low interest rates on the other.

It is also unclear to what extent the preferential tax treatment in favor of small savers encouraged household savings. The household saving rate may not be responsive to after-tax, after-inflation interest rates, particularly when consumers have a lifetime saving target. Japanese consumers are motivated to save to "prepare for unforeseen circumstances" (top motive), to finance "children's educational and marriage expenses" (the second), to "prepare for old age" (the third), and to "purchase land and houses" (the fourth). More generally, Japan's household saving rate has apparently been influenced by three "macro" factors: the growth rate of income, demographic changes, and the social security system. During the high growth period until the early 1970s, the saving rate rose from 12 percent to 23 percent. First of all, income growth was higher than expected, and even accelerated. Second, the Japanese population remained young. Third, the social security system was underdeveloped. Since the mid-1970s, the household saving rate has declined, as was noted. The three factors have also changed significantly. The growth rate of real income has halved. In terms of the ratio of labor force to retirees, the Japanese population, though still the youngest among the industrial countries, has been aging rapidly and will be the oldest among the advanced economies by 2020-2025. The social security system, such as pension and medicare, has advanced so much that reforms are now required to prevent the system from going bankrupt in the near future.

Lessons to be Drawn from the Japanese Experience

First, foreign exchange and import controls would have retarded Japan's industrial development by cutting off foreign competition, if private enterprises had not fiercely competed with one another on the domestic market. Tough domestic competition for greater market shares among a significant number of firms in an infant industry holds the key to continued improvement of efficiency and productivity in the sheltered market.

Second, realistic views on dynamic changes in comparative advantages in the foreseeable future should be the basic criterion for selecting the infant industries to be protected. In Japan, no ambitious projects for industrial development were selected that deviated far from comparative advantage. Equally important, the advance announcement of the timely liberalization of trade and direct investment policies forced private firms to be prepared for foreign competition by accelerating their efforts to control costs and innovate.

Third, only high rates of both business investment and domestic savings can promote the dynamic transformation of comparative advantage through the steady accumulation of capital and skills. High government savings also helped to finance the development of social infrastructure in accordance with the rapid accumulation of private capital stock. Only in this broadly favorable macroeconomic environment and disciplined fiscal and monetary policy framework could policies such as low interest rates, preferential tax treatment for small savers, and accelerated depreciation for targeted industries act as catalysts and accelerators of high investment and savings.

Finally, the close working relationship between the government on the one hand and business and labor unions on the other may be unique to Japan, where government bureaucracies have maintained their authority over the private sector. Bureaucracies both broadly define industrial policies and prepare (and continually revise) indicative medium-term economic plans (consisting of projections and broad policy directions). More important, bureaucracies utilize such a planning process to keep open the lines of communication between the government and the private sector. The consensus-building process is particularly important in disseminating information as to broad directions of the industrial, financial, and external development of the economy and associated necessary policy changes in the medium term.

Notes

1. Strong demand for loanable funds stemmed from buoyant private business investment, which grew by nearly 15 percent per year throughout the 1950s and 1960s. Retained profits accounted for 35-40 percent of total sources of investment

funds used by corporations during this high growth period, as compared with 60-70 percent in the U.S. and the U.K. Therefore, corporations' demand for external funds remained very strong throughout the period. Bank loans and inter-firm credits accounted for another 40-50 percent, stock issues another 8-9 percent, and bond issues around 2 percent (their small share due partly to strict controls on coupon interest or issue rates in order to keep the low capital costs of enterprises). Government finance to the private enterprises under FLIP accounted for only about 3 percent of the total (higher than in the case of the U.S. and the U.K., where government finance amounted to about 1 percent or less).

10

Liberalization in Korea and Taiwan

Yung Chul Park

South Korea (henceforth Korea) and Taiwan have been widely acclaimed as the two most successful cases of development in recent history. While their rapid growth and industrialization over the past three decades have undoubtedly been the result of a number of interacting economic, political, and social factors, many studies have shown that an outward-looking development strategy with emphasis on export promotion has played a key role in the development of the two economies.

Journalistic accounts and occasionally even serious studies identify an outward-looking strategy with liberal policies of laissez-faire. It is true that both countries undertook a major policy reform at an early stage of export promotion, whereby tariffs and quantitative restrictions on imports were reduced, and the exchange rate and the interest rates were adjusted to reflect their equilibrium values. Since then, both Korea and Taiwan have introduced a series of policy reforms aimed at liberalizing their trade and financial regimes and at opening up their capital markets to foreign competition. Nevertheless, it is also true that in both countries the government has played a leading role in the process of industrialization. Neither Korea nor Taiwan, therefore, provides a good example of an economy following its comparative advantage or operating close to a free trade regime. Instead of relying on the free functioning of the market system, the governments in both Korea and Taiwan have been actively involved in managing the economy.

The purpose of this chapter is to examine the experiences of the two countries with economic liberalization. In particular, this study will focus on the question of how important it is to pursue liberal policies to success-fully carry out an export-promotion strategy and will assess the extent to which the interventionist regime has interfered with growth and industri-alization in Taiwan and Korea. The next section sets out an analytic framework in which the relative advantages of export promotion and

147

import substitution are discussed. This is followed by a discussion of trade liberalization and its effects. The fourth section analyzes the liberalization of finance in Taiwan and Korea. Brief concluding remarks are found in the final section.

Economic Liberalization and Export Promotion: An Analytical Framework

In trade and development literature, export promotion and import substitution are often described as two alternative trade and development strategies, though in reality both policies can and in fact do coexist within a broad framework of an outward-looking development strategy in most economies (as noted in Chapter 5). One could define the two policies in terms of the degree of bias of the industrial incentive system. That is, a trade regime is biased toward export promotion if the incentive system favors production for sale in the foreign market rather than the domestic market; it is biased toward import substitution when relatively more incentives are given for sale in the domestic market, replacing imports. Taking a free trade regime as the norm, the degree of bias may be measured by "the difference between the domestic price received for export sales relative to sales of goods produced for the home market and the same price ratio internationally."[1] Likewise, an import-substitution bias could be defined as the divergence between the domestic price ratio of importables and exportables to the foreign price ratio of these goods.[2]

Although these definitions based on the overall bias of incentives are logical and appealing, their practical application is rather limited because of the difficulties in quantifying incentives. The problem is more serious in an import substitution regime, where controls such as non-tariff restrictions of imports, rather than incentives, are employed to protect domestic industries. Furthermore, the presence of price controls in the domestic market makes it difficult to estimate a true discrepancy between domestic and international market prices, an important element for measuring the protection of domestic industries. Given these measurement difficulties, it is possible to create a situation in which the thrust of industrial policy may favor export sales, even though the economy's overall incentives, including those elements that are not easily quantifiable, favor domestic sales. Therefore, an operational definition of export promotion may have to be supplemented by an actual performance measure on the assumption that exports do respond to incentives.

Outward-looking strategies, characterized by their emphasis on export promotion, can differ among countries and among different time periods in a given country, in terms of the bias of the incentive system, the goods and services selected for export support, and the policy measures adopted to carry out the strategies. In this study, we define an export promotion strategy rather broadly as a strategy in which incentives, the main thrust of industrial policy, and the mode of government intervention all favor exports rather than domestic sales.

Relative Advantages of Export Promotion

There is considerable empirical evidence showing that export-oriented developing countries have outperformed those pursuing restrictive trade policies or attempting to develop their industries through import-substitution policies. Despite the voluminous and growing literature on the experiences with export-led industrialization, not much is known about the set of factors that could explain the relative superiority of export promotion over import substitution.

One difficulty of ascertaining the relevant determinants is that economic development is a complicated process, the result of a number of interacting economic, social, and political factors. Their relative contributions cannot be easily quantified and are likely to differ from country to country and change over time in the same country. Another difficulty is that conventional trade theory sheds little light on the causality between trade on the one hand and economic growth on the other, and the role of trade policy in promoting economic growth.

Within the neoclassical framework, one could argue that the policies adopted under export promotion allow the economy to operate close to a free trade regime in which static optimum conditions are satisfied. One could also argue that this feature explains economic performance. According to this view, export promotion is a trade strategy in which the free play of internal and external market forces determines the speed and pattern of development. The role of trade policy is to constrain policymakers to minimize their market intervention. This argument, however, cannot explain why a free trade regime produces a higher rate of growth in comparison to a restrictive regime, because trade and growth theories have very little to say either about the quantitative contribution of trade to growth or why a deviation from a free trade optimum affects rate of growth.

Aside from theory, only Hong Kong, and possibly Singapore, among the Asian NICs qualify for such a free-trade policy interpretation. Taiwan and particularly Korea should be characterized as inverventionist regimes in which the governments actively promote exports and intervene extensively in a number of markets, including the financial and foreign exchange markets.

The successful experiences of interventionist and export-oriented economies can be accounted for by the application of the infant industry argument to export promotion.[3] If infant industries require some stimulus for growth, then it is argued that export promotion rather than import substitution is a far more efficient way of developing low-cost industries in developing countries.

Although this interpretation may be applicable to some of the present-day NICs, it appears to be at odds with the experiences of Taiwan and Korea. Both countries—Korea somewhat later—completed a primary import-substitution phase by the end of the 1950s. By then some of the infant industries might have grown up to adolescents, efficient enough to provide a competitive industrial base from which labor-intensive exports could take off. Although this is a matter of judgement, one should not overlook the fact that primary import substitution may be important for a successful transition to the export-orientation subphase in that it provides the physical infrastructure and expands entrepreneurial capacity.[4]

It is difficult to explain in terms of conventional trade theory why export promotion produces better results than import substitution. This is because, as far as trade theory is concerned, from an allocative efficiency point of view, a bias in favor of exports is as bad as a bias against them. Therefore, some of the answers for differences in performance under export promotion and import substitution must be sought outside the realm of conventional theory, which opens the door to a variety of explanations.

Krueger advances three propositions purporting to explain several possible reasons for the relative superiority of export promotion.[5] Some of these propositions are consistent with both the free trade and the infant-industry interpretation. They have been noted by several authors and shown to be relevant in the context of the industrialization experiences of both Korea and Taiwan.

The first proposition focuses on the relative advantages of an incentive system that characterizes export promotion over import substitution. The incentive system eliminates some of the costs associated with quantitative restrictions under import substitution. Incentives make more apparent to policymakers the cost of encouraging different industries. This feature of the incentive system allows policymakers to reallocate resources readily whenever the costs become excessive, and thus to avoid allocative inefficiencies.

Export incentives do not discriminate between activities and exporters and are often determined contingent upon export performance, which provides a market test for the potential recipients of incentives. Incentives are also better than controls in inducing desired economic behavior. Because of these advantages, policies under export promotion are likely to be better and more realistic than those under import substitution in the sense that they result in smaller deviations from free trade optimum.

The second proposition is related to international competition, which makes firms more X-efficient than does a sheltered domestic market. As exporters face competition abroad as well as from other domestic firms, monopoly positions arise less frequently and monopolistic or quasi-monopolistic behavior, which is a pervasive feature of import-substitution regimes, is avoided. Under competitive conditions, firms face an elastic world demand that allows efficient firms to grow at rates commensurate with their inherent competitive position. Under an export-promotion strategy, foreign competition functions as a constraint on the economic behavior of both firms and policymakers and provides feedback to them as to the success or failure of policies in terms of their objectives.

The third proposition emphasizes the gains from trade as an important source of growth. Export promotion strategies present opportunities to exploit such technological factors as the minimum efficient size of the plant, increasing returns to scale, indivisibilities in the production process, and factor proportions and comparative advantage.

All three propositions essentially argue that a bias in favor of exports is better than one in favor of import substitutes because policies under export promotion are less distortive. The efficiency gains from trade, whatever their sources may be, can be substantial. However, because the gains tend to be once and for all in nature, they are not easily translated into high rates of growth unless they exert a positive influence on domestic savings and capital accumulation. Following this line of reasoning, one may add a fourth proposition that places emphasis on "dynamic gains" from trade.

For developing countries with abundant labor, export promotion provides a channel through which a surplus factor (labor) can be traded for technology and intermediate and capital goods. The access to world technology and capital markets continuously improves labor productivity. Although real wages rise, productivity increases maintain a high rate of profit, which in turn stimulates domestic investment. Export growth can also bring about structural changes that induce domestic saving.[6] A rising propensity to save, together with a high rate of profit, results in a high rate of growth.

Trade that exploits differences among countries in factor proportions may be one of the most significant sources of growth in export-led developing countries. In theory, any developing country with surplus labor can develop its industry if it can profitably sell labor-intensive products abroad. In practice, only a handful of developing countries in Asia with a similar factor endowment have been able to do so. The crucial question, then, is why some countries can do this whereas others can not. To answer this question, one may have to consider factors other than the relative superiority of policies under export promotion.

Potential export lines consist of a number of products. Success is as much a matter of choosing the right entrepreneur and right specialized product as it is choosing the right industry in terms of comparative advantage. In this view, the problem of industrialization in many developing countries may be the lack of an entrepreneurial class which perceives profitable opportunities, especially abroad, and takes the necessary risks in order to take advantage of those opportunities. The presence or absence of an institutional and organizational structure that supports industrialization can make a difference.[7] The successful implementation of an export-oriented strategy may thus require some initial preconditions. Size, geographic location, natural resource endowment, the general level of education, and cultural heritage may be more important than any economic policy prescription.

Trade Liberalization

Korea and Taiwan are often regarded as classic examples of economies that have followed liberal economic policies in the process of pursuing an outward-looking development strategy to which their economic success is always attributed.[8] Taiwan carried out a policy reform during the latter part of the 1950s, and Korea in the early 1960s, to strengthen the role of the price mechanism in the allocation of resources. Many studies have established that those policy reforms were crucial to the successful implementation of the outward-looking strategies with which the two economies are closely identified.

Since the early 1980s, both countries have set liberalization as the major objective of economic policy—i.e., to reduce the scope and degree of government intervention in trade and finance and to open up their money and capital markets to foreign competition. Indeed, few other developing countries have managed more durable and far-reaching policy changes toward economic liberalization than have Korea and Taiwan in recent years. In spite of this, the two economies have hardly followed classical liberal principles of laissez-faire.[9]

A recent article characterizes Taiwan's trade regime as mercantilist.[10] The economic policy regime that has supported Korea's industrial growth is also claimed to be mercantilist.[11] A number of studies have also shown that the governments of the two countries have intervened extensively in all sectors of the economy. This suggests that liberal policies of laissez-faire are not necessarily essential for a successful outward-looking strategy.[12] In fact, the experiences of Taiwan and Korea demonstrate beyond any reasonable doubt that an export-led industrialization could be as interventionist as an import substitution strategy is often claimed to be. But, it appears, government intervention has not impaired the allocative efficiency of the two economies as much as it could have under different circumstances. A brief history of economic liberalization in Taiwan and Korea will show that policymakers have been by and large passive and conservative in liberalizing the economies, in that they have implemented reform measures mostly when they were forced to do so by internal and external developments. Even when they were compelled to liberalize, they were reluctant to make policy changes unless disruptions to the economy could be minimized. Ever since the outward-looking strategy was launched, liberalization has been carried out on most occasions to attain certain policy objectives, such as improved growth or stability, and seldom for the sake of improving the allocative efficiency of the economy.

Mode of Trade Liberalization

During the latter part of the 1950s, Taiwan reduced tariffs and quantitative controls on imports and introduced an exchange rate and interest rate reform. Korea followed a similar policy of reform in the mid-1960s. Import liberalization in Korea was mainly directed to reducing tariffs and quota restrictions on imported intermediate inputs used in export-oriented industries so that domestic exporters could better compete on international markets. For the next fifteen years, Korea had made little progress toward further import liberalization until around 1978, when it initiated the second round of trade liberalization, which has continued into the 1980s and in recent years has broadened in scope.

In contrast, Taiwan set out a second round of import liberalization much earlier, in the early 1970s, in order to reduce the costs of imports. It should be pointed out, however, that the import liberalization effort did not meet any serious domestic opposition because Taiwan's current account by then had developed a structural surplus. However, the second round of liberalization lasted only four years. With the promotion of secondary import substitution in 1974, Taiwan put a large number of imported raw and industrial materials and capital goods on a restricted list to provide domestic market protection to the domestic producers of these products. Since then, Taiwan has continued to accumulate huge trade surpluses year after year. To cope with the mounting surplus, and under foreign pressure for opening up the domestic market, since 1984 the authorities have committed themselves to an extensive import liberalization program. Except for agricultural commodities, imports of most manufactured products are now approved automatically. By the early 1990s, Taiwan's average tariff rate is expected to come down to the OECD level.

Korea also intensified its import restriction during the 1970s, when heavy and chemical sectors were promoted as infant and import-substitution industries. However, the economic slowdown with a high rate of inflation and burgeoning foreign debt in the early 1980s was blamed on the intervention-oriented regime and set the stage for overall economic liberalization. The emergence of a trade surplus by 1986 has made it easier to open up the external sector of the economy.

The experiences of Taiwan and Korea show that policymakers have always been constrained by balance-of-payments developments in their attempts to liberalize their trade regimes. Efficiency improvement through import liberalization has never been a serious policy objective. In implementing import liberalization, policymakers in Taiwan and Korea have taken a conservative approach. They first lifted QRs and lowered tariffs on imports of those groups of commodities that they had already learned to produce and to export competitively in world markets. This import liberalization was often offset by imposing new restrictions on imports of those commodities they began to produce for the domestic market. Only when the domestic producers of these products were able to meet international competition were these items later liberalized. As a result, the simultaneous pursuit of export promotion and import substitution has always limited the scope of import liberalization. Export promotion has altered the commodity composition of imports from labor-intensive to capital-intensive and finally to skill- and technology-intensive ones. But if the strategy had not expanded the share of the export-oriented industries, import liberalization would have been much more difficult. Success in export promotion has contributed to trade liberalization mostly because it has increased the size of the external sector and improved the current-account position. Export success has also facilitated the transformation of import substitution industries into export-oriented ones within a relatively short period of time.

Can we observe ex post facto any favorable effect of import liberalization on the allocative efficiency of the economy? One study finds no evidence in Korea that the removal of import restrictions increased total factor productivity of the affected industries.[13] A recent study of Taiwan's import liberalization shows that between 1981 and 1986, the across-the-board tariff cuts affected only 37 out of the 104 import competing industries.[14] These empirical results are hardly surprising in view of the mode of import liberalization, in which imports of particular groups of products are allowed in only when the domestic producers of the same products have established themselves as efficient exporters in international markets. One interesting question, also addressed in the previous chapter by Yoshitomi for Japan, is this: Why have such interventionist trade regimes not incurred large deadweight losses as have other economies pursuing protectionist policies?

In general, developing countries with export orientation have, at an early stage of development, comparative advantage in exporting labor-intensive manufactures, mostly consumer goods. The accumulation of capital and technology, together with a trained work force, subsequently enables them to produce other more skill- and technology-intensive manufactured products, which they used to import. They will, with a time lag, begin to export these products. That is, the shift of comparative advantage in the process of industrialization induces import substitution and export promotion simultaneously or in sequence.

Allocative Efficiency of Outward-Looking Strategy

Export Promotion and Government Intervention

For more than three decades, Taiwan and Korea have emulated Japan's pattern of industrialization. In terms of changes in the commodity composition of trade, the pattern goes through four subphases of development, which in turn are lumped into two major phases.[15] In the first subphase, developing countries export mostly primary products. This is followed by the second subphase in which import substitution of labor-intensive consumer goods is attempted. During the third subphase, countries become capable of exporting the consumer goods they succeeded in producing for the domestic market in the previous subphase. With the further development of manufacturing, they engage in import substitution of durable goods for producers as well as consumers, that is, heavy industrial and chemical products (the fourth subphase). When developing countries succeed in establishing an export base for these products, they then cross the demarcation line dividing countries between developed and developing ones (the fifth subphase). Ohkawa and Kohama argue that by the late 1980s, both Korea and Taiwan have reached the end of the fourth subphase of economic development.

According to this classification of the development process, export promotion and import substitution are carried out in sequence as developing countries are transiting from one subphase to another. That is, import substitution in the second and fourth subphases helps expand the domestic manufacturing base for future exports in the third and fifth subphases. In the process, developing countries adjust continuously to changes in their comparative advantage in trade. The length of each subphase differs from country to country. In Taiwan and Korea, beginning around the third subphase, export and import substitution have been carried out almost simultaneously.[16]

The development experiences of Taiwan and Korea show that their policymakers have intervened extensively in the allocation of resources for the sake of both export promotion and import substitution, although intervention has been more apparent in the case of Korea. Since the late 1960s, Korean policymakers have not made any strategic differentiation between import substitution and export promotion. Any domestic industry that is given priority status for import substitution has been accorded protection on the domestic market. This reflects the belief that to move up the ladder of comparative advantage, an essential foundation for successful export promotion is successful import substitution in earlier periods.

To be sure, one could always argue that Korea and Taiwan could have done better had they followed laissez-faire policies. For such a conclusion to be persuasive would require a counterfactual analysis, which is beyond the scope of this chapter. Instead, I will attempt to provide several reasons why their intervention-oriented regimes have been able to sustain rapid growth, whereas in other economies excessive intervention has been the primary cause of poor performance.

Perhaps the most important reason is that although import-substitution industries have been subsidized as infant industries, they have from the beginning been developed as the export industries of the future and not just for meeting domestic demand. As a result, firms in import-substitution industries have been encouraged to build large plants without being constrained by the size of the home market so that they would not sacrifice economies of scale. Given the incentive system favoring sales abroad and the relatively small size of the domestic market, import-substitution firms had early on found it to their advantage to sell abroad as soon as they began operating. That is, the export-incentive system reduced the length of the import-substitution period.

The incentive system was structured in such a way that the firms in import-substitution industries had to go out of business if they failed to meet the export-performance test after a period of protection. With the necessity of competing and surviving in international markets, they had no choice but to undertake investments to acquire the technological capability for improving productivity and for developing new export products. In the two import substitution subphases, Taiwan and Korea both began their industrialization efforts with QRs and high rates of protection. But they were able to make a quick transition to exports and to terminate government support when industries failed to compete in international markets.[17]

Another reason for the relative efficiency of import substitution in Korea and Taiwan is that successful export promotion cannot be achieved without fostering import-substitution industries that are efficient. In the third subphase of development, both countries began domestic production of imported intermediate inputs and capital goods needed by domestic exporters. But the strategy of backward integration raised the costs of intermediate inputs and capital goods to the exporters and undermined their competitiveness on international markets. This was not acceptable. Import substitution therefore met with opposition from the downstream producers, mainly those that produce for foreign markets. Thus, for an export-promotion strategy to be successful, it cannot shelter inefficient import-substitution industries for any length of time.

A third reason is that the rapid expansion of export industries has created a relatively large domestic market for capital goods and intermediate products, such as components and parts that enter into the production of export goods, and also for consumer products. The large domestic market increased the probability of success for import substitution industries because it made it less costly to adopt modern technology. Thus, the expansion of export-oriented industries enlarges the size of the domestic market in other sectors, including import-substituting ones. Such spillovers suggest that the coordination of investment across sectors by the government could be essential for industrialization.[18]

The fourth reason is that the successful promotion of exports contributes to an easing of the foreign-exchange constraint that is typical in the early phases of industrialization. Import substitution generates a large demand for imported intermediate inputs and capital goods. The improved availability of foreign exchange through export growth supports larger investment and facilitates the adoption of "increasing-returns" technologies in import substitution industries. Increased capability of import financing increases the range of investment choices available for the import-substitution industries.

Pitfalls of Import Substitution

Although the incentive system for export promotion serves as a means of improving the efficiency of import-substitution industries, the simultaneous pursuit of export promotion and import substitution has not always been successful. Taiwan's planners were as anxious as those of Korea to develop heavy and chemical industries. But unlike Korea, their efforts at import substitution of capital and intermediate goods were frustrated because they could not find private entrepreneurs willing and able to make large capital investments with long gestation periods. To bypass these difficulties, in the 1970s the government entrusted certain public enterprises with the task of developing the automotive industry. But the attempt did not succeed.[19] In retrospect, Taiwan was fortunate that its planners were not able to push through such an import-substitution program. Otherwise,it would not have been spared the disastrous consequences that Korea had to suffer.

Financial Liberalization

One of the most striking features of the economies of Taiwan and Korea is that their financial systems still remain greatly underdeveloped, characterized by outdated financial practices and government controls of day-to-day operations. Their undesirable situation has remained unchanged in spite of the decade-long liberalization efforts in both countries. This raises two questions: Why did the development of the financial sector lag behind that of other sectors, and to what extent has this inflicted damage on the two economies in terms of allocative inefficiency?

After three decades of rapid growth and industrialization that has elevated Taiwan to the ranks of semi-advanced countries, private enterprises still depend heavily on the curb market for their finance.[20] Credit rationing, collateral requirements, and selective credit controls are widely practiced by financial intermediaries. Entry to financial industries is strictly regulated, and most of the major domestic banks are government-owned.

Although in the 1980s Korea's monetary authorities have divested their holdings of equities of major nationwide commercial banks and relaxed entry controls, they have hardly succeeded in developing a market-oriented financial system in which the price mechanism reigns and the financial system is open to foreign investors.[21]

Despite certain positive efforts at liberalization in both countries, there has been only limited progress toward a fully liberalized financial regime. In fact, in Korea there is a widespread feeling that the process of financial liberalization has come to a standstill, largely because the government has not been able to give up its intervention into the asset-management of banks and even non-bank financial institutions; the government still practices a policy of "directed" loans.

The monetary authorities in Korea and Taiwan have not actively promoted financial deregulation because they do not believe that the underdeveloped financial system has, at least until now, interfered with the performance of their economies. Other possible explanations are that the governments of Taiwan and Korea have not relinquished the idea of directing investment activities and protecting certain industries, or that the purpose of control over the financial sector is their safety and stability.

A well-functioning financial system is alleged to contribute to a better economic performance because it helps induce households to save more if they can invest in convenient and high-yielding assets. However, some argue that neither theory nor empirical evidence can establish the validity of this proposition.[22] In spite of relative inefficiency, the holdings of financial assets as a proportion of GNP have risen markedly in both Taiwan and Korea by the 1980s, reaching the level of those of the developed countries. The two countries have also seen the rise of their savings to almost 40 percent of GNP, among the highest in the world.

Propositions about the allocative efficiency of the financial system are more controversial than are statements about its contribution to savings mobilization. In developed countries, one might argue, financial intermediation works so well that a complete liberalization of the financial sector may be optimal. However, when Taiwan and Korea embarked in the early 1960s on a course of export-led industrialization, their financial systems were dominated by a handful of commercial banks whose liabilities constituted a large fraction of the money supply. Their money and capital markets were fragmented, disorganized, and extremely unstable. In the eyes of policymakers at that time, it was clear that whatever incentive system they could devise for exports, the private financial system would not be able to allocate much of the limited domestic resources to export-oriented industries. In the case of Korea, the financial system could not mobilize much needed foreign savings without the direct assistance of the government because there were few financial institutions with a credit rating acceptable to foreign lenders. These structural deficiencies, concerns about safety, and other considerations may have induced and justified direct intervention on the part of the government in the financial markets. It is more difficult to explain why the governments still insist on retaining their control over finance.

Has the financial inefficiency stood in the way of shifting the economy from one subphase to another and adjusting to external and internal shocks? There are three possible answers: (1) when a country saves more than 35 percent of its GNP, as Taiwan and Korea do, financial inefficiencies short of a complete financial breakdown may be disregarded; (2) Korea and Taiwan could have done better with a liberalized financial system; and (3) financial intermediaries and markets have been reasonably efficient even under government control, as evidenced by the fact that they have allocated a great deal of resources to export-oriented industries which have been the most rapidly growing and profitable opportunities for investment. The correct answer is likely to be a mixture of these three views.

Conclusions

The development experiences of Korea and Taiwan over the last three decades stand out as two of the most successful recent cases of economic growth and industrialization through export promotion. It is often argued that an export-led development strategy as opposed to an import-substitution one tends to free the economy from government control and allows market forces to function. This view implies that the policy regime that characterizes an export-led strategy is close to that of laissez-faire; hence the success of an export-oriented development strategy should largely be attributed to the liberalization of the trade and financial sectors. This essay has argued that the experiences of Korea and Taiwan do not support this proposition.

Starting from a highly protected economy, both countries have, to be sure, managed not only to promote exports but also to remove many trade restrictions and financial regulations. However, the role of the government in the two countries has been much more active than that of primarily correcting market failures and imperfections. In reality, until recently export promotion has been accompanied by import substitution in all subphases of development. Import-substitution firms were accorded domestic market protection and other government support until they developed into efficient exporters. The coexistence of export promotion and import substitution may then in part account for the active role of government and the sequential approach to trade liberalization in which imports of particular products were allowed in only when the domestic producers of the same products could withstand foreign competition on the domestic market. If there is one important lesson to be drawn from the experiences of Korea and Taiwan, it is that the success or failure of export promotion is not correlated with the nature of the policy regime.

Judging from the record of rapid growth and stability, the interventionist policy regimes of Taiwan and Korea do not appear to have produced as large inefficiency losses as they would have in other economies. Being relatively small economies that inevitably depend heavily on imports, policymakers in Taiwan and Korea have set their sights on expanding their producers' world market shares. To survive in the world market, they have had to become efficient. And as long as they remain competitive internationally, distortions in the domestic market cannot be very large and do not matter very much.

Notes

1. Anne O. Krueger, "Export-led Growth Reconsidered," in W. T. Hong and L. B. Krause (eds.), *Trade and Growth of the Advanced Developing Countries in the Pacific Basin* (Korea Development Institute, 1981), p.10. When intermediate goods are taken into consideration, a measure in terms of the value-added ratio may be preferable to the price ratio.

2. *Ibid*, pp. 8-10.

3. *Ibid*.

4. Diaz-Alejandro, "Trade Policies and Economic Development," in P. B. Kenen (ed.), *International Trade and Finance: Frontiers for Research* (Cambridge University Press, 1975), pp. 51-94.

5. Anne O. Krueger, "Trade as an Input to Development," *American Economic Review*, May 1979; and Anne O. Krueger, "The Experience and Lessons of Asian Super Exporters," in V. Corbo et al. (eds.), *Export-Oriented Development Strategies* (Boulder, Colo. and London: Westview Press, 1985).

6. Yung Chul Park, "Export-led Development: The Korean Experience, 1960-1978," in Eddy Lee (ed.), *Export-Led Industrialization and Development* (Asian Employment Program, ILO, 1981).

7. M. K. Datta-Chaudhuri, "Industrialization and Foreign Trade: The Development Experiences of South Korea and the Philippines," in Eddy Lee (ed.), *Export-Led Industrialization and Development* (Asian Employment Program, ILO, 1981).

8. Anne O. Krueger, "Models and Issues of Pacific Growth and Macroeconmic Performance," paper presented to the 18th PAFTAD Conference, Kuala Lumpur, Malaysia, December 1989; and L. E. Westphal, "The Republic of Korea's Experience with Export-led Industrial Development," *World Development*, 1978.

9. Paul Kuznets, "An East Asian Model of Economic Development: Japan, Taiwan, and South Korea," *EDCC*, April 1988, Supplement 511-544.

10. Kuo-Shu Liang, "Financial Reform, Trade, and Foreign Exchange Liberalization in the ROC," *Industry of Free China*, December 1987.

11. S. K. Young, "Trade Policy Problems of the Republic of Korea and the Uruguay Round," Korea Development Institute Working Paper, No. 8913, April 1989.

12. Kuznets, *op. cit.*; and Yung Chul Park, "The Role of Government: Experiences of South Korea and Taiwan," *American Economic Review*, May 1990.

13. K. S. Kim, *Economic Impact of Import Liberalization and Industrial Adjustment Policy* (Seoul: Korea Development Institue, 1988).

14. Chaw-Hsia Tu and Wen-Thuen Wang, "Trade Liberalization in the Republic of China (Taiwan) and the Economic Effects of Tariff Reductions," paper presented at the 1988 Joint Conference on the Industrial Policies of the ROC and ROK, Korea Development Institute, 1988.

15. K. Ohkawa and H. Kohama, *Lectures on Developing Economies: Japan's Experience and Its Relevance* (Tokyo: University of Tokyo Press, 1989).

16. Chi-Ming Hou, "Strategy for Economic Development in Taiwan and Implications for Developing Economies," Conference on Economic Development Experiences of Taiwan and Its New Role in an Emerging Asia-Pacific Area, Taiwan, Institute of Economics, Academia Sinica, June 1988; Yung Chul Park, "Export-led Growth and Industrial Transformation in Korea, 1970-1980," Institute of Economc Development Discussion Paper, No. 7, Korea University, December 1983.

17. H. Pack, "Industrialization and Trade," in H. Chenery and T. N. Srinivasan (eds.), *Handbook of Development Economics*, Vol. 1 (North-Holland, 1988).

18. K. M. Murphy et al., "Industrialization and the Big Push," *JPE*, October 1989.

19. Yun-Han Chu, "The State and the Development of the Automobile Industry in South Korea and Taiwan," paper presented to the Conference on State Policy and Economic Development in Taiwan, December 1989.

20. Jia-Dong Shea, "Internationalization of the Financial Sector in Taiwan," paper presented to the 1988 Joint Conference on the Industrial Policies of the ROC and ROK, Korea Development Institute, 1988; Jia-Dong Shea, "Financial Development in Taiwan: Macro Analysis," unpublished manuscript, Institute of Economics, Academia Sinica, Taiwan, 1988.

21. Yung Chul Park, "Economic Stabilization and Liberalization in Korea, 1980-1984," Proceedings of the Seminar Commemorating the 35th Anniversary of the Bank of Korea, *Monetary Policy in a Changing Financial Environment* (Bank of Korea, 1985).

22. R. Dornbusch and A. Reynoso, "Financial Factors in Economic Development," *American Economic Review*, Vol. 79 (May 1989).

11

Mexico's Liberalization and Eastern Europe

William R. Rhodes

Let me begin with a startling but accurate statement: Mexico is speeding up the liberalization program it began in the mid-1980s because of developments in Central and Eastern Europe.

The first clear sign that Mexico and the rest of Latin America were going to face unexpectedly stiff competition for global risk capital came in November 1989 at a conference sponsored by the Inter-American Development Bank and the Export-Import Bank of Japan in Nagoya, Japan. During a series of conversations with Japanese officials from both the public and private sectors, Mexican Finance Minister Pedro Aspe and his Under Secretary for International Affairs, Jose Angel Gurria, became concerned that in the wake of the sudden opening to the world of the countries of Central and Eastern Europe, Japan was starting to shift attention away from Latin America and towards Eastern Europe. That perception was reinforced at the highest level of the Mexican government three months later when President Carlos Salinas attended a meeting of the World Economic Forum in Davos, Switzerland. Salinas came away from that meeting and others in Europe convinced that the best chance Mexico had of competing for risk capital with Eastern Europe and other parts of the world was to move swiftly with its economic reform package, including the privatization of formerly state-run businesses. The steps taken by Mexico during 1990 suggest that its president's conviction has been translated into action.

External Shocks and Liberalization

To appreciate Mexico's economic epiphany as well as the other trends in capital availability and investment flows, especially in emerging economies, we have to look back over the last 10 years at three political and economic shocks that affected the world:

- the international debt crisis;
- the collapse of communism and Soviet domination in Eastern Europe;
- and the recent Middle East crisis and its effect on oil prices.

Apart from all of the political, economic and social dislocation brought about by these shocks, the debt crisis and the collapse of communism have produced the same important side effect—each has accelerated the pace of economic reform and liberalization in many of the emerging countries. And we are seeing evidence that the rise in oil prices is doing the same. These shocks have also illustrated that those countries with market-based, open economies—those nations that are creditworthy and competitive— are in a much better position to weather such events than countries with closed and centrally planned economies. The former are, therefore, much better positioned to attract investment and capital.

In the midst of the trend toward economic opening and reform, some countries have been implementing needed stabilization programs—for example, balancing the budget and devaluing the currency—without simultaneously undertaking structural economic adjustments, including privatizations. The track record of developing countries, especially those in Latin America, has shown that any viable adjustment strategy must go beyond economic stabilization efforts to spell out a feasible process that leads to the revival of growth and investment. During the early 1980s, economic stabilization programs in Mexico, Venezuela, Brazil and Argentina failed because of weak structural adjustments.

It was not until late 1985, for example, that the De La Madrid government in Mexico successfully applied for membership in the General Agreement on Tariffs and Trade—a clear sign that the country intended to modify its trade restrictions to be more competitive in the international marketplace. At the same time, the Mexican government began taking serious measures to reduce the role of the public sector through privatizations and the closing of some inefficient and money-losing state companies. Another country which has successfully implemented structural adjustment reforms, including privatizations, is Chile, which started even earlier than Mexico and which since the mid-1980s has had an admirable record of stable, sustained growth.

Recent Lessons in Latin America for Eastern Europe

In Eastern Europe, Poland is an example of a country that has not simultaneously implemented stabilization measures and structural adjustments. While its stabilization program has apparently succeeded in substantially reducing inflation, the lack of structural adjustments has made it difficult to create markets for labor and capital. I mention the situation in

Poland for this reason: There is no modern precedent for the transformation in Central and Eastern Europe from a command economy into a market economy, while at the same time opening the way for democratic pluralism. I would suggest, however, that one of the most interesting comparisons for Eastern Europe is Latin America in the 1980s—a time when many countries moved from authoritarian to democratic government and then began opening up and privatizing their economies. For that reason, I think Eastern Europe could learn some lessons from the recent past in Latin America.

Key Components of Mexico's Program

Of all the Latin American countries, Mexico is one of the best examples of a country that is adopting reform measures in order to attract the necessary foreign investment. Mexico's progress is even more remarkable considering that in the summer of 1989 the country's debt negotiations were stalled. Finance Minister Aspe and Under Secretary Gurria advised Citibank chairman John Reed and myself that they were planning to break off negotiations because they didn't think an agreement could be reached. Fortunately, those negotiations continued and today the Mexican government believes that the financial package it signed with its creditor banks in February 1990 was a crucial part of its overall economic program. The package and its economic reforms helped bring Mexico's internal interest rates down to below 24 percent in 1990, the lowest since 1982 and less than half the peak reached in the spring of the previous year. These rates could save the government $10 to $12 billion in expenditures annually, which in turn would help Mexico put its public finances in order, and reduce its budget deficit to two percent of GDP. In addition, economic growth reached nearly 3 percent in 1989, the highest since 1982.

During 1986-1990, Mexico also implemented many more privatization projects than anyone would have predicted a few years ago. There has already been a series of major privatizations in the airlines, copper, and trucking industries. In 1990 alone the government announced $20 to $25 billion worth of additional privatizations in such industries as banking, telecommunications, steel, fertilizers, and insurance. Foreign investment is also rebounding. The government announced that during the first nine months of 1990, new investment reached over $2.7 billion, equal to the total for the entire year of 1989. Mexican borrowers in both the private and public sectors are returning to the capital markets where in recent years they completed a number of voluntary transactions.

Liberalization and the Global Demand and Supply of Capital

The pace of Mexico's economic reform program is, in many ways, related to its awareness of the strong demand for global risk capital—a demand that is likely to become even more considerable in the future. The amount needed for privatizations alone in Latin America, Eastern Europe, and Southeast Asia could easily reach $500 billion over the next two years. This doesn't take into account the privatizations that would be included in the Gorbachev/Yeltsin attempt to open up the Soviet economy. Given the recent history of the problem many developing countries have had of servicing their debts, many of the world's largest commercial banks have not been inclined to lend to the emerging economies for balance-of-payments purposes. However, despite this fact and the shortage of global risk capital, those countries that take substantive steps toward becoming competitive and creditworthy should be able to count on a core group of international banks to help finance their growth and privatization plans. The agreements in 1990 between the governments of Venezuela and Chile and their commercial-bank creditors demonstrate that this core group does in fact exist. Mexico is also an example of a country that is returning to the voluntary markets.

The need to encourage these banks is recognized by, among others, Enrique Iglesias, President of the Inter-American Development Bank (IDB). He is working with a group of bankers, including myself, to develop a new program of co-financing between the IDB and commercial banks, to encourage a core group of banks to continue their lending relationships with those Latin American and Caribbean countries that have viable economic programs. This effort is part of Mr. Iglesias's plan for the IDB to offer increased leadership and financial support for economic growth in Latin America and the Caribbean. The plan is consistent with the initiative of President Bush, spelled out during his December 1990 trip to five Latin American countries.

Arrearages and New Capital

I should caution that the arrearages situation is a continuing impediment to a core group of banks wishing to offer their support. Toward the end of 1990, arrearages on interest payments to commercial banks from restructuring countries totaled over $24 billion. This development may reflect a perception by some countries that the current strategy condones the use of arrearages as a form of external financing. The international financial institutions have in some cases broken with previous policy and disbursed funds to countries that are in substantial arrears to commercial bank creditors. However, I think that the international financial institutions are beginning to realize that arrearages to commercial banks can also stimulate arrearages to them. I am concerned that continuing arrearages will make it increasingly difficult to complete future commercial bank financing packages—packages that are essential elements of the countries' economic reform program.

Latin America versus Eastern Europe

As Mexico discovered early on, a great deal of attention is being focused on Eastern and Central Europe these days. The emergence of democratic pluralism and open economies in these regions is startling. Nonetheless, Latin America has certain distinct advantages in the competition for global risk capital. It has an existing legal, auditing and economic framework, including commercial banking systems. And many countries in Latin America have a head start in the competition for that scarce capital.

In its 1990 report, *Economic and Social Progress in Latin America*, the Inter-American Development Bank notes that the structural reforms of the 1980s, if continued, would allow the region to look forward to improved prospects and a resumption of growth. The report states:

> Even if the attention of the world's policy makers during the 1990s shifts to solving the economic and social problems of Eastern Europe and the Soviet Union, this shift will not necessarily be detrimental to the interests of Latin America, which may actually benefit from the incorporations of these formerly centrally planned economies into a more open system of world trade.

I believe the need for developing countries to implement reforms and privatization is heightened by the scarcity of global risk capital. Those countries that adopt the necessary reforms should have the support of a core group of banks.

As we look ahead, some countries will come out winners and some won't. The determining factor will be how well a country can implement economic reforms and meet its financial obligations. Capital will flow to those countries that are competitive and creditworthy.

PART THREE

Hungary's Experiences and Policy Options

12

Transforming Commercial Relations within the CMEA: The Case of Hungary

András Köves

Transforming commercial relations with its CMEA partners is an important part of the Hungarian reform process. Liberalization and the transition to a market economy would have little chance of success if in this highly foreign-trade-dependent country almost half of the exports and imports continued to be administered using non-market methods according to the traditional system of CMEA trade that follows the logic of the economic system based on mandatory plans and the central allocation of resources. In such a case, a significant part of the Hungarian economy, which has been nurtured in a glass house, and which is thus able and prefers to meet only the requirements of the CMEA market, would not be forced to have its products evaluated by the world market.

Transforming Hungary's trade relations with the CMEA countries is not merely a logical and unavoidable step in Hungary's reform process; it is a step that cannot be further postponed without severe negative consequences. This follows from the critical economic situation of the CMEA countries (primarily that of the Soviet Union), from the increasingly grave disturbances in the operation of these economies, and hence from the growing instability and unavoidable reduction of intra-CMEA deliveries. What we have to face today is not only the structural problems of this trade, its low and deteriorating efficiency, but also that, owing to the deterioration in the capability and willingness of its partners to supply commodities, Hungarian exports will have to be cut back significantly in any case.[1]

But within the present system of trade and payments this cannot be achieved, as attested to by Hungary's large but unusable surplus on the clearing account. Whereas Hungary's debt to the West amounts to more than $20 billion, with a deficit on the current account of about $1.4 billion in 1989, in the same year the ruble surplus on the current account was on the order of transferable ruble (TR) 1.6 billion. Calculated at Hungary's cross exchange rates, this equals more than $800 million; at the official TR-USD exchange rate the sum would amount to about $2.4 billion. Half of this surplus came about in Hungarian-Soviet trade. Because a TR is not automatically convertible either to a usable currency or to goods, it is a negative phenomenon, quite in contrast with trade among market economies. Considering the economic trends and political difficulties in the partner countries, the situation for Hungary may rapidly deteriorate further.[2]

The implications of the current political changes in Eastern Europe for Hungary's economic strategy and intra-CMEA trade policies are immense. As late as the end of 1988, when the previous government's Reform Committee began its work on reforming the country's intra-CMEA trade, Soviet opposition seemed to be the biggest obstacle. Today, however, the external political conditions are more favorable than ever. The evolving new political framework and economic transformation under way in several of the countries will demand a new type of economic relationship among the CMEA countries. Chances for the CMEA to survive in its present form are negligible. In this sense, renewal in Eastern Europe gives an enormous stimulus to Hungary's efforts at creating a new system of relations with the CMEA countries.

The general international environment also favors the Hungarian reform process. This is indicated by the cooperation of the 24 Western countries that has been unfolding since mid-1989, offering economic and financial support, initially to Hungary and Poland. At this point, however, it is far from certain whether this assistance will be large enough and appropriate enough to end, at least temporarily, the decade-long net resource outflow from Hungary.

Reforms and Orientation: What Is To Be Done?

As of July 1990, trade among the CMEA countries is, in essence, a system of peculiar bilateral clearing relations. Settlements are effected in TR. Prices are determined—at least in principle—on the basis of the average world market prices of an agreed past period (presently the five years preceding the year in question). Intra-CMEA trade is based on long-term (five years) intergovernmental agreements on plan coordination and on five-year and one-year bilateral trade agreements. The governments mutually undertake commitments to supply and purchase the commodity quotas specified in the agreements, expressed in kind. An intricate web of price and commodity tie-ins interweaves this trade. The delivery of a given export commodity (or group of commodities) is regarded as an offset for specified deliveries of the partner country; that is, a given commodity is sold because a certain product (or products) can be purchased in return, and it is sold at the given price because that is the price that is in line with the price of the product received in exchange. Thus, a sales transaction is not brought about merely on the basis of mutually acceptable conditions for the seller and the buyer alone. It is realized as part of a larger package. Hence its conditions (e.g., the prices, or the profitability of the deal) cannot be evaluated in themselves but only as a function of what other product can be obtained in return for the given commodity, and under what conditions. Because these price and commodity tie-ins are of macroeconomic significance, it cannot be questioned that, within this system, the ultimate responsibility for reaching an agreement on prices, quotas, and other conditions of trade lies with the authorities.

In this way, even in Hungary's modified centrally planned economy that was in place at least until 1990, the roles, responsibilities and risks assumed by government bodies and enterprises cannot be separated. The exporter and the importer regard their activities not merely or mainly as trade, but as the performance of a definite state task. Therefore they consider it natural that they cannot incur losses; if needed, they would get sufficient subsidies from their government to make the activity profitable. On the other hand, the government may, with the same justification, believe that eventual profits made on export to or import from the CMEA countries are not due to the efforts of the enterprises alone, since the government has not only established the necessary macroeconomic conditions of trading but also the individual terms of the deal for the enterprise. Therefore, this or that part of the profits generated in intra-CMEA trade shall routinely be drawn into the state budget.

Even this sketchy description reveals how this system disorients the economic agents and why it has proved to be an impediment of adjustment to the world market requirements. The factors to be changed are self-evident. A situation should be created in which the logic of the Hungarian economic system—that of an evolving market economy—should prevail. Business decisions should be made by the enterprises; only macroeconomic regulation should be the field and duty of the government. Hungarian enterprises should, even in intra-CMEA trade, decide on a business basis with whom they wish to trade, what they want to purchase or sell, how much, and at what terms, and they should assume the consequences of all their decisions. The government should not assume itemized commitments in kind for the purchase or the supply of individual commodities. Achieving these objectives requires that a new system replace the present trade and payments arrangements.

Defining the ways and means of the transformation of trade relations among the CMEA countries is a most complicated issue. The Reform Committee of Hungary, in its deliberations early in 1989, suggested changing the system of Hungarian-Soviet trade first. Several alternative solutions were envisaged: (1) trade in a convertible currency (dollars), implying the use of (world) market prices; (2) clearing settled in a convertible currency; and (3) ruble-clearing (following the pattern of Finnish-Soviet trade). In contrast to the radical version mentioned first, which would not exclude the possibility of a transitory mechanism and measures to dampen the shock effects of the transition, the third option (the Finnish model) was considered the most likely moderate solution. This would be a system wherein trade would continue to be conducted on the basis of long-term and annual intergovernmental (clearing) agreements, but the commodity quotas determined therein would not contain governmental commitments to supply or purchase the goods in question. As far as Hungary (and not necessarily the Soviets, given their different foreign-trading system) is concerned, only enterprises would take on supply or purchase commitments after an agreement had been reached by them on prices and other conditions. In such a system there would be no need for declaring any new principle of settlement or pricing. Although settlements would continue to be made in TR, without intergovernmental price and commodity tie-ins, market prices different from the TR prices currently applied within the CMEA would gradually evolve.[3]

A fourth version would leave the major part of the present system—namely, the intergovernmental agreements on quotas, pricing and settlements—intact. Only transactions above the quotas would be freely permitted in any currency—hard currency, national currencies, or TR—but with the limitation that in the case of non-convertible currencies there would be no official guarantee for their conversion to forints. Instead, the currencies earned would have to be auctioned to their highest bidder.

In theory, Hungary's choice among the different versions should be based on a comparison of their short-term costs (primarily manifested in the deterioration of the convertible-currency balance of payments) and of the benefits expected in the long run as a result of the new pressures on and opportunities for enterprises to reorient their trade from the CMEA to the world market. In any case, however, the choice is made difficult by the fact that the costs of transformation appear concentrated in time immediately upon the introduction of the change, while the benefits accrue over a lengthy period and to the extent that the process of economic adjustment is successful.

The more radical the solution chosen, the larger will be the initial shock—namely, the foreign exchange burden and all the known domestic costs that are concomitant with discontinuity, restructuring, and market switching. The moderate solution would reduce the initial extent of the burden and leave more time for adjustment.

The shock effect, as well as the lack of it, can be both advantageous and disadvantageous, depending on the timing and the actions taken. Under certain conditions, the shock could lead to a paralysis of the economy as much as it could, under a different set of conditions, trigger a massive and inevitable transformation and reorientation. The absence of such a shock or its moderation may equally provide an opportunity for gradual adjustment as for its postponement, if graduality remains a slogan. The dilemma of making the change immediately versus gradually is a problem well known in the literature on liberalization, and is discussed ably in the contributions in this volume by Halevi and Langhammer.

Costs and Risks of the Transformation

As important as it may seem in Hungary's present financial situation to opt for a moderate, less costly solution of abandoning the TR system, the Nemeth government (1989-1990) had opted for Solution 1 (with Solution 4 as its second choice, in case the necessary conditions for transition to hard-currency trade with the Soviet Union, as of 1991, could not be created). Two basic arguments explain the choice. First, hard currency trade is the alternative acceptable to the Soviets.[4] Second, this is the only realistic way of abandoning the traditional CMEA trade system. Given the vested interests of the participants in the trade—including, of course, the enterprises in Hungary—in maintaining the old patterns, structures, preferences, and familiar arrangements, less radical solutions could be counter-productive because they may not trigger the changes in behavior that are desperately needed. Changing to real hard-currency trade seems to many to be the only way to convince Hungarian enterprises, the Soviets, and the West that the Hungarian government means what it says: it is serious in its determination to reform and reorient the country's CMEA trade relations. Credibility is a crucial problem here; 1990 is not the first year for a Hungarian government to tell the enterprises that the possibilities of exporting to the CMEA are limited and that there is an urgent need to export to alternative markets as well. Because the government has never followed this warning with serious and consistent policy action, the message so far (with a few exceptions) has not been effectively received.

The costs and risks of transition for Hungary arise from the one-sided CMEA (Soviet) orientation of a large part of the Hungarian economy. According to the Hungarian foreign trade data calculated at the official Hungarian rates of the forint to the ruble and other currencies (which differ substantially from the official TR/$ rate), even in 1989, 45 percent of Hungary's total exports of manufactures went to the CMEA countries, 27 percent of which went to the Soviet Union. One-sidedness is even more pronounced in machinery exports, where the share of the CMEA countries is 70 percent, and the Soviet Union is 45 percent of that. This is much higher than these shares were even in the 1970s.

A significant part of the products that Hungarian enterprises export to the Soviet market for rubles cannot be sold in the world market at all, or only at significantly reduced prices or after substantial additional expenditures for improvement. Therefore, the transition to the new system of trade and settlements would have negative consequences on Hungary's balance of payments in the short run, primarily because this circumstance would then influence behavior on the Soviet side also. Presumably, after the change the Soviets would be willing to buy only products that meet world market standards if they are to pay world market prices in dollars. They would buy the other products—regarded as "soft" in the CMEA—only at reduced prices or not at all. The dollar cost for Hungary of this "problem" can only be alleviated, not eliminated, by opting for the moderate solution of transition. The import policy of the Hungarian enterprises will be similar. But the share of the "hard" goods (those that can be sold for dollars at world market conditions, such as energy and other raw materials) in the Soviet Union's exports to Hungary is higher than in Hungary's export to the Soviet Union.[5] That is why it is realistic to assume that after the switch-over the present Hungarian surplus in Hungarian-Soviet trade would turn into a deficit in dollars.

On this Hungarian economists generally agree, although the details of their views, and the results of their calculations as to the expected magnitude of the deficit, differ. A marked dissenting opinion is represented by Nagy:

> Certain official calculations keep frightening us that this transition would mean an annual loss of USD 1.5 billion for us. . . . If we accept that we enjoy such or similar price advantage today, then that will be lost not only in the case of and primarily not because of the change to a settlement in freely convertible currencies, since such a matter depends not on the mode of settlement but on the power relations, on the negotiation positions, and on the skills [of the parties].[6]

Others also believe it probable that the position of Hungarian exporters on the Soviet market is stronger than what is generally assumed. The reasons include knowledge of the language and of the country, their contacts, and the fact that Hungarian firms and products are well established there and have a well-defined role in meeting shortages—especially today, given the critical state of the Soviet economy. This could limit the projected decrease in the export volume and in prices due to the transition.

The future development of Soviet import policy could also be an influencing factor. To be more exact, the question is, what kind of import intentions or pressures will the collapse of the domestic market for consumer goods give rise to in the USSR?

While numerous other risk and uncertainty factors could be mentioned, there is a single circumstance of fundamental importance that must drive Hungary's economic policy choice: there is no alternative that would render the elimination of the tensions accumulated in intra-CMEA trade without grave costs to Hungary in the short run. Hungarian-Soviet trade will plummet not because of the switch-over to dollar trade. The reasoning should be just the opposite: the timeliness of the policy change follows from the unavoidability of the certain decrease and possible collapse of trade. The macroeconomic necessity of reorientation obtains in any case; it does not depend on which of the alternative solutions is selected. Nevertheless, it is only the radical version that conveys this macroeconomic necessity to the enterprises authentically and decisively, by exerting tough pressure on them to reorient. At the same time, abolishing the intergovernmental contracts that are binding on enterprises gives firms a wider range of possibilities of reorientation.

Hungary's import policy will also have to be changed. Although Soviet energy and raw material deliveries have stagnated throughout the 1980s and even decreased in a few areas, so far the highest economic priority has remained to spare no effort in importing the largest possible quantities of Soviet raw materials and energy. This policy of import maximization[7]— forming the basic content of plan coordination and having long been pursued at the highest political level—is responsible for the fact that little trade reorientation has taken place in Hungary through the end of 1989, even though Soviet economic performance in general and export performance in particular have been deteriorating since the mid-1970s. Hence, Hungary's import dependence on the Soviet Union should have been reduced rather than increased. In addition to political considerations (the "inadmissibility" of depending on non-CMEA countries for energy imports), the grounds given in support of the policy of import maximization were that energy and raw materials could be purchased from the Soviet Union at prices below those on the world market and, even more important, for transferable rubles, which means that they could be exchanged for Hungary's manufactures. And "of course," the usual argument for a Soviet-oriented development of industrial production was that the industrial goods produced could then be offered in exchange for energy and raw material purchases from the Soviet Union. To this day, Hungary's economic policy has been unable to break out of this erroneous circle of reasoning.

However, with the rejection of the TR system, the ground would be pulled out from under the policy of import maximization. This applies in particular to trade settled in convertible currency. The Soviet Union would have no reason to make its deliveries dependent on Hungary's behavior—political or economic. The Hungarian government would also not have any reason to finance activities aimed at increasing exports to the Soviet Union merely in the hope of a future increase, maintenance, or minimization of the decrease of Soviet energy deliveries. This factor would be of major significance in rendering possible the reorientation of Hungary's strategy of economic development.

The Need for a Safety Net:
Difficulties and New Opportunities

It follows from the above that a one-step switch-over to hard-currency trade with the Soviet Union can responsibly be suggested only in case a safety net for financing the deficit can be established.

It should be noted that the need for a safety net is not confined to the switch-over to hard-currency trade with the Soviet Union. Hard-currency losses would result from switching to any of the three alternative systems mentioned. The sums involved in the transition to hard-currency trade are perhaps larger than the costs of alternative versions, but so are the potential medium- and longer-term benefits of a more decisive restructuring process which could be the consequence of the radical change of the trade system.

Hungary endeavors to reach an agreement with the Soviet Union on the transition that would make possible an orderly switch-over, the reduction of the resulting short-term burden on Hungary, and a minimization of the risks involved, such as huge unforeseen changes in trade volume that the Soviets might initiate. Certainly, certain changes in the Soviet system of planning and financing foreign trade with respect to Hungary are necessary if the TR system were to be abandoned in Soviet-Hungarian relations. But in this respect, a two-fold problem has to be faced. First, relying on Soviet support seems to be illusory, first of all because of the weak state of the Soviet economy. Second, striving for too many guarantees from the Soviets would perpetuate the very system that is intended to be abolished.

It is important to note that the Soviet proposal about the switch-over to hard-currency trade is basically different from the Hungarian one. Whereas, according to the Hungarian position, trade should be on a business basis and, as a condition for this, the present system of the country's trade and financial settlements with the CMEA countries should be abolished and replaced by a new one, the Soviets do not envisage any systemic changes. What they want is to change the currency and the price basis of their trade with the other CMEA countries, and to do accounting in dollars, at current world market prices. A bilateral clearing settlement can mean very different things, depending on the technical solutions applied. At one extreme, it can be an effective business-based trade among the firms of the countries involved, under the umbrella of an agreement between the competent authorities (governments, central banks) of the respective countries regulating the framework and perhaps imposing selective quantitative restrictions, with the trade balance to be settled in convertible currency. At the other end, there is the CMEA-type state trading, with very strong government involvement in microeconomic decisions, and without the possibility of using the trade balance for either buying commodities or obtaining hard currency. Soviet ideas concerning dollar clearing seem to be much closer to the second type. Bilateral trade would remain largely centralized, and the "market" would mean no more than setting prices in dollars instead of rubles. This, according to Soviet understanding of the distribution of advantages and disadvantages of trade within the CMEA, would discontinue the big price losses for the Soviet Union in intra-CMEA (Soviet-Hungarian) trade.

The apparent Soviet unwillingness to establish—parallel to changing to accounting in dollars—a trade system essentially different from the traditional one may be explained by their belief that insisting on a clearing relationship can effectively limit Hungary's withdrawal from the CMEA and the country's foreign economic reorientation (and of course, that it is in the Soviet interest to limit Hungary's reorientation). The second kind of explanation, one may speculate, is rooted in the centralizing tendencies in Soviet economic management, especially that of foreign trade. Soviet planners and policymakers, faced with growing economic chaos and disturbances in their domestic economy, as well as growing shortages of both foreign exchange and exportables, would see maintaining the existing institutions of bilaterally managed trade as a means of blocking those negative tendencies.[8]

The Soviets may be mistaken on both counts, for two reasons: first, because they seem to be impervious to what has already happened in Eastern Europe; and second, at a time of disruptions in the economy, centralized channels of trade management may work even more poorly than decentralized ones. The last point is crucial from Hungary's perspective. We suppose that whatever happens in the Soviet economy, ample possibilities for Hungarian-Soviet trade will remain. But it is essential that Hungarian firms participating in this trade should have the option to explore new, decentralized trading channels. These could be established as a consequence of the changing political and economic situation in the Soviet Union; they could be substituted for the old ones, which would cease to function.

Even irrespective of the future developments in the Soviet Union, maintaining the traditional CMEA system while switching to accounting in dollars would make no sense for Hungary because it would have major negative implications for the country. Hungary would pay for imports of Soviet energy and raw materials more than it pays now, in terms of export volume. At the same time, the commodity pattern of its exports would largely be determined by how the Soviet central authorities assess the needs of their economy. It is easy to understand that this approach would leave little chance for effective restructuring and reorientation of the Hungarian economy.

From the point of view of macroeconomic rationality, as distinct from the other reasons mentioned, there is no reason for the Soviets to insist on maintaining clearing relations with Hungary. What they are effectively interested in is getting the most (in terms of foreign exchange or imports needed by the economy) for their exports of oil, other energy, and raw materials. To sell oil for hard currency and to get the world market price for it is certainly the best way of both maximizing the revenues from exports and maintaining a free hand to decide the optimal mix of imports. Deliveries of oil to Hungary would make it possible for the Soviet Union to obtain the same amount of free foreign exchange for the given volume of exports as it can get from the oil exports to Western Europe. It could decide on its own whether to spend the money obtained in Hungary on buying Hungary's food, industrial consumer goods, or machinery, or buying the commodities of any other country.

The important point is, of course, that what the Soviets have to maximize is total foreign exchange revenues and not their volume of trade with Hungary. But it is also important to add that insisting on clearing in Soviet-Hungarian trade is not the proper way to maximize bilateral trade. As the experience of recent years suggests, with Soviet export capacity constrained and unreliable, Hungary would have no option but to continuously limit and administratively cut its own exports. This would have negative implications for the Soviets as well. Given the Soviet Union's economic situation and trends, the undesirability of further unusable surpluses for both sides is a key argument against the clearing solution.

All this means that even the reconciliation of the conflicting Hungarian and Soviet positions won't be that easy, although we believe that the creation of an asymmetrical trade system (with Hungary applying the logic of the market economy to its relations with the Soviet Union and the latter the logic of its economic system to trade with Hungary) is feasible—just the same way as trade between market economies and centrally planned economies is practicable.

In spite of these problems, it is important to mention that according to the preliminary Hungarian-Soviet agreement on switching to hard-currency trade as of January 1991, an arrangement concerning the 1989 Hungarian surplus was reached. The TR 800 million surplus in Hungary's trade with the Soviet Union has been recalculated at an exchange rate of TR1 = USD 0.92. The resulting $700 million or so will be credited to Hungary's account, with the changeover to dollar trade as of 1991. However, there is no agreement as of July 1990 on the precise ways in which this dollar credit can be used.

Although the above arrangement, Hungary assumes, will ease significantly the burden of transition in 1991, many uncertainties do remain. For example, will the trading be conducted in clearing or regular convertible currency? If the latter, will the Soviets have the money to import, and if yes, will they wish to spend it in Hungary? Even more fundamentally, a great uncertainty is caused by the emerging economic and political disintegration of the USSR. Hence it would be important to establish the needed safety net in international cooperation, within the framework of the Western support for the Hungarian reform process.

Although it would be irresponsible to suggest that this problem (being a part of the complex issue of balance-of-payments financing) is easy to solve, we believe that the idea of the safety net is more than just wishful thinking if Western governments and international economic organizations will realize that reforming Hungary's commercial relations with the Soviet Union is a precondition for opening up and liberalizing its economy. It is for this reason that it is in their interest to support the establishment of a necessary safety net.

What is needed is guarantees that should depend on fulfilling certain conditions, making it possible in Hungary to finance the eventual additional hard-currency deficit that would occur in the coming years as a consequence of the transformation of Hungarian-Soviet trade. Further, the IMF should regard this additional deficit as a consequence of the process of restructuring. This deficit should be handled as a separate problem of Hungarian adjustment and not as non-compliance with the balance-of-payments targets previously agreed to by the IMF and the Hungarian government.

It is also worth mentioning the new business opportunities that might be opened to foreign capital as a result of the switch-over to hard currency in Hungarian-Soviet trade. These could be of interest primarily to those contemplating foreign direct investment in Hungary. It is well known that one of the main impediments is Hungary's small domestic market. Investment in Hungary could be much more attractive if it could serve a much larger market, as noted by Inotai in Chapter 6. At the same time, Hungarian enterprises mainly affected by the transformation of Soviet-Hungarian trade, owing to their one-sided orientation to the Soviet market, will require strategic and business policy changes, the renewal of the technologies used as well as their organization and management, in order to make them competitive in the world market. We believe this is another opportunity not to be underestimated by Western investors, especially if the "reorientation program" of these enterprises were to be supported by the Western governments and international organizations.

Conclusions

This chapter addresses the problems of transforming Hungarian-Soviet commercial relations. Of course, as a consequence of economic and political developments, transformation is topical in Hungary's trade with the other CMEA countries also. Because of the German monetary reunion of July 1, 1990, change to hard-currency trade with the GDR is already an established fact. As of July 1990, negotiations with other countries have also progressed.

Change to a new system of trade with those countries is also imminent. Because the problems and structures in those bilateral relationships are different from those of Hungarian-Soviet trade, the evolving new trade systems may also involve various solutions.

A more important problem is whether Hungary's approach to transforming trade with the Soviet Union is relevant to the other East European countries. As a matter of fact, some of them are much more reluctant to change the trade system with the Soviet Union than Hungary seems to be. Differences in economic situations, such as the large Polish ruble debt to the Soviet Union, partly explain this. Basically, however, the problems and options for all of the East European countries are very similar. The Soviet insistence on changing to dollar trade is but one—and not the most important—factor in explaining this situation. More fundamentally, all the reforming countries agree that there is a pressing need for the discontinuation of the one-sided dependence on trade with the Soviet Union, for reorientation and restructuring as a part of the process of the transformation of their economic systems. Maintaining the traditional CMEA-type trade system with the Soviet Union is incompatible with the aims mentioned. A country cannot wish to reorient and maintain its traditional trade flows and structures. A choice must be made.

Notes

1. For a discussion of the problem see András Köves, "A New Situation in Hungarian-Soviet Trade: What Is To Be Done?" in *The Challenge of Simultaneous Economic Relations with East and West* (London: Macmillan, 1990).

2. In early 1990, a considerable additional surplus was accumulated on the ruble account, forcing the Hungarian government to introduce severe administrative controls on exports to the CMEA countries.

3. The radical solution was first proposed by Sándor Richter, the Finnish-Soviet type of clearing by Gábor Obláth, "A rubelforgalom szabályozása—a gyökeres reform szükségessége és lehetösége" ["The Regulation of the Ruble Trade—The Necessity and Possibility of Radical Reform"], manuscript prepared for the working committee on "Opening to the World Economy and the Development of Market Relations" of the Economic Reform Committee of the Hungarian Government, 1988.

4. As a matter of fact, at the Sofia meeting in January 1990, the Soviets not only agreed to but insisted on a switch-over to hard-currency trade with all CMEA countries, and, at the end of June, abrogated the decades-long agreement of the CMEA countries concerning accounting trade in transferable rubles.

5. The share of machinery in Soviet exports to Hungary is much lower and is sharply falling: from 27 percent in 1980 and 22 percent in 1985 to 11 percent in 1989.

6. András Nagy, "Külkereskedelmi orientációváltást!" ["A Change is Needed in Foreign Trade Orientation!], *Közgazdasági Szemle*, September 1989, pp. 1033-1046, 2045.

7. For details, see A. Köves, "The Import Restriction Squeeze and Import Maximizing Ambitions: Some Connections of East-West vs. Intra-CMEA Trade," *Acta Oeconomica*, Vol, 34, Nos. 1-2, pp. 99-112. Reprinted in *Soviet and Eastern European Foreign Trade*, Vol. 23, No. 2, Summer 1987, pp. 78-93. See also, A. Köves, "Some Questions of Energy Policy in East European Countries," in *Energie, Umwelt und Zusammenarbeit in Europe* (Vienna and New York: Springer-Verlag, 1987).

8. I am indebted for this explanation to László Csaba.

13

Foreign Trade Liberalization (1968-1990)

János Gács

In centrally planned economies, the mere notion of trade liberalization raises a number of questions. In the early stage of development in this system, even the chance of trade expansion was questionable. Autarkic tendencies were reinforced in every planned economy partly on grounds of ideology (menace from abroad as a justification for discipline and the autocratic, command economy, thus presenting foreign trade as an element causing disintegration and dangerous exposure) and partly as a consequence of the essential factors of a planned economy (such as minimizing the effects of foreign trade, outside the control of planners). This policy entailed a systematic cutting of all international links in production, cooperation, development, trade, and capital ownership established before central planning. This process characterized the first decade of the socialist economy in Hungary.

According to the national plans, in the 1950s the centrally specified requirements of forced industrialization were to be supplied increasingly by domestic production. However, this only worked for a short while; this kind of industrialization devoured energy and materials and caused a rapid growth of imports, with a corresponding expansion of export targets that had to be built into the national plans to ensure equilibrium of the balance of foreign trade.

The rapid growth of intra-CMEA trade began in the early 1960s, developing the dual nature of Hungarian foreign trade in which a large part was conducted with market economies, another substantial part with centrally planned economies. These two kinds of foreign trade were interconnected by many links. However, they were predominantly segregated from each other—especially after 1968—as far as the method of decision making in trade and production, contacts with foreign partners, and the macro level control of such trading activities were concerned.

Thus an initial autarkic stage of the development of the Hungarian economy was followed by a growth of the importance of foreign trade, gradually making Hungary, by the 1970s and 1980s, one of the most open East European economies—at least in terms of trade volume. But was the high degree of openness indicated by the exports/GDP ratio accompanied by an equally high degree of openness of the institutions and trade policy? Did the decisive role of foreign trade imply that Hungarian business units responded quickly and flexibly to world market changes—that the domestic resource allocation was directly influenced by the shifts in external demand and supply? Did it mean that competition in internal and external markets with foreign goods and services became a performance measure for Hungarian firms, or that the structure of foreign trade contributed substantially to the long-range balanced growth of the Hungarian economy? The answers of Hungarian economists to all of these questions tend to be, no.

The closed nature of the Hungarian economy is shown by the following incomplete list of factors. Central planning kept strict control over foreign trade activities, whether directly or indirectly, of most state-owned business units. The key instrument of control was the isolation of production from foreign trade. The profitability of neither imports nor exports was subject to calculations at the enterprise level; firms were expected to absorb input shortages and output surpluses in the system of national balances, according to plan breakdown. Under state ownership, trade could develop only in traditional forms, transparent and easily controllable by the center. Direct international cooperation in production, joint ventures, capital flows, or capital combinations was not given much chance. Development decisions were mostly issued in the framework of grand national projects expressed in physical terms, with their trade implications more or less ignored.

Was there any sign of development towards opening up Hungary to the world economy, establishing integral relations with external markets, or dismantling the protectionistic barriers? And if there were reforms in the field of foreign trade, did reversals or temporary retreats assert themselves, as they did in other countries? This chapter tries to answer these questions for Hungary's trade with market economies. First, it outlines the major characteristics of foreign trade and control under traditional central planning. Then a summary table shows the dimensions in which liberalization attempts could or did take place. A separate section discusses import liberalization and control, followed by conclusions.

The Early Period

In 1967-1968, when real trade reforms began, Hungary's economy was fairly advanced as compared to an average developing country that starts to liberalize trade. Foreign trade was conducted by two to three dozen specialized state foreign trade companies (FTCs). For Hungarian producers of exports and purchasers of imports, the points of departure, in addition to plan targets, were the fixed domestic prices at which products were delivered to and imports were received from the FTCs. A foreign trade price equalization system was in use at the FTCs. Incentives associated with plan targets or other artificial indicators were supposed to encourage producers and salespeople to fulfill the foreign trade targets set by the planners.[1]

The exchange rate was unknown as an active, adjustable economic policy instrument. There were as many de facto exchange rates as goods in trade. Crossborder flows of information, cooperation, and competition of the local producing and trading companies with the outside world were negligible or limited to physical quantities and a few technical parameters. Economic decision makers (central planners and managers of industrial and foreign trade companies) were driven by powerful forces in this system towards import substitution and export expansion to the CMEA markets.

Trade Liberalization

Table 13.1 summarizes the key changes of the last 40 years on Hungary's foreign trade liberalization. Hungary's inward-oriented development strategy was determined by the intrinsic isolationism of a centrally planned economy. This tendency was reinforced by the evolution of CMEA cooperation in the 1960s and 1970s (Table 13.1, row 1). By the end of the 1970s, substantial debts were built up, so that Hungary was no longer in the position to remain apart from world market changes. The adjustment necessary for the economy required the application of at least one of the usual elements of liberalization, i.e., to put an end to the subordination of export incentives and the encouragement of import substitution. The Kádár administration, finding its legitimacy in a consensus based on a gradual improvement of living standards, refused to permit the pain that would have accompanied radical structural changes. Rather, it took the easier way: introducing strict import controls and furthering import substitution. Export promotion efforts were also numerous but too weak to have much effect. The pressure to reduce the debt burden required adjustment to world market changes via drastic structural changes. One reason for the slowness of the adjustment was the strength of the industrial lobbies and employee groups. It is also true that the significant restructuring required by the debtor status of Hungary would have necessitated giving up old dogmas, such as full employment, steady increase of living standards, and price stability, and building new, market-type institutions.

The first significant step in foreign trade liberalization was taken in 1968, when economic decision making was decentralized under a comprehensive though still partial reform known as the New Economic Mechanism (NEM). Producers were free to decide where to purchase inputs and sell output. The perfect isolation of world market prices and domestic prices was discontin-

TABLE 13.1 Major Elements of Trade Strategy and Institutions in Hungary and the Approximate Period When They Were in Effect, 1950-1990

	1950	1960	1968
Development policy: Inward or outward looking	Autarkic targets, forced industrialization.	Expansionary policy based on self-sufficiency and CMEA cooperation.	Bold expansion continues, based mainly on large investment programs in framework of CMEA cooperation. Growth financed by growing indebtedness to West and Soviet Union.
Institutions conducting foreign trade	Small number of specialized foreign trade companies work according to national plans, decomposed to the level of enterprises.	As before, plus some industrial companies market their products abroad according to detailed national plans.	Small number of specialized FTCs work with greater independence, according to many rules and under informal central control. More industrial firms receive right to export their own products.
Export control		National plan targets broken down to enterprise level. Incentives attached to plan targets employed in FTCs and industrial firms. Periodic export campaigns.	Some central targets or informally transmitted expectations from center. Incentives: subsidies and other advantages attached to products, projects and firms. All exports licensed.
Import control		Foreign exchange allocations broken down to enterprises according to national plan. Incentives attached to plan targets used in FTCs and industrial firms. Periodic campaigns.	Some central targets or informally transmitted expectations from center. Informal control through consensus among licensing authority, monopolist foreign trade firms, indigenous producers and buyers. Moral pressure. Licensing. Stricter quotas for consumer and investment goods.

TABLE 13.1 (continued)

	1979	1990
Development policy: Inward or outward looking	Policies of import restrictions and import substitution. Pressures and campaigns to limit imports from West, with temporary success. Less emphasis on CMEA cooperation, granting preferences for investments to expand convertible exports.	
Institutions conducting foreign trade	Granting 8 existing FTCs and some new ones the general license for parallel foreign trading in manufacturing export to West. Right to export given for many more production firms.	Gradual move toward declaration of general right to engage in foreign trade: each company allowed to trade any product or service, provided item not on special list of exceptions.
Export control	As before, complemented by price system designed to stimulate exports to West (first only efficient ones, then less efficient ones). Demand management intended to boost exports. Campaigns. Bargaining between government and firms to export more in return for advantages.	As before, but artificial "export stimulating" price system abolished. Exchange rate policy beginning to be used. Incentives become more transparent. Easier access to import for firms with additional exports.
Import control	Strict item-by-item licensing, often delaying license granting. Different regimes of import control approximately every two years; all based on distribution of funds for firms or groups of firms. Depending on status of balance of payments, funds used more or less freely.	As before. Emergence of formal linkage between additional imports and additional exports. Liberalization of first 35 to 40% and then 70% of imports. Monetary restriction and exchange rate policy used to control imports.

ued and an embryonic exchange rate was introduced under the name of "foreign trade multiplier." By the expanded—though often mechanical—use of commission accounts, the chances were improved for building and intensifying relations with foreign partners. This was the first step toward removing the artificial barrier between production and trade.

To be sure, the foreign trade multiplier was not a real exchange rate; it was supplemented by several subsidy and tax-like tools—the so-called "financial bridges." Domestic price formation was kept largely independent of world market prices as well as local demand conditions. Even when in the 1980s a so-called "competitive price system" did build a link to world market prices, the rules of this new system still resulted in rather artificial prices.[2]

Nevertheless, if the prices of imported goods rose, the changes were usually felt by the industrial companies using the imports: there was no automatic mechanism to compensate for such impacts (except for a few years following the world market price explosion). The situation was the same also in the case of exports. The new system enabled industrial firms to get closer to the world market through the mediation of foreign trade companies; they could exchange information with their foreign partners, join the negotiations, and begin to understand the signals, the habits, and the actions taking place on real markets.

Despite their enlarged freedom of decision making, Hungarian companies were treated by the 1968 reform as infants in such fields as investments, wage setting, and foreign trade. The authorities were afraid that the staff of the FTCs would be corrupted by "rich and sinful foreigners" and that only the iron-handed guardianship of the state could prevent Hungarian traders from being "taken" by selfish foreigners. Accordingly, the routine activities of foreign trade were minutely regulated by central directives and instructions. Central approval was needed to begin negotiations with a new partner; central directives specified the number of offers an FTC was supposed to obtain before finalizing an import deal, as well as the composition of the boards authorized to select from the offers; travel and representational budgets were fixed as a percentage of its turnover; and so on. The chapter by Lányi provides additional details about the overregulation of foreign trade.

Until the early 1980s, this distrust and the belief that fewer units were easier to control stood in the way of increasing the number of foreign trading units and the development of any degree of competition among FTCs, each retaining a monopoly in its area. The new winds began to blow in 1981. The exact reason for the turn is not clear. Deterioration of the non-ruble balance of trade, the emergence of a liquidity crisis, and a parallel campaign of decentralization in industry, retail trade and services were probably contributing factors.

TABLE 13.2   Export and Import Concentration in Trade with the West:
Share of Companies with Largest Turnover in Total (percent)

Export Concentration

Share of	1982	1983	1984	1985	1986	1987	1988	1989	1990*
Largest 5	49	48	50	46	38	32	34	33	31
Largest 10	65	62	62	60	54	50	52	51	48
Largest 25	87	84	84	82	80	76	76	75	72
Largest 50	96	95	96	95	93	91	90	89	86

Import Concentration

Share of	1982	1983	1984	1985	1986	1987	1988	1989	1990*
Largest 5	42	43	42	40	36	35	35	32	24
Largest 10	63	61	61	60	57	55	53	48	39
Largest 25	92	90	90	88	86	83	79	72	64
Largest 50	99	98	98	98	96	95	92	86	81

*As of July 1990.
Source: Author's calculations from data found in the various publications of the Department of Information, Ministry of Foreign Trade and Ministry of Trade.

Many more industrial companies were authorized to sell their own products abroad (20 to 30 licenses a year compared to the previous two or three). Eight FTCs were granted the general right to sell manufactured products in Western markets, and several FTCs with comprehensive scope were established upon central initiative. This so-called parallel foreign trade meant that, although under strict supervision, these companies could start to compete with each other domestically as well as on foreign markets.

As this trend of liberalization steadily expanded after 1981, general foreign trading licenses (i.e., the right to trade in all kinds of products) were granted to 38 companies in 1986 and to as many as 101 companies in 1987. Since 1988, any business unit may pursue foreign trade in a range of goods not included in the so-called exception list, provided that the staff is competent. The number of units engaged in foreign trade increased from 350 at the end of 1987 to 500 in April 1988, to about 2,000 in November 1988, and then to 7,000 by mid-1990, including state companies, joint ventures, private companies, and private entrepreneurs.[3]

The exception list is shrinking year after year. Whereas in 1987 it covered 54 percent of non-ruble exports and 58 percent of imports, in 1989 it covered only 36 percent of exports and 20 percent of imports. At the same time, the concentration of trade also diminished and still continues to do so (Table 13.2). Although free foreign trading is still obstructed by a great deal of red tape, the trend just noted can be considered the second decisive measure in the liberalization process.

One may note also a significant decrease in the level of tariffs since 1968—from 34 percent in 1968 to 16 percent in 1989.[4] However, if we consider the roles of the rigorous import control system and of the institutional and personal connections often needed to obtain an import license (see below), it will be obvious that a certain percentage decrease in tariffs cannot explain the extent of trade expansion, the range of import competition, the level of protection, and the bias in favor of import substitution versus export expansion.

Of some importance also were the efforts aimed at increasing or unifying the export incentives. However, here the signs do not point unambiguously to liberalization. Even after acknowledging the importance of increasing non-ruble exports, the central management alternated its export policy every two to three years—first encouraging the increase of the volume of exports, then the improvement of efficiency of exports, then again the volume, and so on. The instruments applied for increasing exports or for enhancing export efficiency were most often individual ones, or soon became differentiated by industries, products, producers, or were based on some artificial concept that could be maintained only for a short time. The type of export incentives actually applied was influenced by the strength of pressure on the balance of payments, by the prevailing popularity of reform ideas, and by the power of the relevant lobbies. Experience shows that no matter which system of export incentives was actually in vogue, the funds for export promotion were regularly channeled to existing big exporters or big firms.

It is difficult to measure the incentives for import substitution. Although during the 1970s and 1980s some kind of quantitative import restriction was always in effect, the rules of price formation on the domestic market did not allow for those having obtained import licenses to realize a surcharge on scarce imports. For this reason, the producers of goods substituting for imports similarly could not realize a price advantage. Nevertheless, excessive import substitution existed, stimulated by the looser and poorer terms of delivery that producers get away with owing to the dominant (monopoly) positions enjoyed by local suppliers, and by the fact that import substituting operations had easy access to scarce resources, such as investment finance, opportunity to raise wages, and foreign currency.

Import Control and Liberalization

The formal system of control of non-ruble imports underwent substantial changes in 1968. Before then, producers were allocated quotas of import according to a plan breakdown; after 1968, companies requiring imports, after formally applying for and automatically receiving an import license, were free to convert their income in local currency to hard currency for that purchase.

However, the system operated only for a few months, if ever, in this declared form. It gradually became a Potemkin village of import regulation. At the given overvalued exchange rate of Hungarian forints and with the countless benefits of Western imports (up-to-dateness, reliable quality, favorable terms of delivery, dependable supply), the likely increase of import demand would have been impossible to finance without upsetting the balance of trade. Thus, along the officially declared system (whose operational validity was accepted by international organizations), a specific system of import regulation, tailored to Hungarian conditions, developed and was operating between 1969 and 1981.

In an earlier study, I called this system of control "regulation based on consensus."[5] In this system, the authorities informally delegate a good part of the task of import regulation to the FTCs and the companies trading in the means of production. These trading companies, enjoying monopoly positions, have a fairly good insight into the import use in their respective fields and, owing to their position, are more or less capable of assessing the import requirements and of influencing the importing behavior of the user industrial enterprises placing the orders. Besides the task of import restriction, however, they also are informally responsible for the smooth supply of materials and parts in their respective fields. The user enterprises and the monopolist trading companies are engaged in nonstop bargaining for imported materials and parts. These arguments do not turn into an open struggle because industrial enterprises are interested in maintaining cordial relations with the monopolist trading companies. Therefore, importers show considerable self-restraint in forming their import requirements.

Since 1968, the system of import control has depended mainly on the concept of base-year consumption of companies: the level and distribution of imports among companies has been strongly determined by the past level of imports. The acquisition of imports above this level was influenced by the bargaining power of the user companies, their ability to document the bottlenecks that the absence of imports would cause, national economic priorities, personal relations, and amount of time and effort that managers at user enterprises were willing to devote to fight for their requests.

In 1982, when a balance of payments crisis threatened, this Kádárian policy of "restrictions through consensus" was no longer sufficient to successfully implement drastic import restrictions. At that point, the administration made it clear that it started to use formal commodity quotas and to restrict imports by a comprehensive system of item-by-item licensing. During 1983-1988, somewhat less rigorous import regulation regimes were in use. However, all the basic features of the previous systems of import control were left unchanged.

The evolution of import control between 1968 and 1988 may be considered a sort of liberalization. Firms obtained more say in making decisions about their import purchases, and they could not import without having the domestic means of payment. In most periods, the rigidities of the central control of imports were eased. On the other hand, the prevailing system could not be considered a liberalized one as long as the access to imports was determined only in part by the income of the purchaser, by the price of the importable, by the exchange rate, and by tariffs and other costs.

In July 1988, at an important meeting of the ruling party's Central Committee, a proposition was made to begin liberalization of imports in the next year. This was the first time a proposition of this kind had ever appeared publicly and officially. It is still not clear what made the party and the government ready in 1988 to consider the idea of liberalization. The arguments for it were just as valid, say, ten years earlier. Moreover, at that time much larger reserves were available to finance import liberalization.

Nor does the timing of the decision to liberalize fit in the picture that emerges from international experience—i.e., that in many cases national economies are at the deepest point of a crisis when they make up their minds to implement liberalization cum stabilization programs. In the summer of 1988, although the Hungarian economy was not well off, it was not at a point of crisis. In fact, the liberalization package was not connected with an economic stabilization program.

Considering the motives of the government between 1978 and 1988, a restrictive policy has been pursued (except for a short interval), entailing a gradual decline of business activity, especially in the state sector. In mid-1988, the government assumed that while maintaining the restriction by explicit monetary instruments, it could lift certain restraints, hoping that by liberalized wages, prices, and imports it could jump-start the economy, with the efficient ones leading the charge.

The government finally adopted a liberalization program targeting a gradual replacement of the four or five systems of import control in existence. In three years time, 80 to 85 percent of imports from the West would be liberalized. This concept of liberalization, made public just before its implementation, has been criticized mainly on the grounds of failure to support it with a substantial real devaluation of the forint. Critics also challenged the failure to combine import liberalization with additional export promotion, such as the removal of existing bureaucratic barriers before new exporters and easier export financing.

Another point of criticism was that no thought was given to protecting certain industries. In spite of decades of a de facto high degree of protection and import substitution, the authorities in Hungary had no concept of the selective protection of certain industries. Rather, the protection was ad hoc and, of course, often undeserved. Liberalization provided a good opportunity to define, on the basis of a concept of industrial policy, what sectors, for what period, and at what level to protect against the possible sudden surge

TABLE 13.3   Distribution and Growth of Liberalized Imports
              (Computed in Hungarian Forints)

Products of	Distribution %		Growth %	
	Year 1989	Jan-July 1990	Year 1989	Jan-July 1990
			(Previous year = 100)	
Mining	0	0	0	97
Metallurgy	0	5	0	90
Engineering	83	53	148	136
Building materials	2	1	664	57
Chemicals	1	25	104	105
Light industry	2	7	195	114
Food	11	6	116	78
Other industries	0	1	0	346
Industry Total	**98**	**97**	**145**	**117**
Agriculture	2	2	173	217
Forestry	0	1	0	216
Total Convertible Imports	**100**	**100**	**146**	**118**

Source: KOPINT-DATORG data base, author's calculations.

of imports, as well as what preferences should be offered for the development of exports of certain industries or products. In this case, the selection was based on the assumption that restructuring the Hungarian economy would need up-to-date equipment; this is why machines and parts were liberalized. The liberalization of consumer goods imports began because this was emphatically demanded by the IMF.

On January 1, 1989, import licensing was cancelled for liberalized goods, although a bureaucratic reporting procedure was maintained and a procedure similar to an import deposit system on all imports was added to contain the demand for imports. As of 1990, imports had not surged, although the import of liberalized products increased faster than those of non-liberalized imports. Restrictive monetary policies did play a role in limiting imports. A number of Hungarian companies faced liquidity problems due to the strict monetary policy applied by the National Bank of Hungary and to climbing interest rates.

In 1989, the first year of the program, liberalization was concentrated in the engineering sector. About 85 percent of the increment of liberalized imports fell into this category (Table 13.3). Interestingly, consumer demand for liberalized goods increased at a substantially higher rate than the demand of business organizations. For example, the import of certain building materials (e.g., tiles) increased by four- to sevenfold; that of deep freezers and color television sets increased twelvefold and twofold, respectively. The total 1989 import of durable consumer goods was nearly three times the volume imported the year before, whereas the equipment and components imports of enterprises increased by only "a paltry" 38 percent. A likely explanation is that in the consumer goods market there were absolute shortages (such as tiles and deep freezers) that were met by imports.

Another fear was that the weakening of protection for industries might push too many local manufacturers into difficult situations. We cannot evaluate this because information is insufficient. But so far there have been relatively few complaints in the media and in public forums about displacement of domestic production by import competition, even though there must have been such cases.

In 1990 there was a significant increase in the range of liberalized goods, affecting another 20 to 25 percent of convertible imports. Items that were added to the list included mainly raw materials of the metallurgical industries, building materials, chemical and light industries. Hungarian price experts claim that the prices of local raw materials tend to be much lower than those imported from convertible currency markets. It is still a point of contention how far this will be able to compensate for the higher quality, shorter delivery times, and better after-sales service of imports. If the powerful lobby of Hungarian raw material producers feels threatened by import liberalization, then the program will probably be exposed to severe attacks.

Conclusions

Thinking over the zig-zagging reform process under way in Hungary since 1968, I conclude that since its inception from a very deep base 23 years ago, foreign trade liberalization has shown a slow but palpable progress, especially in 1968 and again since the mid-1980s. Between these two periods, the prolonged process of implementing the previous reforms was accompanied either by abortive make-believe reforms or an open standstill. In fact, considering the 23-year time span, the number of genuine liberalizing actions was not really that significant.

The three essential elements of foreign trade liberalization were:

1. putting an end to the isolation of foreign trade and production in 1968;
2. allowing the emergence of competition in foreign trade and giving the freedom of independent foreign trading to every business organization;
3. beginning the liberalization of imports from the West as of 1989.

The first two of these cardinal changes meant discarding certain principles of a CPE: the principle of the hermetic isolation of foreign trade and domestic production in the first case and of the dogma of the state monopoly of foreign trade in the other. At the same time, both changes included elements that are typical characteristics of trade liberalization in economies under any system, e.g., reduction of state control, removal of bureaucratic rules, or increasing the role of prices and of market factors generally. To began liberalizing a significant part of imports was an exceptionally radical step, especially in light of the low level of genuine integration of the Hungarian economy with the world market.

Notes

1. A comprehensive account of trade institutions and policies in traditional CPEs can be found in Thomas A. Wolf, *Foreign Trade in a Centrally Planned Economy* (Chur, Switzerland: Harwood, 1988).

2. For details, see Paul Marer, "Exchange Rates and Convertibility in Hungary's New Economic Mechanism," in *East European Economic Assessment*, Part 1, a compendium of papers submitted to the Joint Economic Committee, U.S. Congress (Washington, D.C.: GPO, 1981), and Paul Marer, "Economic Reforms in Hungary: From Central Planning to Regulated Market," in *East European Economies: Slow Growth in the 1980s*, Vol. 3, selected papers submitted to the Joint Economic Committee, U.S. Congress (Washington, D.C.: GPO, 1986).

3. A comprehensive analysis of this process was made by Péter Nyitrai in "The End of the Foreign Trade Monopoly: The Case of Hungary," *Journal of World Trade*, 23 (6), December 1989.

4. Unweighted average of tariffs under the "most favored nations" category.

5. János Gács, "The Conditions, Chances and Predictable Consequences of Implementing a Step-by-Step Liberalization of Imports in the Hungarian Economy," *Acta Oeconomica*, Vol. 36, No. 3-4. See also János Gács, "Import Substitution and Investments in Hungary in the Period of Restrictions (1979-1986)," in A. Rába and K. E. Schenk (eds.), *Investment System and Foreign Trade Implications in Hungary* (Stuttgart: Fischer Verlag, 1987).

14

Visible and Invisible
Trade Regulation and Deregulation

Kamilla Lányi

This chapter concerns primarily the problems of deregulation of foreign economic relations in Hungary. But it also tries to call attention to the fact that Hungary still has a dense mesh of regulations and compulsory procedures, which I call conditionally invisible regulations, and which will be exceedingly difficult to break with the usual tools of deregulation. This phenomenon may play a great role in explaining why the reform measures that have been undertaken so far have not had the effects that could have been expected.

The essay first summarizes the hesitant steps the government took in the 1980s to partially deregulate foreign trade, and then outlines briefly the deregulation program of the Reform Committee of the Nemeth Government (1988-1989). The second part of the essay gives examples of how invisible regulation affects the everyday practice of foreign trade and how it impedes current reforms.

In the literature, deregulation usually refers to a process whereby the state decreases its intervention in the functioning of the market to assure free entry and to promote competition. In some cases this involves privatization; in every case it eliminates or decreases considerably the regulations concerning price setting, the quality of the goods and services, the designated sources of suppliers and distribution, the legal conditions of entering a market, and so on.[1] I am using this definition of deregulation. Because the previous chapter by Gács provided a detailed discussion of the history of foreign-trade liberalization, on this topic I can be very brief.

Partial Deregulation in the 1980s

The 1974 foreign trade law, although it recognized the right of the enterprises to choose, according to their own economic interests, between domestic or foreign sales and sources of purchase, and although it gave the

Minister of Foreign Trade the right to order the signing of contracts only in exceptional cases, was nevertheless based upon the principle of the foreign trade monopoly of the state. This law stated that foreign-trade activities could be carried out only by those who obtained a special license from the state; granting such a license could have certain preconditions, and could be revoked. At the same time, the state placed foreign-trade activities under special direction and control so as to transmit to the participants the foreign-trade policy of the state. Among the tools of this special direction and control were the so-called licensing system (until the early 1980s practically every export and import contract needed a license from the Ministry of Foreign Trade) and the state monopoly of foreign currency loans, debts, and payments (which is still maintained, almost fully, by the National Bank of Hungary [NBH]). The law also covered the preparation, signing, and implementation of foreign-trade contracts, which meant that the Minister could require a license even to conduct preliminary discussions concerning trade. Only very few producing or service enterprises had received foreign-trading rights. The usual rule was that only one Hungarian company was allowed to export and import a given product or service. Thus, a manufacturer could not enjoy the right offered by law to choose its own business partners. This system was maintained—with few modifications—until the early 1980s.

Since the beginning of the 1980s, the establishment of mixed-profile foreign-trade companies (commercial houses) has been permitted, mainly for serving the new exporters. Since 1985, producing companies can receive independent foreign-trade rights in a much more liberal way, primarily for the export of their own products. Producing and service enterprises can obtain occasional or time-limited export rights practically without limits, and among the foreign trade enterprises (FTEs) the machinery export for convertible currency has been liberalized. Most of the joint ventures with foreign partners, which have become numerous, have asked for and received export rights. Thus, during the second half of the 1980s, the number of companies with their own foreign-trading rights has increased from about 100 to more than 1,000. (The number of occasional export licenses, which used to be granted by the hundreds, has decreased because in early 1990 they became more difficult to receive, especially to countries of the CMEA.) Obtaining an export license has become somewhat simpler for the regularly exporting large firms, and the requirement to license the sale of very small items, of tools related to customer service, and of exhibited goods and other similar items has been eliminated.

As of January 1, 1989, engaging in foreign trade (in convertible currencies) has become a basic right for every Hungarian economic organization, limited only by two circumstances. One is the so-called lists of exemptions (separately for exports and imports), which contain those products and services whose trade still requires special permission (accounting for about 36 percent of convertible-currency exports and 20 percent of such imports). The other limitation is that those who intend to conduct foreign trade must give assurance that they have the "necessary conditions for foreign trade activities." This refers mostly to the qualifications of the personnel, but are quite restrictive, in terms of what diplomas are accepted and so forth, so that they could never be fully complied with even by the huge FTEs that are under the supervision of the Ministry of Foreign Trade itself. The new system encompasses private companies and associations as well, but they can export only their own products and import only those goods necessary for their production. As for the state monopoly of foreign currency, the only measure taken so far is that a few commercial banks have received the right to manage the foreign-currency accounts of their clients. These banks have begun to take part in financing the foreign trade businesses of their account holders.

The Reform Committee set up by the government in 1988 published its recommendations in 1989, with the following major elements: economic policy should aim at opening Hungary to world market and expanding exports; trade, especially of imports, should be liberalized and deregulated (including the elimination of the foreign-currency monopoly of the NBH); all regulations, procedures, and incentives should be made public and transparent. As of mid-1990, the new government has not as yet had the opportunity to prepare and discuss their own program in this area, so a great deal still needs to be done.

Invisible Regulation

In contrast to the above-mentioned visible regulations, what I shall call invisible regulations include (1) those parts of compulsory procedures that are not even written down so that they are spread around by word of mouth only, and (2) those that are written down but are not readily accessible, especially to those who are new in the business. Some examples of invisible regulation follow.

Legal Measure with an Uncertain (Sinister?) Outcome

Obtaining export and import licenses for signing contracts is still necessary except, for the most part, for the imports that have been liberalized. Licensing is regulated by an Order of the Minister, modified several times, and by a Ministry Instruction. One section of one of the articles of the Instruction says that the applicant must fill out a printed form prescribed by the license giver. This is clear so far. The next section says the applicant must prove that he also has the "permissions and certificates prescribed by other legal measures." Even this is not unusual. But according to another section, the applicant may be "required to enclose further supplementary information and certificates." Then further on it states that the company can be required to "provide additional information before the application is handed in." For this purpose, the licensing organs can have a "starting meeting, a preliminary consultation, or can set up a committee." Whether such will be required can be determined only by trial and error. Yet another article states that "the licensing organs . . . may regulate within their jurisdiction . . . the questions to be answered in the course of the procedure."

And what is the license giver committed to? Practically nothing. The Order says that the preparation, signing, and realization of foreign trade contracts not mentioned by the Order can be put under licensing requirements; one of its articles states that the already issued licenses can be modified or revoked by the Minister; and another article of the Instruction states that the license given to sign a cooperation contract does not empower the company to carry out exports and imports necessary for the fulfillment of the contract.

This highly touted law on liberalizing the licensing of trade more or less says to the companies or to the individual citizens: "You must do everything I can think of, but this does not obligate me to do anything." Thus, a great deal more deregulation remains for the future.

What Makes the Guidelines Compulsory?

Generally every year, the Hungarian National Bank issues its Guidelines for Financing in Foreign Currencies. These guidelines are published in its official bulletin, but this does not make them legal measures. There are two Orders of legal force that empower the Bank, the foreign-currency authority, to supervise the companies carrying out foreign trade activities.

A simple circular of the Bank says that, by the force of the legal measures (that were still valid as of mid-1990), before a company signs a foreign contract, it must obtain a written license from the Bank if it does not intend to offer to the Bank for purchase the full amount of the foreign currency that will enter its account. Otherwise, according to the circular, if a company signs a contract, it will have deviated from the current guidelines of financing in foreign currencies. Furthermore, companies must ask for a written opinion from the Bank before they pay a foreigner for any kind of goods or services in national currency (forints). In both cases the applicant must pay a fee. Although there are some exceptions to these rules, they are valid for most companies and transactions.

Regulations Involving Foreign Currency

Because of the NBH's monopoly of foreign currency, the Bank considers any foreign money entering and leaving the country as its own, using it mostly free of charge and requiring the companies to give a full accounting of all their foreign-currency transactions. This means that companies must inform the Bank, in advance and also subsequently, of all foreign-currency incomes and expenditures and of all possible circumstances that can increase or decrease them. They must hand in copies of all vouchers and documents to the Bank; within certain deadlines they must compile a summary of these and send it to the Bank, often together with written explanations. There are certain documents whose originals belong to the Bank, and the addressee is authorized only to take a look at them.

The Role of the Invisible Regulation in Business

Why do companies consider these and similar measures (such as the ones related to traveling, use of cars, advertising and promotions, and hundreds of other expenses—not necessarily only in foreign trade) so tough? Mainly because the vouchers and other required documents related to these rules must become a part of the company's accounting and record-keeping system. But to comply with all regulations fully, including recording everything under the proper number and code and with license numbers, is very difficult and time-consuming. The responsibility lies, in the first instance, with the company's own specially licensed accountant. The books are then examined by inspectors of the Ministry and of the NBH. At that stage, the "economic police" and (until fall 1989) the Central People's Control can intervene to check for shortcomings and irregularities from which they can deduce either criminal or only inadvertent intent of the companies and their managers, the difference being often only a matter of interpretation. In some cases, infractions in recording fall under the jurisdiction of the Criminal Code. These examples illuminate that a somewhat modified interpretation of deregulation, especially concerning foreign trade, must be accepted than what is usually put forward in the literature.

Interpretation of Deregulation

If one reads only the legal measures, especially the higher-level summaries, it is not immediately evident what a tangle an enterprise gets into when trying to enter foreign trade. The major problem with these regulations is not just the fact that they involve several stages, are incredibly complicated, and are impossible to learn other than by trial and error. The bigger problem is that often the seemingly simplest procedure can lead to a dead end; meanwhile, the enterprise can go bankrupt.

There is an agency, called the Tradeinform Office (which operates under the auspices of Kopint-Datorg), where the new exporter or importer can buy a few volumes of legal measures with explanations and obtain sets of sample forms and a few booklets containing the 60 to 70 forms that are needed for the start (there are more than 700 types of forms used in foreign trade). The enterprise may also subscribe to the Bulletin of Foreign Trade, which until 1990 could only be obtained by those already in the trade, and which updates them continuously about what they must know, perhaps only by saying that further information can be obtained at this address or at that telephone number. Appendices to the volumes appear one after another, and there are no guarantees that something important is not left out. This is the least lucid area of Hungary's business environment, and neither research nor practical experts have mastered it to the degree necessary to convey all required information to a newcomer.

All foreign companies and Hungarian-foreign joint ventures established in Hungary as of January 1, 1989 must function under the same regulations and conditions that are applied to the Hungarian-owned companies. Thus, they too will enjoy the blessings of the coming deregulation. But until then they are under double pressure: they are considered to be Hungarian companies, but their managers and some of their employees are foreigners to whom a separate set of regulations apply.

Deregulation and Reform

I remember well—and so do many others—the enthusiasm when, in 1968, as part of the New Economic Mechanism, enterprises theoretically (and actually in practice as well) were no longer given compulsory plan directives; when theoretically (and much less in practice) they could choose among alternative sources of purchase and sale; and when theoretically (and only a very little bit in practice) they could spend their profits according to their own decisions and for their own purposes. We remember that most of the companies suddenly came to life and tried to exploit their new liberties to the utmost. This is also true of foreign trade, where within the framework of the declared exchange rate and commissioned contracts it seemed worthwhile for the producer to wage a life-and-death struggle for a bargain with a foreign-trade company over export and import prices. Together with the planned instruction system, many procedures and regulations were also eliminated, and the number of new regulations was small. Thus, companies were busy with each other and with creating their own—perhaps fragmented and imperfect—markets. Understandably, they hardly visited the offices of bureaucracies, where the phones were silent for days at a time, at the beginning.

The new reform measures introduced in the 1980s did not evoke a similar response among the companies, even though quite large steps were often taken. (The only exception is the small enterprises, which increased in number and economic importance from 1982, when the so-called second economy was legalized, until 1989, when their boom was exhausted). A number of explanations have been offered for this seeming inertia: that there is a contradiction between statements and practice regarding economic policy ("one cannot believe in the reforms"); that the reform has not yet reached the "critical mass"; that companies are insensitive and their managers are incapable or egoistic; that the market does not function; and so on. On the basis of what I have said about deregulation, is it not possible that companies do not try harder because they are not really allowed to? Every law is accompanied by an order of execution, by an instruction about who is empowered with what authority regarding which details. The bureaucrats immediately issue their instructions, notices, prescripts, and circulars, which have the function of ensuring that before a company takes a step, it must ask the authorities.

More than two decades after the 1968 reforms in Hungary, there is such a huge mass of all kinds of obligatory measures and regulations, within or outside the legal system, published or confidential, generally valid or individually applied, that in their totality they would not be acceptable even in a strictly centrally planned economic system, and that had not existed in Hungary before 1968. Indeed—and this is a supposition—these regulations and practices were established as a counterbalance to the 1968 reform, to ensure that companies remain in continuous contact with the authorities. That way, the authorities not only justify their existence but also maintain the illusion that the economic processes, especially foreign trade and possibly every individual business, are all "in their hands."

The enthusiasm of the authorities concerning these matters is alive and well even today. A more and more common slogan concerning deregulation is, "Of course it's necessary, but let's make it impossible to abuse." But what happens if the authorities consider something an abuse simply because they are left out, or because something is not done according to their own business ideas? Unfortunately, not only is the opposition of the bureaucratic apparatus strong, but certain groups of reform economists still think we must hold off on legal deregulation, especially regarding foreign trade, until the reform of ownership (privatization) becomes much more advanced; otherwise, companies would use their bigger freedom for all kinds of bad things—more Western imports, more Soviet exports, wasting national assets, and so on. This could make the reform fail just as much as an inconsistent economic policy could. The fact is, companies as well as households would gain enormously from deregulation via the elimination of something very nonproductive, which has tied down large resources and too much of their energy. If these resources and energy were liberated, they would surely be utilized better than in shuffling the masses of paper that are paralyzing everyone. Let us deregulate right now!

Notes

1. Albert Pera, "Deregulation and Privatization in an Economy-Wide Context," *OECD Economic Studies*, Spring 1989, pp. 159-204.

15

Trade Policy Recommendations

Gábor Obláth

The aim of this essay is twofold: to discuss certain timely issues related to the external liberalization in Hungary, with reference to the experiences of the liberalizing developing countries; and to present certain Hungarian peculiarities that call for special solutions when opening up the economy.

Recent Steps toward External Liberalization

In January 1989, the Hungarian government launched a program for liberalizing imports from the West. The method chosen for liberalization, discussed earlier in the chapter by Gács, was drawing up a (positive) list of readily accessible imports. The list covered around one-third of imports from the West and consisted mainly of certain machines, components, semi-products, and some electronics (among them consumer goods). The scope of liberalization was widened in 1990 (e.g., chemicals, steel products were added) so that about two-thirds of Hungarian imports from the West became liberalized. In January 1988 the government liberalized tourism for Hungarian citizens (and granted a hard-currency quota for each citizen to purchase for travel abroad every third year). Since September 1989, hard currency held by households can legally be placed on currency accounts with Hungarian banks, without having to explain the origin of the currency. Regulations concerning joint ventures as well as previous rules concerning the repatriation of profits were also liberalized.

Recent Hungarian economic policy is thus characterized by a series of measures aimed at external liberalization. Hungary accumulated a huge external debt during the 1970s and 1980s, without using the money to promote the opening up of the economy. The major part of the credits were used to service the accumulated debts; today the pressure stemming from the level of indebtedness has become a major constraint to liberalization.

The other problem is related to policy matters. The necessary steps that should have accompanied trade liberalization have not been taken. True, several developing countries began their liberalization programs in a state of crisis—in much deeper trouble (higher inflation rate, larger balance-of-payments deficits, more marked decrease of living standard, etc.[1]). This can certainly be a reason for optimism for Hungary. The experiences of other countries[2] can contribute to finding solutions for problems related to Hungary's trade liberalization. But quite often it is not so easy to establish what the relevant experiences are.

Although I believe that the developing countries' liberalization experiences are relevant for Hungary's policymakers, those that are especially relevant cannot be applied to Hungary directly, without modifications that take into account certain unique features of Hungary's economy.

Dual Structure of Hungary's Foreign Trade

Hungary's level of development is higher than most of the countries whose experience the vast literature on external liberalization discusses. Its industry's (and within that, manufacturing's) share in total output and employment is close to that of many developed market economies. However, these indicators conceal the dual nature of the Hungarian economy, which is closely related to the dualism in its foreign trade structure. Throughout 1990, Hungary has had two rather different types of trade: a clearing system with countries belonging to the CMEA, and hard-currency trade with the West and most of the developing countries.[3] Although its trade structure in clearing trade is that of a developed country, its structure on the world market resembles those of the developing countries.[4] This dualism is closely related to the fact that Hungary's economy has been highly protected, at least until recently, with an excessively inward-looking commercial-policy orientation.

Although quantitative comparisons of this sort are very difficult, the extent of the "inward orientation" of Hungarian policy has—at least until recently—probably exceeded those of the most protectionist, inward-looking developing countries. That is why lessons of the developing countries' liberalization attempts are important for Hungary.

However, before discussing why the lessons of experience cannot be applied directly to Hungary, it is necessary to make some remarks on Hungary's commercial diplomacy and on the attitude of international economic organizations toward the external liberalization of the country.

Commercial Diplomacy "Presents" Hungary to the West

During the 1970s and 1980s, one of the major aims of Hungary's foreign economic diplomacy was to try to "sell" the Hungarian economic system in general, and its foreign trade regime in particular, to international organizations (during the 1970s to the GATT, and in the 1980s to the IMF and the

World Bank) as if it were basically similar to those of the developed market economies. This attempt was successful in the sense that Hungary became a member of the GATT and other organizations as a country having an effective tariff system. These organizations accepted—or rather, acted as if they accepted—the notion that, except for tariffs and some quotas for consumer goods, no impediments existed in Hungary to the free inflow of foreign goods. This thrust of Hungarian commercial policy certainly had its merits in the early 1970s and perhaps even in the early 1980s. True, the picture presented to the outside world of the Hungarian economy was much more attractive than reality. But it was important to persuade Western partners that the post-1968 reformed economic system was different from the traditional centrally planned model. The differences were perhaps exaggerated, but the direction presented to the outside world was not inaccurate.

As a sign of goodwill toward Hungary, the international community accepted the picture offered by the Hungarian government. A sort of consensus emerged on not discussing certain peculiar aspects of Hungary's economic system, especially those related to the foreign trade regime. It is difficult to evaluate the balance of the cumulative costs and benefits of this consensus for the Hungarian economy. Be that as it may, the concern of this essay is not so much the effects of past policies, but rather the constraints the above-mentioned consensus places on future liberalization policies.

Presenting the Hungarian economic system to the Western world as if it were an open market economy has, over time, become more and more counterproductive. It is imperative for Hungary to open up its economy. In order to do this, the country needs assistance from the West. However, if the image of the Hungarian economic system is built upon a fiction—and especially if both the Hungarian government and the West have interests in maintaining this fiction—neither the policies of opening up nor the necessary forms of assistance can be designed in an economically rational way.

Therefore, in my view, one of the preconditions of further policies aimed at external liberalization is that the Hungarian government acknowledge, and the West recognize, the actual state of Hungary's economic system. It is important that Hungary's trading partners, creditors, and the international organizations understand the workings of the Hungarian economy, and that future Hungarian policymakers should not be constrained by incomplete or inaccurate information given by previous governments.

Let me give an example. When the Hungarian government liberalized about one-third of the country's Western imports, after a long-lasting period of restrictions, one would have thought it logical that some measures making these imports more expensive accompany the removal of non-price restrictions. However, nothing of the sort happened; it took some time even for devaluing the currency. Not devaluing right away was a mistake. Not increasing tariffs was another. But since the Hungarian government stated, and international organizations accepted, that quantitative restrictions did not exist in Hungary for some time, then the removal of these "non-existing" restrictions could not be legally compensated for by an increase of tariffs. All the more so, since international agreements signed by Hungary specified the timing of the reduction of its tariffs.

The international agreements, however, were negotiated based on inaccurate notions about the role of QRs in Hungary's foreign trade. It might easily turn out that with initially higher but subsequently decreasing tariffs, as well as fewer QRs, Western exports would have had better access to Hungary's markets than in a situation characterized by lower tariffs and more intense, though not always transparent, applications of QRs.

The message of the above is straightforward: the formulation of rational and sustainable liberalization policy measures should not be blocked, either in Hungary or in the West, by incomplete or inaccurate information about Hungary's foreign trade system.

The Nature and Consequences of Protection

Until recently, Hungarian firms were almost totally protected from foreign competition. Protection was exercised not by tariffs or even by explicit quotas, but rather by means of a complex and informal system of import rationing. Though tariffs were, and still are, high by international comparisons, neither the nominal nor the effective rates reveal the true extent and effects of protection in Hungary.[5] Before the liberalization measures in 1989, the licensing system functioned as a means of making imports from the West just as unreliable a source of supply as goods originating on the domestic market. In the latter, dates and conditions of delivery have always been characterized by a shortage economy. By making supplies from both markets almost equally unreliable, the effect of the licensing system was to reduce the attractiveness of foreign supply to the level of domestic supply. This task of the licensing system was not so designated officially, but by making the availability of foreign products for Hungarian companies uncertain, this was its de facto microeconomic effect.

But owing to formal and informal domestic price controls, the scarcity of imports was not expressed in the higher prices of imports or importables (converted at the current exchange rate) than those of products on the domestic market. This is an important difference between Hungary and other inward-looking countries. By comparing prices on the domestic and foreign markets, one cannot get a clear view of the strength of protectionism in Hungary. Protection meant (and, in the non-liberalized groups of products, still means) administrative barriers to the availability of imports, not their higher prices. These characteristics of protectionism in Hungary have significant impact on the position exporters; they also have implications for exchange rate policy.

Hungary's exporters to the West are at a disadvantage as compared to supplying the domestic (and the CMEA) market as well as in relation to their Western competitors. This is because selling to the protected home market is always easier than exporting to the competitive Western markets. Furthermore, foreign competitors are certain to operate under freer trade conditions and have readier access to more reliable, better, and, in many cases, cheaper imports than do Hungarian exporters. That is, actual and potential Hungarian exporters are in a way victims of the domestic shortage economy. These effects of the trade system constrain exports just as in inward-looking developing countries.

These constraints have been effective in spite of the subsidization of a significant part of Hungary's exports. In fact, one of the reasons for subsidization of exports to the West has to do with trying to counteract the mentioned constraints. But the latter cannot be interpreted without reference to the exchange rate.

If a significant part of exports has to be subsidized, and if there is an excess demand for imports (restrained by QRs), that certainly suggests that the domestic currency is overvalued. However, purchasing power parities (PPPs) suggest an undervaluation of the Hungarian currency—the official exchange rate has continually been roughly twice as high (forints/dollar) as the exchange rate warranted by PPPs. This finding concerns comparison of both consumer prices and producer prices.[6]

It is clear from the literature on comparisons between PPPs and exchange rates that there is a rather close negative empirical relationship between PPPs and exchange rates on the one hand and the level of development on the other.[7] That is, the lower the level of development, the larger the difference between PPP and the exchange rate. However, in Hungary's case neither the magnitude nor the explanation of the difference fits into the generally accepted model. The roughly 100 percent difference is much greater than one would expect based on Hungary's relative per capita income level. The conventional explanation focuses on the relative price of tradeables and non-tradeables. Prices of traded goods are supposed to be roughly equalized internationally (except for tariff and other restrictions, which should push up the prices of domestic tradeables relative to international prices). The difference between PPPs and exchange rates boils down to differences in the relative prices of tradeable and non-tradeable goods.

In Hungary there is a very large difference also in the prices of traded goods in Hungary and abroad (expressed in a common currency). This needs special explanation. Why are traded goods prices, on average, much lower in Hungary than in the West, if converted at the official exchange rate?

This, in my view, has to do with two factors. On one hand, the development strategy of the past forty years has led to establishing an industrial macro-structure similar to those of developed Western countries. But a large part of the output of this structure is not marketable in the West at the prices of similar Western products. Within these conditions, whatever the exchange rate, there has to be a difference in the relative domestic price of comparable goods at home and abroad. This difference reveals that an unfounded presumption is involved in PPP calculations: namely, that if a product or a group of products has the same name, they really are the same. In fact, this is the most explicit indication of the inward-looking nature of Hungary's economic and trade policies. For decades a number of industries and their products could very well survive without having been challenged by Western competition. In the case of products whose relative prices would indicate the existence of a competitive advantage, this advantage immediately disappears when an attempt is made to sell the products. Those products in turn, in which Hungary has no price and/or cost advantages (these are nonmanufactured goods in general), can be sold relatively easily to the West.

This is the basic reason for the difference between the PPP of traded goods and the exchange rate. However, to maintain this difference, both import and price controls are necessary. These controls were very widespread indeed, probably much more so than in most developing countries wishing to liberalize their foreign trade.

Before trying to interpret the Hungarian system and compare it with those of the developing countries, a caution is in order. Average and macroeconomic indicators concerning the Hungarian economy conceal a much wider dispersion of microeconomic performance than in most developing countries. But a comparison of international and domestic prices at the official exchange rate do not, in and of themselves, express on average the extent of the isolation of the Hungarian economy from the outside world. It is not easy to decide whether the problem lies with the concepts used for categorizing different types of foreign trade regimes (and strategies), or with the Hungarian economy.

Although I sympathize with the conceptual framework proposed by Liang, Marer, and Battat in Chapter 5, I am afraid that even their extended interpretation of foreign trade strategies is unable to capture certain features of the Hungarian model. Liang et al. term the situation in which neither exports nor import substitution are promoted as "de facto import promoting" (DIP) strategy. Although this certainly was a characteristic of Hungarian economic strategy in the 1970s, its importance, as well as modifications of this strategy, would probably not be revealed by calculations of effective rates of tariffs and of protection. For example, the move in the early 1980s toward a much stricter control of imports would not be revealed by such standard computations, nor would conventional computations show that a major liberalization of imports has occurred in recent years. This is because protection in Hungary is not value-based but takes the form of implicit quotas via administrative intervention and price controls.

In conclusion, there is a great deal of similarity between the inward-looking developing countries and Hungary. An important step toward reducing the inward orientation of Hungary's economy would be if mainly the price system and not QRs would convey the macroeconomic scarcity of imports. This could be done through a reduction of extremely high and an increase of unreasonably low tariffs. For liberalization to continue, it will be necessary to increase the role of the price system in implementing foreign trade strategy.

Import Liberalization and Protection: A Proposal

Most important at this stage of Hungary's systemic transformation would be to have more intense competition on the domestic market and for prices to express, to a larger extent than now, economically justified protection. This requires some combination of protection based on instruments affecting prices and further liberalization of imports. In what follows, I outline some rather general ideas about the further liberalization of imports in Hungary, building upon the experiences of the liberalizing developing countries, while also trying to capture the special features of the Hungarian system.

The first step toward a liberalization of imports could be an increase of tariffs of those particular products whose QRs are decreased, an idea also proposed by Nagy in Chapter 16. I have no strong views concerning which product groups should be liberalized first, next, and so on. But I am afraid that without making them more expensive at the initial stage, the process of liberalization might get into trouble owing to its adverse impact on Hungary's already precarious balance of payments. The increase of tariffs should be done in such a way that a schedule of annual tariff reductions is announced simultaneously. I recognize the fact that in certain product groups, such as investment goods, Hungary's tariffs are strikingly high, without any justification, and have a rather negative effect on investment in new technology, where Hungarian supply is lacking. Therefore, I do not recommend a general, non-selective increase in tariffs. What I have in mind is a very pragmatic approach involving the conversion of non-tariff (quantitative) protection into price signals.

There is a major difference between liberalization in developing countries and in Hungary. In the case of the former, a transition from quotas to tariffs generally does not involve large changes in prices because such a transformation means that quota rents are captured by the government.[8] In

Hungary, this type of transformation should (with exceptions) lead to higher prices of the products involved. This is not a disadvantage; an increased price (and profit) incentive for import-competing domestic production at the time of liberalization is not a drawback. Nor is the fact that readier access to foreign products is accompanied by an increase in their prices. Both factors can contribute to restraining the demand for imports in a market-conforming manner.

The most important aspect of the proposal is the transitory nature of tariff increases. The system would be transparent; the changes would be foreseeable and calculable for the enterprises. My proposal has implications for the treatment of exporters as well as for exchange rate policy. Exporters to the West would, of course, receive a refund of the tariffs they paid so they would not be affected. More generally, as an important element of liberalization, exporters to Western markets would have more ready access to imported inputs, quite apart from the timing of the general liberalization measures. The point is to establish a system in which exporters to the West are treated in such a way that their double disadvantage, discussed earlier, would disappear.

The implication of the proposal for exchange rate policy is that it would allow a smaller devaluation of the domestic currency than would otherwise be necessary to accompany import liberalization measures. This is all the more desirable since a large devaluation is far from being warranted by PPP comparisons. In due time, as a result of the general development of the Hungarian economy, the large difference between PPP and the official exchange rate should decrease.

As a practical matter, inflationary expectations in Hungary are rather overheated, which implies that devaluation is likely to have rather short-lived effects. This does not preclude the necessity of devaluation as an accompanying measure of import liberalization. But by applying the proposed tariff increases, the magnitude of the devaluation (and the resulting increases of the prices of primary products, and thus, in domestic prices) would be smaller than would otherwise be the case. Furthermore, it can be argued that whereas changes in the exchange rate are instruments for solving macroeconomic imbalances, the proposed measures concerning tariffs are intended to affect, in a preannounced way, specific sectors and enterprises.

The proposal seems to involve some kind of an industrial policy or planning in terms of selecting sectors or product groups for protection. In fact, no such presumption is made. Although if it turns out to be economically justified, certain preferences to certain sectors or product groups may be granted, the increase in tariffs I recommend can just as well be achieved in a mechanical way, by applying uniform surcharges on imports to replace QRs, without having a clear view on the desirable industrial structure. The essence of the proposal has nothing to do with the final outcome in terms of some desirable industrial structure, but rather with sequencing the process of opening up, and giving time and the possibility for firms to adjust to the process of import liberalization.

Liberalization of Western Imports and Trade with the East

Eastern Trade Practices

Through 1990, trade with the East has been conducted within a formally multilateral but effectively bilateral framework with countries belonging to the CMEA, as is detailed in the chapter by Köves. Two characteristics of this trade are relevant from the point of view of liberalizing trade with the West. First, market conditions in CMEA trade are much "softer" than in Western trade. Also, many Hungarian industries were established and expanded with the explicit purpose of supplying this particular market. Such manufacturers have no alternative markets, in the short run.

The other feature of Hungary's Eastern trade is that foreign trade price relatives have little to do with world market prices. The findings of Ausch[9]— that never in the history of clearing arrangements did prices differ from those on the world market by more than the extent experienced in intra-CMEA trade—are still valid. The departure from world market prices is most marked for manufactured products, especially machines, which constitute the major part of Hungary's exports to the East. These products are overpriced, which, naturally, is a source of macroeconomic advantage for Hungary. The price to be paid for this advantage is the existence of a large manufacturing industry whose products are obsolete and cannot be sold on Western markets, or if sold, only at a large discount as compared with foreign trade prices in CMEA or even in West-West trade. It should be noted that, as a result of Hungarian foreign trade regulations, the firms involved in CMEA exports could never actually realize the extra profits so generated; these were taxed away by the government. At the same time, other exports to the CMEA, mainly light industrial and agricultural products, were subsidized.

A major implication of the tax system applied to manufacturing exports to the CMEA is that the protection offered by the Eastern markets was not (or rather could not) be expressed in higher than average profits of companies exporting to this market. Thus, the protection received by clearing trade resembles the protection that domestic industries receive by means of QRs. Both imply (or rather, used to imply) guaranteed markets for Hungarian products. But in neither case was the fact of protectionism expressed in relative prices and profits.

Liberalization of Western Trade
and Options in Eastern Trade

Trade liberalization leads to wider opportunities and stronger pressures at the same time. Domestic firms will have more possibilities in terms of selecting among suppliers, but they will also be placed under more competitive conditions. Trade liberalization toward the West does not automatically lead to similar effects in Eastern trade. Therefore, liberalization toward the West should be accompanied by changes in the regulation of trade with the East as well. True, Hungary's Eastern trade needs to be reformed, quite apart from liberalization of Western imports, for the reasons elaborated by Köves. The two, however, are interrelated. Depending on the alternatives of changing the framework of Eastern trade (also discussed by Köves), different solutions are called for.

If there is a rapid transition to hard-currency payments in trade with the CMEA countries—that is, clearing is replaced by convertible currencies—liberalization toward the West might have no direct implications for the management of Eastern trade. In this case, the differences between the two types of trade and their consequences for Hungarian industry would lose their present importance.

However, the actual interpretation of "hard-currency payments" with the Soviet Union (and other East European countries), slated to be introduced as of 1991, is far from clear. If the actual interpretation of hard-currency payments turns out to be some sort of a dollar clearing arrangement,[10] then special regulations should be designed to counteract the potentially unfavorable macroeconomic effects of liberalization of Western trade on trade with the East. The unfavorable macroeconomic effects would arise from the conversion of Western imports into "quasi-convertible" or directly non-convertible claims on the Soviet Union and Eastern Europe.

To avoid this danger, it might turn out to be necessary, as in Finland's case in its clearing trade with the Soviet Union, to control the hard-currency-import content of Eastern exports. (The Finnish regulation limits the hard-currency-import content of clearing exports to 20 percent.) However, it is essential for the Hungarian government to reach an agreement with the Soviets and other East European partners on the payments system, in which clearing arrangements (calling for special regulations for Western inputs in Eastern exports) have only a partial and limited role. The latter is important because, lacking this, foreign investors wishing to bring capital to Hungary with the aim of reaching Eastern markets would be seriously discouraged.

Conclusions

The liberalization of Western imports since 1989 is generally considered to be a successful part of Hungary's foreign trade policy. In mid-1990 this general assessment can be accepted, but with reservations. The partial liberalization of imports accompanied by monetary restraint and minor devaluations of the domestic currency have turned out to be sustainable so far. This policy, at least by mid-1990, has not led to a significant displacement of domestic production nor to balance of trade problems.

However, it should be clear that serious dangers are involved in a trade liberalization policy that does not try to compensate (at least initially) by increasing the prices of liberalized goods that were previously controlled via QRs. The simplest way of implementing such compensating price increases is by augmenting certain tariffs. This option, however, meets several obstacles, because international agreements were entered into by previous governments that were based on inaccurate information concerning Hungary's import regime. It would be logical that these previous agreements not block rational steps of economic policy. The less so, since large devaluations, implying major increases in the price of primary imports, might be excessively inflationary in the face of the inadequate monetary control characterizing the transforming Hungarian monetary system.

In Eastern trade, special safeguards will be necessary to avoid the conversion of Western imports into Eastern exports until the trade and payments system of Eastern trade becomes the same as Hungary's trade with the West.

Notes

1. World Bank, *World Development Report* (Oxford University Press, 1987).

2. Described, for example, by W. M. Corden, *Protection and Liberalization: A Review of the Analytical Issues* (Washington, D.C.: International Monetary Fund, 1987); and M. Bruno, "Opening Up: Liberalization with Stabilization," in R. Dornbusch and F. L. C. Helmers, ed., *The Open Economy* (Oxford: Oxford University Press, 1988).

3. This distinction is not exact since Hungary has some free-currency trade within the CMEA as well as clearing arrangements outside the CMEA. But for reasons of exposition, this is disregarded.

4. F. Jánossy, in "Widersprüche in der Ungarischen Wirtschaftsstruktur—wie sind sie entstanden und wie können sie überwunden werden," *Acta Oeconomica*, Vol. 4 (1969), was the first to point to this dualism; he called it "quasi development."

5. That is why I have doubts concerning the findings, based on input-output computations, of the effective rate of protection in Hungary, as computed, for example, by A. Simon and I. Hercegh in "Effektiv vámvédelem Magyarországon" ["Effective Protection in Hungary"], *Kopint-Datorg*, Budapest, 1989.

6. The first investigation of this sort to include Hungary can be found in I. Kravis et al., *International Comparison of Real Product and Exchange Rates* (Johns Hopkins University Press, 1975). Further works by these and other authors—for example: "CEE, Comparisons mondiales du pouvoir d'achat et du produit réel en 1980," *Eurostat*, Théme 2, Série D, Bruxelles-Luxembourg, 1987; and Marer, *Dollar GNPs of the USSR and Eastern Europe* (Baltimore: Johns Hopkins University for the

World Bank, 1986)—reinforced their conclusions. Most recently a publication by a representative of the Hungarian Price office, A. Bodócsy in "Csodák márpedig nincsenek" ["There are no miracles"], *Figyelő*, 31, August 1989, discussed the magnitude of the difference between the official exchange rate and PPPs.

7. See B. Balassa, "The Purchasing Power Parity Doctrine: A Reappraisal," *Journal of Political Economy*, December 1964; Marer, op. cit.; and the large literature on this reviewed by L. Officer in "The Productivity Bias in Purchasing Power Parity: An Economic Investigation," IMF Staff Papers, November 1976.

8. J. Bhagwati, *Foreign Trade Regimes and Economic Development: Anatomy and Consequences of Exchange Control Regimes* (New York: NBER, 1978); A. O. Krueger, *Foreign Trade Regimes and Economic Development: Liberalization Attempts and Consequences* (New York, Cambridge: Ballinger Publ., 1978); M. Michaely, "Trade Liberalization Policies: Lessons of Experience," in *Trade Liberalization: The Lessons of Experience*, Internal Discussion Paper, The World Bank, April 1988.

9. S. Ausch, *Theory and Practice of CMEA Cooperation* (Budapest: Akadémia Kiadó, 1972).

10. Details in G. Obláth and P. Pete, "Trade with the Soviet Union: The Finnish Example," *Acta Oeconomica*, No. 3-4 (1985).

16

Lessons of Market Economies for Hungary

András Nagy

The advantages of trade liberalization are well known: it leads to a rational specialization of the economy according to its comparative advantage, to a high level of allocational efficiency, and to a better use of the country's resources. As a consequence, productivity increases, output and income expand, and growth is accelerated. The greater the distortions on the domestic market in the pre-liberalization stage, the more restricted the competition, and the higher the level of protectionism, the greater are these advantages. As is well known, Soviet-type economies went to the extreme, with no historical parallel, both regarding the monopolization of practically all economic activities and—closely related to this—the protectionist isolation of these countries in the process of an introverted, import-substituting industrialization. It could be concluded, then, that both the stakes and the risks of trade liberalization are greater in these countries than in other societies or in other periods because both the suppressed advantages and the probable shocks of transformation are larger than in countries where monopolistic protectionism was not as pervasive, as in the case of the Central and East European countries.

From the point of view of the economic agents, one of the most important advantages of liberalization is that it eases or relieves the shortage of foreign exchange and the scarcities created by various import-control systems, such as licensing, QR, and the like. Opening up the economy means the gradual elimination of protected import substitution and the anti-export bias, resulting in an easier adaptation to world market conditions. This in turn leads to a boosting of exports, foreign exchange revenues, and imports. But there is, of course, a high price to pay: changes of products and technologies as well as in trade orientation are always painful, bringing about failures, losses, and unemployment. Even if these are but temporary, they create social tensions and resistance.

For this reason, even if the superiority of free, or freer, trade is accepted by policymakers—as is increasingly the case in several Central and East European countries—the real problem to be faced is how the transition can be made irreversibly.

Experiences of Attempts at Trade Liberalization

There is a lot to learn from the experiences of other countries, and several good analyses are available.[1] Let us review briefly some of the main conclusions of international investigations and comparisons.

• Liberalization of trade was never achieved, and quite probably cannot be achieved, at once. It has to be gradual, the question being how fast or slow the process should be. The experiences of several countries tell us that the likelihood of success is significantly higher when the initial changes are substantial and policy actions are resolute rather than hesitant. This is probably more true for non-market economies than for market ones, because the former have a long and more pervasive history of trade restrictions. The decisive point is the credibility of the new policy: minor changes are usually regarded as ephemeral and inconsistent, whereas a very slow liberalization is more likely to halt or collapse. Sudden and major changes can create a pressure group benefitting from the new policies, which is badly needed to overpower the resistance of the previously protected activities.

• The replacement of quantitative restrictions by tariffs is the major step during the early stages of successful liberalization. The use of tariffs instead of quotas is more advantageous in several respects even when it grants the same level of protection. It was found, quite surprisingly, that even when only the form of the protection was changed, it has led to a quicker and better adaptation to market demands, to a greater uniformity of the system, and to substantial changes in the volume and structure of imports. Such a change is of special significance in economies with a long history of mandatory planning and a strict foreign exchange control, because it increases the "monetization" of the economy and shows that certain objectives can be attained by financial means rather than by orders and coercion. However, it is not easy to acknowledge that many quantitative restrictions were in practice previously that were officially denied. As a result, it is not easy to have the trade partners accept the necessity of tariff increases.

• Liberalization fails if it is not linked to strong export promotion and to the containment of import growth. The most appropriate way to achieve this is a substantial depreciation of the real exchange rate—i.e., a stronger initial devaluation than the domestic rate of inflation. Several liberalization attempts failed because their fate was sealed by an unsustainable deterioration in the balance of payments. Import liberalization itself is obviously a strong promoter of exports because the removal of restrictions and barriers diminishes the bias against exports. However, this is usually insufficient, especially during the initial phase of the transition; therefore, a stronger push of exports and curb of imports is needed. Neutral means such as devaluation have proved to be more efficient than differentiated subsidization and tariff schemes.

• A firm, consistent, and reliable policy is needed, in which the different stages of the liberalization process should be clearly pre-announced. Only a relatively strong and determined government can influence the expectations of the different economic agents in favor of the survival of the new policies, and can resist the pressures of those groups that are negatively affected by those policies. Nevertheless, the use of authoritarian measures—in which certain policymakers still believe—is neither necessary nor feasible, in my opinion, because neither liberalism nor economic rationality can be expected from dictatorships in this part of the world. In addition, it is not acceptable to people liberated after a long period of oppression. It is crucial for the enterprises to be granted time to prepare for the changes in prices, abolition of subsidies, removal of quotas, reduction of tariffs, and so on, in order to reduce the shocks, to reallocate their capacities and labor, and to change their R&D and marketing policies. If time is too short or the enterprises don't trust the authorities to be able to carry into effect the policies announced, their resistance can grow strong enough to make the implementation of such liberalization measures politically impossible.

• In order to continue the liberalization process, once started, it is of extreme importance that positive results should materialize relatively early to compensate for the negative effects. This is not an easy task to achieve. As a consequence of liberalization, certain import-competing activities have to contract, whereas others, including exports, have to expand. Usually it is not feasible to immediately channel the resources of the contracting sectors or firms to the expanding activities. For this reason, much depends on how much assistance can be given to this reallocation process; how contracting is phased and, if necessary, curbed; and how expansion is supported by economic policy measures. Unfounded export-pessimism is quite frequent in the stage before the radical changes are introduced. It is usually impossible to recognize before liberalization the activities that can expand fast and increase their exports. But it is an important lesson of international comparisons that the scale of export expansion as a result of liberalization has in many cases been much larger than expected. The speed of the appearance of positive results can be strongly influenced by exogenous factors, such as changes in world market demand and in terms of trade, and the behavior of the capital markets. All of these play a role in determining how fast a given economy can adapt to new conditions. In a non-market, or semi-market, economy, the variance in efficiency levels among firms is much wider than in market economies because of extreme market distortions created by monopolies, arbitrarily fixed prices, and extreme protectionism. As a consequence, both the contracting of inefficient activities and the expansion of efficient ones have to be of a much larger scale. Thus, both gains and losses of the transition process will presumably be greater, and it is more difficult to achieve a maximum of benefits at a minimum of costs. Consequently, there are more risks in change even if the reasonably expected gain is higher.

• One of the major reasons for resistance to liberalization by policymakers is their fear of mass unemployment. Both physical and human capital have a number of specificities and rigidities that hinder the reallocation of the factors of production. The relatively slow responsiveness of expanding activities and the time involved in the construction of new and up-to-date capacities contribute to a temporary unemployment in branches whose protection must be decreased or discontinued. However, it came as a surprise when the results of the studies comparing the experiences of different countries showed that the size of gross unemployment caused by liberalization has generally been small. In most cases, the reason for this was that labor discharged from inefficient activities was in great part compensated for by its absorption into other expanding activities. It was observed that shifts of resources within branches or even within firms were common and contributed to the relatively small-scale aggregate unemployment. This does not mean that these shifts, reallocations, and unemployment— where in the case of unsuitable skills or locations it could not be avoided— did not cause serious social tensions. Employment considerations are legitimate reasons why the government may not immediately adopt a discriminatory, non-uniform policy of liberalization; in the case of labor-intensive activities hit by the removal of protection, a slower process of liberalization may be warranted. Cautious policies in this respect have contributed to the fact that even in cases in which the liberalization process was aborted, the reversal was not caused primarily by the emergence of unemployment.

Lessons from Liberalization Experiences

It is clear even from this brief summary that much can be learned from the successful and unsuccessful liberalization attempts of other countries, both developed and underdeveloped. Nevertheless, even if there are many similarities, one should not forget some basic differences between market and non-market economies that will have a strong impact on the applicability of foreign experiences to them.

Protectionist and import-substituting economic policies use similar methods in quite different economic and social systems: exports are subsidized, prices are controlled, imports are licensed, tariffs are high and their variance great, foreign exchange is strictly controlled and there is no market for it, the local currency is overvalued, and a multiple exchange rate system is likely to exist even if it is declared to be uniform. The basic differences lie in the motivation of state-owned versus privately owned enterprises and in their relation to party and state bureaucracies—in other words, differences in property rights.

In Hungary, a peculiar relationship has developed between the central administrative organs and enterprises during the last twenty years.[2] The central organs are controlling and orienting the activities of the enterprises mainly by indirect financial means instead of direct mandatory interventions. Thus, the outcomes of the bargaining for wage increases, import licenses, tax reductions, investment funds, credit reliefs, subsidies, price changes, and—last but not least—managerial bonuses play a more important role than profit motivation.

As long as enterprises are not cut off from the umbilical cord of the state and are not subject to the control of private or public owners of capital and the capital market, and while competition does not exert a strong pressure to improve their efficiency, all liberalization and decentralization attempts tend to be dangerous. They may extend the field of maneuver of the enterprises, helping them to adapt more easily to changing conditions and opportunities. But this does not mean that they will be using the factors of production in a more efficient way if their protected monopolistic position on the domestic market does not change.

Large-scale trade liberalization should be introduced only in parallel with creating or extending the market and competition. Without the latter, the former is not recommended: economic management could become more flexible while the efficiency of earning and spending foreign exchange would not improve and could deteriorate. There is also a considerable risk that it will become even more difficult to maintain the balance of the current account, which is, of course, not permissible at the present state of Hungary's indebtedness.

Basically there are but two main courses open: (1) either the suggested changes in the forms of ownership will be carried into effect and enterprises will in fact become independent of the central organs and interested in profits, or (2) the system of indirect controls and bargaining over the regulators remains. It is only in the case of the former that a gradual liberalization of foreign trade and a gradual development of a foreign exchange market can be successful. As regards the latter, the adequate form of foreign trade and foreign exchange policy would be a strict control by the government and by the central bank, which must be maintained even if only a partial liberalization takes place.

Changes in the forms of ownership take time; their effect on the management and business policy of enterprises is usually not felt immediately. In the initial period of transition, efforts must be concentrated on this change.

As long as the desired effects are not achieved, only moderate improvement can be expected from liberalization. Care should even be taken that the easing of restrictions and the increased independence and scope of movement of enterprises should not strengthen their monopolistic positions or the possibilities of misusing such positions. In addition, the extension of the market and competition should increase the pressure to improve efficiency.

According to official estimates, the liberalization of 40 percent of imports from convertible-currency areas in 1989 was regarded as one of the most important liberalization measures introduced by the last (communist) government. It took this step to show how much its policy differed from that of all previous governments and from those of all other East European countries. It is difficult to judge how far the intention was to favorably impress Western banks and international financial authorities to improve the conditions and availability of credits, and how far it was part of a package of liberalization measures, of which only a small part had been implemented. The beginning of the liberalization process created a difficult situation for the government concerning continuity and consistency with earlier policies. In order to gain admission to GATT in the early 1970s and the IMF in the early 1980s, previous governments gave the impression that Hungary was already an open economy and imports were liberalized. Those who were intended to be impressed knew well, of course, that this was not true. Subsequently, it became painful for both the government and the international institutions to acknowledge that fact, to state that, contrary to earlier declaration, the liberalization of trade only began in 1989.

It is also difficult to analyze the results of the import liberalization attempt of 1988-1990, since it is hardly possible for a research worker to get all the necessary information on such details as the hidden strings attached to the measures introduced. What an outside observer can note is that neither the positive nor the negative expectations concerning import liberalization were fulfilled; subsequent contributions in this volume discuss this in detail. Some experts have estimated that because of the lack of proper preparation and especially because of its not being linked to a significant devaluation, the liberalization effort will miscarry, creating an intolerable balance of payments deficit. Advocates of the liberalization package expected that by liberalizing Western imports on such a scale, a substantial opening and the extension of the domestic market would be achieved, exerting a strong competitive pressure on enterprises. They also expected it to facilitate and increase Western exports, since it would be easier to import the necessary intermediate products and materials of good quality.

What actually happened was neither a spectacular increase in Western imports nor a serious "threat" of competition. Not many complaints were voiced by enterprises about their domestic sales being threatened by import competition. The reasons for this are not yet fully clear, but some explanations can be offered on why the liberalization measures so far have not made much impact on either the volume of Western imports or on domestic competition.

Most of the imports liberalized were complementary and not competitive to domestic production. Moreover, a serious brake was introduced suddenly for Western imports: prepayment was required (without interest) for all import orders at a time when a severe money and credit squeeze already created serious liquidity problems for many enterprises. As a result, shortage of money, not licensing, became the major barrier to imports. To freeze a substantial amount of money without interest at a time when the general interest rate was about 20 percent and when credits were hardly available obviously represents a serious obstacle for most firms. To use financial means instead of administrative ones is, of course, highly recommended and advantageous. The disadvantage in the Hungarian case is that the liquidity conditions of the firms are not—or not much—related to their profitability. The financial authorities still exert too much influence on it through tax exemptions, subsidies, price controls, differentiated credit conditions, and resource reallocations,[3] while the entry of new firms and the exit of inefficient ones, the breaking up of monopolies, and the introduction of competition are not much supported by the authorities.

It is of prime importance to recognize that very strong social forces, pressures, and conflicting interests operate—overtly or covertly—in the background of trade liberalization. It is obviously not some neutral economic rationality that determines the measures taken, and when and how far liberalization can advance. Pointing out the examples of harmful discriminations, it seems obvious that the fact that intermediate and capital goods had been liberalized without the liberalization of finished products was in the interests of enterprises producing finished products. These were usually large firms, mostly in a monopoly position, exerting great influence on how the liberalized list of products was established.

Competition, especially import competition, goes against the interests of producing enterprises, because it is more difficult to collude with foreign firms than with domestic ones. It forces producers to continuously develop technology, to improve their products, to reduce costs, and to take into account the changing requirements of the consumers. Enterprises do not favor competition, and in fact do their best to circumvent it. Competition is in the interest of the consumers, enabling them to obtain better and more suitable goods at more reasonable prices.

Thus, one cannot expect capital owners to wholeheartedly support competition, including the liberalization of trade. Because in Soviet-type economies the state is the owner of much of the capital stock, it is not surprising that state authorities are reluctant to do anything harmful to the enterprises that belong to them. And the more reluctant the authorities are, the less influence consumers have on the dealings of the state. Thus, liberalization can progress only in parallel with democratization and with depriving the state of property rights. Only when the consumers understand that competition, the opening up of the domestic market, decentralization of monopolies, and trade liberalization are in their interest not only because they will increase their satisfaction as consumers but also because they will increase the efficient use of resources (hence, their income)—and when their influence will increase on policy decisions of the state organs—only then can one expect that decisive steps will be taken in the direction of effective and substantial liberalization.

But is this a realistic alternative at a time when producers have strong lobbies and are intertwined with the central authorities, while consumers are unorganized and in many instances unconscious of their long-term interests concerning competition, market opening, and liberalization? We cannot be certain—even if we wish—that the answer is yes. However, it is now generally admitted that Hungary, after nearly forty years of communist rule, is in an extremely grave and critical situation, and that there is no possibility of recovering from this predicament without fundamental changes of the system itself. This rare, general agreement offers hope for breaking up the old political and economic power structure, as well as ossified habits and fears, including the past policy of protecting producers to the detriment of consumers. But in an unstable and historically untested situation, all predictions are hazardous. Nevertheless, it seems that the necessary changes are feasible. Whether the right policies will be implemented will depend on the balance of social forces in favor of them and against them.

Notes

1. See: B. Balassa, *Trade Liberalization among Industrial Countries* (New York: McGraw-Hill, 1967); B. Balassa, *Policy Reform in Developing Countries* (Oxford: Pergamon Press, 1977); B. Balassa, *Development Strategies in Semi-Industrial Economies* (Baltimore: Johns Hopkins University Press, 1982); NBER (1974-1978), *Foreign Trade Regimes and Economic Development* (New York: Columbia University Press); and NBER (1981-1983), *Trade and Employment in Developing Countries* (Chicago: University of Chicago Press).

2. See: L.Antal, *Gazdaságirányítási és pénzügyi rendszerünk a reform útján* [*Economic Management and Financial System on the Road to Reform*] (Budapest: Közgazdasági és Jogi Könyvkiadó, 1985); T. Bauer, "A második gazdasági reform és a tulajdonviszonyok" ["The Second Economic Reform and Property Rights"], *Mozgó Világ*, No. 9 (1982).

3. See J. Kornai and A. Matits, *A vállalatok nyereségének bürokratikus újraelosztása* [The Bureaucratic Redistribution of Enterprise Profits] (Budapest: Közgazdasági és Jogi Könyvkiadó, 1986).

17

Why We Must Liberalize in a Hungarian Way

Béla Kádár

Legacies and Transformation

The legacies of the Stalinist and post-Stalinist model of previous decades in Hungary and in the other countries of Central and Eastern Europe cannot be ignored during the period of systemic transition. The postwar absence of market mechanisms, and later the weakness of the emerging market mechanisms, the non-competitive environment, the low levels of efficiency of the inherited productive structures, established in isolation from the mainstream of the international division of labor, the non-market linkages in intra-CMEA relations, the "psychological barriers" and behavior of the population grown up in a "paternalistic" environment—all have narrowed the room for maneuvering for post-transition governments that cannot be eliminated in the short run by any kind of political decision or intentions and declarations about changing course. Another requirement that conditions the transformation is the domestic and foreign political necessity of non-violent transformation, which makes the "Schumpeterian" creative storm of limitlessly unfolding hypothetical market disruption not expedient. In other words, it would not be wise to pursue economically rational policies that ignore the various internal and external threshold of tolerance.

In the present situation, the capacity of action of the power structures and the government is, as a matter of course, more limited than in earlier years. However, in the absence of adequate social and political support, the less popular elements of reform strategies can be implemented only with much difficulty, by accepting too great compromises and by all means only in a "diluted" way. As a consequence of this, it is increasingly recognized that the implementation of a modernization and transformation strategy requires, on the one hand, a legitimate and strong government capable of action, of speeding up modernization, since just relinquishing the economic positions of the state will not in itself create markets; on the other hand, it demands a much longer transitional period. This transitional period creates a mixed economy of a specific kind, in which "pure" solutions of management techniques and economic policies may not exist. The transitional characteristics must be accepted as matters of reality both by domestic society and by our foreign partners, because without accepting them there is the danger that a rather explosive situation will occur, undermining the whole of the reform process.

The distance between the heritage of the past and the requirements of the target state of a market economy make it necessary to reckon with a special transitional period in the 1990s. The economic environment of the transitional period will also be a market economy, but of a "Hungarian variety," based on the specifics, the expediencies, and the constraints of the country. This sort of hybrid economic environment will determine the pace, the extent, and the forms of economic liberalization.

The past, and perhaps even post-election, weaknesses of central economic management can partly be explained by the fact that in periods of accelerated political changes, the capacity for action and political implementation, including demanding sacrifices, is usually not particularly great. However, the past weaknesses of economic management were strongly influenced, beyond political considerations, by the neophyte economic philosophy of the economic leadership, the interpretation of its own role. This can best be summed up as a policy of nonintervention, that of "benign neglect" of the economy. This has undoubtedly improved the positions of certain interest groups, especially those of big enterprises, enjoying relatively great bargaining power. At the same time, there was no strong pressure in the real economic processes to improve their performances.

The previous government's laissez-faire type of economic philosophy, wishing to get rid of the heritage of the last decades, did not reckon with the fact that the behavior of economic units can be influenced under the conditions of a shortage economy, as a matter of course, only to a rather limited extent by the monetary instrument of demand restriction. Enterprises were functioning within the various subsectors with profit-rate differentials often amounting to several hundred percent, had low levels of cost sensitiveness and adjustment abilities (owing to the legacies of the past), and were characterized by equally low levels of profit-interests because of the high fiscal burdens and the uncertainties regarding the withdrawal of incomes by the central budget. Monetary management, just like convertibility or an up-to-date system of taxation, is not the cause but the consequence of a sustained healthy development of the economy.

Similar to earlier Latin American examples, the Hungarian "half market" economy coming about in the last two decades has also demonstrated that the means of economic management, well proved in developed market economies, like interest rates, exchange rates, and taxes, have a different impact in a heterogenous economic environment characterized by a strong supply constraint. The more market-oriented segments of the Hungarian economy responded to the income-restricting measures of the last years not by supply expansion or by a more buoyant supply competition involving even price reductions, but by narrowing their scope of activities, by efforts to push up their prices, or by withdrawing from market competition to a more protected state environment, acting either like self-supplying cooperatives or focusing on exports to the CMEA. Hungarian economic history in the past four decades has convincingly demonstrated the uselessness of administrative economic management trying to solve market problems. In recent times, however, the thesis—well known for a long time by those who are dealing with the economics of countries at medium levels of development—has once again been demonstrated: namely, that the "market-conforming" instruments of macro-economic policy are effective only to a limited extent for eliminating the inherited administrative and political distortions of the national economy.

Reflections on a Medium-Term Liberalization Strategy

Hungary's liberalization strategy must, first and foremost, start with and build upon the country's endowments, elbow room, and requirements. In principle, of course, one can envision a kind of "Program Hungary" of an international nature that would provide large amounts of financing and resources to help the country shift to a market economy and liberalize in one giant step. Past and expected developments make this kind of international assistance rather improbable. One can forecast with a high degree of certainty that the size of external resources and preferences obtainable in the framework of international cooperation will be determined first of all by the improved performance of the Hungarian economy, based on its own resources.

The value system of liberalization is and will continue to be influenced by the legacy of past doctrines. What is the proper yardstick of successful liberalization? Those institutional-technical approaches that measure the level of liberalization by such indicators as the share of products with free prices, liberalized imports, and so on do have an impact even today. This yardstick is not irrelevant, of course, in developed market economies established on the basis of a historically organic development during the past several hundred years. However, almost 150 nation-states in the world just do not fit into this category. Thus, the speed of liberalization cannot be measured only by the growth rates of imports or the share of free prices because Hungary has a different economic model than that of a well-functioning market economy. The yardstick of the liberalization of the

Hungarian economy cannot be quantitative. Instead, it must be the qualitative changes taking place in the efficiency, competitiveness, equilibrium, and modernization of the economy—all of these being a consequence of liberalization. These qualitative changes make it possible in economic management to liberate the national economy from the regulating activities of fiscal bureaucracy, and to change from tactical to strategic management. This kind of approach questions the value of a liberalization in which imports grow, though without improving the economic environment, without the genuine price reductions, and without improved international competitiveness.

Because qualitative changes can hardly take place in the short term, liberalization demands a stages approach. According to certain surveys, made with rather wide margins of error, at present 30 to 40 percent of Hungarian enterprises would be able to "hold their own" in a sharp, unlimited market competition, in the case of an immediate and full-scale liberalization. There are strong doubts that import-liberalization of, say, 80 percent within the next two years would offer a sufficient "period of grace" to radically improve the competitiveness of enterprises and to avert their collapse. This danger can be decreased only by powerful promotional measures of industrial protection, by facilitating the improvement of competitiveness and the acceleration of reallocation, and by an active, "offensive" policy of industrial restructuring.

Similar problems of stages appear also in price liberalization. Price liberalization without supply competition, with producers and products in monopoly positions, has a price-increasing effect. The reduction of budget subsidies is a basic requirement. Eliminating the subsidies on agricultural and food prices, house rents, energy prices, those of infrastructural services, and their simultaneous marketization without a previous, comprehensive wage reform and tax reduction of anti-inflationary effect, already touches the limits of tolerance of the population. By now a nation-wide resistance has come about against the "squandering" of state property and the "preferential" property-acquiring activities of the economic and political establishment and their friendly circles. On the other hand, one must not disregard the fact that the combined sum of personal savings both in banks and in cash does not amount to even one-fifth of the estimated value of state industrial enterprise property. Therefore, "property liberalization"—that is, privatization creating real owners—can be developed only in stages. It presupposes the encouragement of personal saving propensities and the substantial improvement of enterprises' profit-interestedness. The presently discussed and property-centered liberalization programs do not devote sufficient attention to this precondition.

The sequencing of liberalization is also important. Given the presence of powerful inflationary pressures and missing real owners, it would not be very wise to advance rapidly in the liberalization of wages. Furthermore, given the tensions in the balance of payments, easing the private imports of the population concentrating on durable consumer goods purchases under the pretext of tourism, would not be wise either. In a distorted scarcity economy, improved returns on savings, investments, and capital generally are the key factors in the rational behavior of the state sector, and they must precede privatization. Privatization and the emergence of real owners and property-interestedness must be the basis of progress in price and wage liberalization. The considerable level of Hungary's indebtedness and the requirements of world economic opening make it quite clear that the pace and possibilities of the country's social and economic progress are basically determined by its external economic performance. From this point of view, a basic priority and candidate for top liberalization is that of capital imports, so as to encourage an export-oriented structural transformation and increased export capability on the one hand, and import-saving and the establishment of an economic and political environment necessary for the acceleration of the influx of foreign capital on the other. Of equal importance with capital imports is the liberalization of the import of technologies, services, semi-processed goods, and raw materials necessary for hard-currency exports. The list of priorities continues then with the imports necessary for advancing on the road to technology-intensive growth, for the market-reorientation of enterprises formerly specializing in the CMEA markets. The import liberalization of consumer goods must thus be postponed. The present, product-oriented version of import liberalization does not satisfy the needs of strategic selectivity.

The deregulation of the economy is of outstanding importance in the rational order of priorities. The classic instruments of economic policies, including import liberalization, cannot result in the genuine improvement of performances in a non-homogeneous economic environment that is overregulated by an economic management serving basically fiscal interests. Only those actors who function in a deregulated economic environment can respond with improved performance to the challenges of import liberalization. Deregulation has been accelerated, rather belatedly, only in 1989. Defiscalization, stronger emphasis on generating the supply responses needed, is also necessary.

The importance of a system-oriented implementation of reforms and coordinated action cannot be stressed strongly enough. A reform policy of small, isolated steps, well known from the past, is inadequate and enhances the danger of reversing the reform process. Recommended instead is a stages approach, together with the rational sequencing and harmonization of the different reform measures. The implementation of a liberalization strategy requires a process segmented into multiyear periods. One of the most important tasks of the new government is to work out a comprehensive liberalization program that helps cope with the present crisis while being an organic part of a longer-term Hungarian development strategy. The establishment of an integrated Hungarian market economy—the Hungarian way of liberalization—presupposes, in the medium run, a strong role for and strategic management by the government, using special techniques during the transitional period, in order to reach the desired target.

PART FOUR

Central and Eastern Europe and China

18

Poland and Eastern Europe: What Is To Be Done?

Jeffrey Sachs

The Basics

There are two basic first steps to the transformation of Eastern Europe's centrally planned economies. One, the Eastern countries must reject any lingering ideas about a "third way," such as a chimerical "market socialism" based on public ownership or worker self-management, and go straight for a Western-style market economy. Two, Western Europe, for its part, must be ready and eager to work with them, providing debt relief and finance for restructuring, to bring their reformed economies in as part of a unified European market.

The main debate in economic reform should therefore be about the means of transition, not the ends. Eastern Europe will still argue over the ends: for example, whether to aim for Swedish-style social democracy or Thatcherite liberalism. But that can wait. Sweden and Britain alike have nearly complete private ownership, private financial markets, and active labor markets. Eastern Europe today has none of these institutions; for it, the alternative models of Western Europe are almost identical.

The process of transformation will be difficult, and a shared vision in East and West of joining in a unified European market will be vital in keeping it on track. Such a market is the key to Eastern Europe's hopes of getting the new technologies, managerial talent, organizational methods, and financial capital needed to overcome the dismal economic legacy of the past 40 years. For the West, the reintegration of Eastern Europe into the market system will offer not only enormous investment and trade opportunities but also the best hope that the unleashed energies of the East will be channeled into peaceful and constructive purposes rather than into a renewal of ancient national rivalries.

This chapter is a revised and updated version of the author's article in *The Economist*, January 13, 1990.

The economic and political complexities of the transition to a market economy argue strongly for a decisive and comprehensive approach, such as the new Polish economic program, introduced on January 1, 1990. Poland's goal is to establish the economic, legal, and institutional basis for a private-sector market economy in just one year. Other countries should pursue programs of similarly rapid transformation, tailored to national circumstances; as one Polish economist has put it, "You don't try to cross a chasm in two jumps."

Reform and Financial Instability

Past attempts at reform in Eastern Europe have had a paradoxical result. The countries that have attempted the most market-oriented reforms—Hungary, Poland, and Yugoslavia—are the very ones now suffering the greatest economic instability. Poland and Yugoslavia have hyperinflation; together with Hungary, they face the worst foreign-debt crises. Obviously, the reform efforts have gone seriously awry.

The basic reason is that, although the "market" reforms did indeed end central planning, they did not create real markets. State enterprises were freed from many central controls (though prices often remained controlled), but were still sheltered from competition. The private sector remained closely circumscribed, and crushed by high tax rates and bureaucracy. Private firms were allowed to fill some gaps left by the state sector—in services, for instance—but not to compete directly with it. International trade, another potential source of competition, was tightly controlled by quotas and foreign-exchange rationing.

This absence of real competition put central governments at the mercy of their own enterprises. The government could not realistically shut any firm down. For a start, a firm's financial position gave little indication of its true performance, since competition was weak and prices still heavily distorted. Second, the firm was most often a monopoly supplier. So firms were kept alive at any cost, including cheap credit, subsidies, tax breaks, and the like; they operated under "soft budget constraints," in the phrase of János Kornai, the path-breaking Hungarian economist who predicted and explained this pathological condition.

Knowing the government would always bail them out, state enterprises acted accordingly. As decentralization increased, workers and managers found new ways to appropriate the enterprise's income for their own benefit. For example, workers pressed for ever higher wages, which their managers routinely granted; both knew that the government would make up for the firm's higher wage costs one way or another.

Similarly, managers were eager to arrange whatever foreign loans they could, whether or not the money could be invested profitably. The loans were a one-way bet: if the project worked, the managers and workers would benefit; if it failed, the state would have to bail out the firm by taking over the loans. Indeed, state enterprises were often allowed to borrow abroad with the explicit guarantee of the central government. The process was an invitation to irresponsibility. Much of Eastern Europe's $100 billion or so of Western debt started out as loans for enterprise investments, and ended up in the hands of central governments.

The Way Ahead

So the reforms under communism were necessarily self-limiting, and thereby self-defeating. But after the democratic revolution of 1989, Eastern Europe can move beyond the failed "market socialism" and create a real market economy with a large private sector and free trade. Countries that have not yet given up central planning, such as Czechoslovakia, may require more time to set up market institutions; but they can also avoid some of their rivals' transition pains, by recognizing the dual need to create real competition and to keep financial discipline over state enterprises.

There should be four simultaneous parts to a program of rapid market transformation. First, let prices find market-clearing levels, in part based on free trade with the West. Second, set the private sector free by removing bureaucratic restrictions. Third, bring the state sector under control, by privatization and by imposing tougher disciplines on such state firms as remain. Fourth, maintain overall macroeconomic stability through restrictive credit and balanced budgets. Thus:

• From the outset, governments should strive to create a set of market-clearing relative prices. Price controls should be ended, subsidies reduced or eliminated, and the economy opened wide to international trade. Sensible prices are vital for efficient resource allocation. And with market-clearing prices and competition from foreign trade, governments will have a strong and demonstrable basis for closing down enterprises that suffer chronic losses. That in turn will send ripples of discipline throughout the state sector. In order to have free trade, the currency must be convertible; importers must be able to receive foreign exchange on demand. Convertibility has long seemed a distant dream to many economists in Eastern Europe, yet it can be accomplished rapidly through sharp devaluation combined with restrictive macroeconomic policies and financial control over state enterprises. It is one of the most vital steps toward market competition. Since the East European countries are small economies close to Western Europe, open trade will provide an immediate source of strong competition for the state enterprises.

• The second part of the program is to eliminate restrictions on private economic activity. New commercial laws must be prepared, or old ones dusted off (Poland will begin by updating commercial codes from the

1930s); company laws should allow for the easy establishment of new enterprises; tax laws should remove the punitively high marginal tax rates that are now common; and various licensing restrictions now applied to international trade and domestic investment should be eliminated.

• The third and hardest part is to discipline state enterprises. Part of the solution is obvious: drastically reduce their number through privatization. But that will take time. Meanwhile, they must be subjected to real market disciplines: by allowing private firms and importers to compete; by eliminating subsidies, cheap credits, and tax concessions; by ending borrowing on the basis of central-government guarantees; by antitrust policies to break up industrial giants; and by forcing loss-makers to close.

• The fourth need is to establish price stability (in the high-inflation countries), or to maintain it (in places like Czechoslovakia, where inflation has been low). This can be done mainly through tight monetary and fiscal policies. In practice that will require balanced budgets, no more cheap credits for state enterprises, and direct controls on wage-setting, given that these enterprises have little incentive to restrain wages.

One part of the economy that will take time to put on a market basis is trade with the Soviet Union. Countertrade will continue, but Finland has shown that some countertrade can be incorporated into an otherwise well-functioning market economy. Still, as soon as possible, the East European countries should take up the Soviet Union's recent offer to trade on a more market-oriented basis, with accounts settled in hard currency. In the short run that may hurt them somewhat, as the Russians cut back on imports of low-quality machinery. But the increased rationality of resource use will easily justify the transition costs.

The Need for Speed

The transition program (except for privatization and Soviet trade) can be decisive and rapid. There are several reasons why it should be.

The first is that reform is a seamless web. Piecemeal changes cannot work, since each part of the overall reform has a role in strengthening the other parts. Financial control of the public sector requires active competition. That in turn depends on free trade and free access to foreign exchange. Currency convertibility at a stable rate in turn requires restrictive monetary and fiscal policies. So macro- and microeconomic reforms must go hand in hand.

A second reason is the state of the bureaucracy. Throughout Eastern Europe mammoth bureaucracies remain in place, ready to continue the mismanagement of the microeconomy. New governments cannot change their course, nor replace them. The solution is to sidestep them, by letting market forces do their jobs. A sharp devaluation, for example, can eliminate bureaucratic allocation of foreign exchange.

A third reason is the sheer scale of the needed adjustments. Some sectors, notably in protected heavy industry, will have to shrink; others, particularly services and housing construction, must expand sharply. These changes will eventually produce great benefits, but they will be opposed by many in the shrinking sectors. Populist politicians will try to hook up with coalitions of workers, managers, and bureaucrats in hard-hit sectors to slow or reverse the adjustment—just as they have, successfully, in Argentina for more than a generation. So it is crucial to establish the principles of free trade, currency convertibility, and free entry to business early in the reform process.

A fourth reason for dramatic action, at least in Poland and Yugoslavia, is that the starting point is hyperinflation—which, if not decisively controlled, ravages societies by undermining tax systems, the budget process, and, in time, the most elementary functions of the state. Argentina, Brazil, and Peru provide stark illustrations of the failures of gradualism in ending it.

The Puzzles of Privatization

Even under the most accelerated timetable, the privatization of a large portion of state enterprises will take years. The macroeconomic control and opening of the economy to the West must therefore precede full-scale privatization. And yet the effort to privatize must proceed with full urgency. Macroeconomic stabilization, and liberalization of the state enterprises without creating real private owners for them, cannot succeed for long. If the enterprises remain in state hands, the industrial sector will fall back into financial chaos, and will create a cascading series of political crises as well.

The problem is straightforward. As central planning is eliminated, the economies will be left with enterprises that operate without any oversight at all, either from central planners or from real owners. Unlike Western firms, in which plant managers must respond to a board of directors representing the owners, the state managers in Eastern Europe will respond to no one at all, or in some cases to workers' councils within the firm. Either way, problems are bound to multiply.

Part of the problem will be the self-serving behavior of the managers, unchecked by a board of directors. Lazy or incompetent managers will face few if any sanctions. Worse still, opportunities will abound for self-serving managers who are freed to operate in the new market environment. Already in Hungary and Poland, there have been many cases of managers who have pocketed the proceeds of their state enterprises by channeling the profits (through transfer pricing schemes and other sweetheart deals) to private corporations in which they own a stake. Some managers have negotiated joint venture deals with foreigners that have sold out the firm at low prices in return for a promise by the foreign partner of a favorable personal contract for the manager. In enterprises with powerful workers' councils, the managers have been unable to maximize the value of the firm—say, by restructuring the labor force—if the workers' councils object.

These problems can lead to a political backlash. In Poland and Hungary, there is already a sharp (and appropriate) attack on so-called "nomenklatura takeovers," and part of the public have the growing feeling that a market economy will be yet another path to enrichment for the former communist bosses. The problems will also lead to a renewed financial crisis on a macroeconomic scale, since managers that are unencumbered by real owners are tempted to borrow recklessly or gamble with the firm's income. It is a sad fact of life that everywhere in the world, the state enterprise sector is prone to financial crisis. Such crises can be contained when the state sector is a mere 5 percent of the economy, but these crises wreak havoc when the state sector is 50 percent of the economy, as in Latin America, or 90 percent of the economy, as in Eastern Europe.

The essential problem, then, is to move rapidly on privatization. But there's the rub. Margaret Thatcher, the world's leading and swiftest privatizer, has overseen the transfer of a mere few dozen major state enterprises in a decade. Poland has more than 7,500 enterprises that should be candidates for privatization, of which the 1,000 largest have 1,000 employees or more. The great conundrum is how to privatize such an array, in a manner that is equitable, swift, and politically viable and likely to create an effective structure of corporate control.

One apparently easy solution, such as giving the enterprises to the workers, is no solution at all. Not only would this be highly inequitable (and therefore politically unpalatable) since industrial workers account for a mere one-third of the labor force, but it would condemn these economies to the inefficiencies of worker control. It would cut the worker-owned firms out from the capital markets, since outside investors would know that workers can vote themselves higher wages out of the firm's profits. As demonstrated in other countries, it would also condemn the workers to excess risk, because both their human capital and their financial capital would be tied up in the same enterprise.

Thus, there is a need to create more widespread ownership. Of course, many of the enterprises—especially the smaller ones—can be sold in an accelerated program of Thatcher-style privatization. But a large proportion will have to be handled differently. The most promising solution, though admittedly one that is quite unusual and untested, is to give away part of the enterprise shares in a free distribution to the public. A strategy might work roughly as follows.

Each of the largest enterprises would be converted into a limited liability company. A portion of the shares of each firm would then be distributed freely to the public. Perhaps 10 percent would go to the workers in the firms. Another 10 percent would go to the state banks, assuming that they too are on a path of privatization. Another 20 percent or so would be distributed into a group of newly created "mutual funds." These mutual funds (or more accurately, investment trusts) would themselves be share companies. The shares of the investment trusts would be distributed freely to the adult citizens of the country. In one swoop, each adult citizen would therefore receive a well-diversified portfolio of the shares of the industrial sector. Initially, the government would continue to hold the balance of the shares, but only under a legal commitment that it sell its shares in a defined time period, perhaps three years.

Based on such a share distribution, it would be possible to compose a board of directors for each firm, appointed by real owners. The managers would be brought under control; widespread ownership would be created; and the gradual development of share trading would lead to a building up of the stock exchanges in these economies. Within a fairly brief and well-defined period of time, the state would reduce its remaining claims, and become a minority shareholder.

Poland as Pioneer

At the beginning of 1990, Poland ushered in the first comprehensive program of macroeconomic stabilization and transition to a market economy. The Polish program, led by the Deputy Prime Minister Leszek Balcerowicz, is remarkable in its scope, with a broad and ambitious agenda on stabilization, liberalization, and privatization. Although the program is less than one year old, the Polish experience already points up several lessons.

The first phase of the Polish program emphasized stabilization and widescale liberalization of economic activity. By mid-1989, when Solidarity took power, the Polish macroeconomic situation had become desperate. Hyperinflation was raging, with price increases topping 50 percent in October 1988. The inflation was fueled by budget deficits on the order of 10 percent of GNP. Shortages were rampant, shops were empty. Industrial production was plummeting, and the prevailing system of wage indexation was threatening an even greater acceleration of prices.

The stabilization program called for an elimination of the budget deficit by sharp cuts in spending and subsidies and improved revenue collections. Energy prices were raised several hundred percent as subsidies were cut. The *zloty* was devalued to allow for instant convertibility on the trade account. At the same time, wages were sharply controlled in the state sector, so that the devaluation and subsidy cuts did not get dissipated in wage rises, a process that would have set off an explosive wage-price spiral.

The liberalization measures were equally dramatic. Almost all price controls in the economy were instantly lifted at the start of the year. International trade was freed by the elimination of almost all quotas, and by the introduction of a low and nearly flat tariff schedule. Limitations on private economic activity were eliminated.

After a sharp increase in prices in January 1990 (around 80 percent), inflation fell off sharply, and shortages were almost instantly eliminated as prices equilibrated supply and demand. By March, inflation was running at about 5 percent per month, and continued to fall to around 3 percent by mid-year. The stores filled with goods, and many consumer durables, long unavailable, were suddenly available and at discount prices.

Measured real wages fell sharply—by around 30 percent compared with the previous year—as subsidies and price controls were eliminated while wage controls remained in place. But this drop in the statistical real wage vastly overstates the actual decline in living standards. Actual living standards probably fell by no more than 10 percent or so. The reasons for the overstatement are straightforward. In 1989, goods were simply not available at the official prices. Queues and shortages were rampant. When prices went up in 1990, thereby eliminating the shortages and queues, the *real* effect on living standards was more modest than would seem from the official price statistics. In addition, during the hyperinflation in 1989, the apparent purchasing power of the wage each month was eroded by price increases during the month. By the time a household made its monthly purchases, prices had risen ahead of wages, and the real consumption power of wages was less than the statistical real wage suggested.

The early effects of Poland's "shock treatment" on production and trade are also notable. First, and of great importance, the exchange rate stability and convertibility have held firm. Poland has run a large trade surplus in the first six months, as a result of a rise in exports to the hard-currency countries as well as a fall in imports. Foreign exchange reserves have therefore risen measurably, strengthening the newly convertible currency. Individual enterprises are adjusting to their new trading opportunities, with many state firms seeking out new markets in the West.

Measured industrial production has fallen sharply, roughly by 25 percent over a year. Once again, however, the statistics must be interpreted with care. Part of the decline is simply a mirage. The official data cover only the declining state sector, not the growing private sector. Another part of the decline, perhaps as much as 10 percent year over year, is the result of dislocations in trade with the Soviet Union, not the result of the economic program itself. All of the countries in the region, even those not undertaking Polish-style reforms, have suffered a sharp drop in output as a result of the Soviet economic crisis. A third part of the decline, perhaps another 5 to 10 percent, is cyclical—the result of the credit squeeze imposed to end hyperinflation. The remainder is the result of some sectors being unable to compete with the new foreign competition, and therefore cutting back on output, a kind of adjustment which is necessary as Poland becomes better integrated with the world economy.

Since the beginning of 1990, unemployment has started to rise. At around 500,000 workers in mid-1990, this level of unemployment amounts to only 3 percent of the Polish labor force. Of that amount, most were new entrants to the labor market, or job quitters, rather than job losers. It is expected that unemployment will grow to between 5 and 10 percent of the labor force, comparable to the rates of Western Europe.

Of course, it is too early to predict the outcome of the 1990 reform program in Poland. There are reasons for profound optimism, but also reasons for worry. It is still possible that populism will take hold, with new demagogues convincing the public that there is an easy and painless way to a prosperous economy. Some of the old communist trade union leaders seem poised to try to play such a spoiler's role. There is also a risk that the growth of the private sector will be unnecessarily hampered.

A rapid and healthy development of the private sector will require two things: a favorable economic environment for new private firms, and a successful move on privatization. New firms are sprouting up—around 120,000 in the first six months. But they remain small, and so far have been cut out from bank credits. Poland urgently needs to develop its banking system, and to make sure that it is responsive to the needs of new private entrepreneurs. With regard to privatization of state enterprises, the big risk is that Poland will become bogged down by attempting to sell the enterprises one by one. That would be too slow, and would lead to too many controversies, while also leaving too many unsupervised managers in the state sector. The need is clear for more dramatic and decisive actions in the area of privatization.

The Role of the West

Western governments are only now beginning to recognize how much they must do to support the changes in the East. They must provide more leadership and vision, and far more generous financial support. The most fundamental support needed is a commitment to incorporate the East European countries into a common European market. As Eastern Europe ends trade restrictions and makes currencies convertible, Western Europe must be prepared to accept new imports from it. That means in agriculture as well as manufacturing: pig-farmers in the EC will just have to accept that free trade in Polish hams is a price to be paid for living in a united and democratic Europe.

At the same time, the Cocom restrictions on exports of most high-technology civilian goods to Eastern Europe can, after a prompt review, be lifted. These restrictions have bizarre and unintended effects. Poland's central bank cannot get the communications equipment necessary for rapid check-clearing, nor its telecoms authority the switching equipment needed to upgrade the notorious Polish telephone system. The Solidarity newspaper cannot buy the Apple computer it needs for efficient typesetting.

As East European economies become more integrated with the West, they will tend to become more integrated with each other, as part of an expanding common market. But efforts to promote East European integration make sense only if they accelerate, rather than try to replace, what will occur naturally in a united European market. The East European common market that some suggest as a precursor to integration with the West would simply be a poor man's club. The answers to Eastern Europe's needs lie mainly in integration with Western Europe, whose market is perhaps 15 times as large.

As well as trade liberalization, Eastern Europe will need financial support. The most urgent kind will be grants or loans directed mainly to building up its foreign-exchange reserves—rather than increasing imports—to help stabilize exchange rates and establish convertible currencies. IMF loans help to do this, but they are too small. From Western governments Poland has received just $1 billion for this purpose, after much haggling among the lenders.

The second kind of support needed will be money to help finance a social safety net for the region. The West moved rapidly to provide food aid for Poland. But when the Poles asked the World Bank for cash to support workers dislocated at the start of 1990, the Bank reacted in slow motion, suggesting that a fraction of the sum requested might be available by next summer.

The third kind of support is cancellation of most of the debt owed to Western governments and banks. Poland owes some $40 billion, Yugoslavia, Hungary, and East Germany around $20 billion apiece—all these figures are pretty uncertain. Any attempt to collect more than a small share of these or the lesser sums owed by other countries would subject Eastern Europe to financial serfdom for the next generation—a plight that would be particularly bitter since the debt is a legacy of communist mismanagement, over which the public had no control.

The debts should be reduced cleanly, not in a long-drawn-out battle. If commercial banks are not pressed by Western governments to accept a straightforward package of debt reduction, they will fight to collect fully; failing that, they will press for debt-equity swaps and other inadequate approaches to debt relief. That would gravely threaten the overall effort of reform.

Germany, of all nations, should champion the cause of debt relief. After each world war the Germans had to grapple with a crushing debt burden. Relief came too late the first time, only after Hitler's rise to power had confirmed Keynes's prophetic warnings to the victors against trying to collect reparations. In 1953 West Germany's creditors showed far more vision, cancelling much of its debt and thereby buttressing the financial basis for its spectacular economic recovery.

The fourth kind of support needed is long-term finance for development. The Marshall Plan provided grants, not loans, for Europe. Grant aid is again needed, for spending on infrastructure and on environmental control. But most proposals from Western Europe are for loans. And the form of these loans could well set back the market reforms. Take a standard official export credit from, say, Germany to Poland. A German supplier contacts a Polish state enterprise, promising finance for a project. Though the loan is guaranteed by the German government, nearly always it must also be cross-guaranteed by the National Bank of Poland—just the sort of soft option for enterprises that Eastern Europe must avoid.

Surely the West can do better than this in the 1990s. If Western governments provide loans, these should be the sole responsibility of the recipient firms, not of their national government. The loans should be directed specially to the new private sector, in particular to small and medium-sized firms. And Western governments should provide finance for an industrial project only when the private market also puts in some risk capital, with the governmental share being a minority of the total.

The French initiative for an East European development bank must be assessed in this light. Debt cancellation must precede new large-scale lending by any development bank. For infrastructure spending the bank should provide grants or concessional finance, rather than loans on market terms. For other projects it should aim its loans mainly at the private sector, and only when private money too is at stake.

Towards Growth

Many recent visitors to Eastern Europe have expressed pessimism over its future, citing outmoded factories, the absence of sensible accounting systems, the shortage of managers, and so forth. The reform process could indeed go off track, with political paralysis or worse in the East and miserliness in the West. But surely we must find ground for hope in the great talents of the East Europeans, exemplified by the dignity with which they have assumed the mantle of political democracy. When we look beyond the region's shattered economic systems at more fundamental features, there are reasons for optimism.

Compared with any region of the world at comparable living standards (around $2,500 per head), the population is highly skilled; the resource base is strong; income inequality—responsible for so much social strife in Latin America—is modest; transport costs for exports are low; and the industrial base is diversified, though outmoded. We can be confident that a highly skilled Polish worker will earn many times his current wage of $100 a month once Poland's market economy is established and closely integrated with Western Europe.

Businessmen, not economists, will determine the new technologies, organizational systems, and management techniques that will be the source of Eastern Europe's reinvigoration. It is they who will develop the new

exports crucial for its growth. But the energies of business must be unleashed, through the combination of market reforms in the East and
financial assistance and open markets in the West. It is up to politicians to
act with vision and daring to create the conditions for Eastern Europe's
economic transformation.

19

Liberalization and Stabilization

Károly Attila Soós

It is conventional wisdom by now that systemic reforms and transformation in communist or ex-communist countries entail open inflation. The reasons include the freeing of prices and wages, shortages (i.e., repressed inflation), a reduction of enterprise and consumer subsidies, and a real depreciation of the exchange rate required by the precarious status of most of these countries' balances of payments.[1] Inflationary pressures are difficult to control because much of the pre-reform institutional setting remains for quite some time, but without being able to function (even) in the old way. The essence of the old system is rigidities—the limited responsiveness of economic agents to prices. In the case of Hungary, the problem is made worse by the country's exceptionally high debt-service obligations. Interest payments alone on its nearly $21 billion foreign debt require the transfer abroad of 3 to 5 percent of GDP. This implies a diminution of the internal absorption, requiring an enormous effort. This is a problem of politics, economic policy, and also of the economic system. A crucial issue concerning the system is whether the foreign economic liberalization can be maintained under these circumstances. The danger is that either the current account will not improve to the extent necessary or inflation will accelerate beyond the controllable level. Such an improvement in the current account may entail strongly accelerating inflationary pressures. Then, with prices and wages liberalized, inflation may get out of control. How can we extract from the economy the necessary surplus with the least inflationary effect?

Surplus Extraction and Inflation

Traditional CPEs

In an economy with perfect central planning, just about any amount of foreign trade (or other) surplus can be extracted without inflation, because in such a system money is totally passive, its functioning subordinated to perfect *in natura* planning via direct controls. Reality, of course, never follows this model exactly. Stalinist planning for the rapid development of heavy industry is a kind of surplus extraction. As we know, pre-war Soviet five-year plans entailed strong, partly repressed, partly open inflation in all sectors of the economy. Similar ventures of the Soviet Union and other communist countries later, in the late 1940s and early 1950s, when striving to make money passive was at its peak, had little or no inflationary consequences within the state-controlled enterprise sector. But in retail trade, repressed, hidden and open inflation all prevailed, and the private sector experienced skyrocketing price increases.

Market Economies

A market economy will always react with greater or lesser inflation to an attempt by the government to extract from it a significant surplus. For example, achieving rapidly a significant export surplus usually requires a substantial real devaluation. This is a demand shock that most probably has an inflationary effect. Of course, this inflationary effect may be rather limited under certain conditions. Devaluation may even be (though usually only partly) substituted for by other, non-inflationary measures aimed at generating the necessary foreign-trade surplus.

The economy may be in a state of Keynesian unemployment and react to a (positive) demand shock with quantity, rather than price, adjustment. However, especially if the demand shock is a very large one, the inventories and idle capacities will probably not be sufficient for the adjustment to be primarily a quantity adjustment.[2]

The inflationary effect of a demand shock may also be limited if the product-mix of supply reacts flexibly to the change in demand. But if big firms, whose price sensitivity is necessarily limited to some extent, have an important weight in the economy, then bigger price shocks will be needed for generating the desired supply response.

In order to counterbalance the positive demand shock of a devaluation, the government can increase the forced savings of economic actors: taxes. But significant tax increases may have undesirable impacts on output and spending. Also, unions will probably fight for higher wages to maintain the workers' previous level of after-tax real wages. Government spending can be cut, but in reality only to a limited extent, and often also with inflationary consequences. Of course, the voluntary savings and the savings-investment gap of economic actors can be boosted by restrictive monetary policy.

Economies in Transition

The economic systems in Central and Eastern Europe are based on a combination of planning (i.e., hierarchical subordination) and market principles. Owing to the structural rigidities inherent in such a mixed system, bottlenecks remain important even if there are—as nowadays there increasingly are—idle resources.[3] Keynesian unemployment, and consequently Keynesian expansion, are out of the question. In other words, short-term possibilities of output growth are rather limited. Moreover, output in many fields has to diminish, because of the contraction of the CMEA market and the difficulty of reorienting elsewhere productions previously sold there. Thus, in order to rapidly bring about an important foreign trade surplus, product-mix changes and adapting to the needs of export markets are required and the internal absorption of the GDP has to be diminished.

At the same time, the authorities no longer have the necessary legal authorization and the required means (such as a sufficiently large apparatus) to implement either of these tasks via direct controls: to order product-mix changes, or to cut back the internal absorption of the GDP—i.e., to extract the necessary foreign trade surplus in an (ideally) non-inflationary way. Meanwhile, those features of a market economy and those above-mentioned means that are usually available for governments in a market economy to counterbalance the inflationary character of the response to the demand shock of a devaluation are missing or operate very problematically in the Hungarian system.

In the highly monopolized organizational structure, with a predominance of large, state-owned enterprises whose sensitivity to relative prices is even much weaker than those of large Western firms, the product-mix will only react to a strong export demand shock. This seems to imply the need for a large devaluation, the inflationary effect of which will be substantial.

And how to reduce the domestic absorption of the GDP? It would be quite problematic to increase foreign savings—taxes—further from their already high "Swedish" levels. Although there are many tax exemptions and reductions, their elimination is difficult because it requires a great deal of struggle with strong interest groups, in many cases for rather small sums.

In Hungary, as in Poland, substantial cuts have been effected in budgetary expenditures. Among them are reductions in consumption subsidies, primarily where the elasticity of demand is low (public transportation, bread, milk); these add to inflation. But there have also been non-inflationary cuts, more of which might be undertaken in investment, administrative, and military spending and in agricultural subsidies (but at the price of seriously jeopardizing the long-term future of agriculture, which must compete with highly subsidized agriculture in the EC). Further possible cuts in budgetary expenditure would affect consumption in areas of low elasticity of demand, with even stronger inflationary effects. Health care, pension, education, and other social systems could also be streamlined. But doing this without causing serious social and political problems is only possible through a comprehensive reform program. This is a medium-term, rather than a short-term, task.

The population's savings have been low—in Hungary, for example, nominally 3.5, 4.2, and 3.6 percent of the GDP in 1987, 1988, and 1989, respectively. The sole factor favorable to the development of savings is the increasing income differentiation of the populations (in Hungary, the ratio of household incomes between the highest and the lowest income deciles was 3.8 in 1982 and 4.6 in 1987, according to the Central Statistical Office), but this of course poses other problems. On the basis of the worsening age structure of the populations and the stagnation of real incomes in most of these countries, a higher propensity to save is not likely. Short-term prospects, because of inflationary expectations and general economic and political uncertainty, are especially unfavorable, and under such conditions it is rather difficult to stimulate savings through increasing the otherwise rather modest real rates of interest. Nevertheless, such increases are unavoidable.

Savings and the savings-investment gap also have to be enhanced in the enterprise sector. Since any large increments of GDP are unlikely in the short run, savings can only be increased through the improvement of efficiency, including that of investments; otherwise their reduction would seriously jeopardize future economic growth.

An important means of promoting the obviously crucially important improvement in efficiency may be restrictive monetary policy, also needed as an anti-inflationary device. As Thomas Wolf states, the effects of a devaluation

> are very importantly determined by the degree of stringency of the credit and monetary policies of the authorities. Specifically, the inflationary impact of a devaluation will be less than the theoretical maximum permitted by the domestic price system as long as the authorities do not fully accommodate the price level increase through expansionary monetary policy.[4]

However, there are several difficult problems with monetary stringency in a transition economy, where it may have rather substantial unfavorable effects.

Attempts at monetary restriction in recent years in Hungary have not led to the hoped-for results. The attempted quantitative control of the money supply entails a wave of indebtedness among enterprises ("queuing"); in other words, the economy creates its own "money," substituting it for the scarce "official" one. This has also been a problem in Poland. In Hungary, during 1989 the total amount of such liabilities increased by 60 percent and reached a large share of the total credit of enterprises. And positive real interest rates on bank credits (which in Hungary in 1988 reached the level of 10 percent) raise the costs of production for many borrowers, and thus contribute to price rises in those field where competition is weak. As we know from the famous Radcliffe report in the U.K. and from Lord Nicholas

Kaldor's works, none of these undesirable effects of tight monetary policies is unknown in Western market economies; but in the specific institutional setting of the countries of Central and Eastern Europe, they are even stronger.

The seemingly uncontrollable growth of inter-enterprise credits can be explained by the extreme weakness of bankruptcy proceedings in these transition economies. In one way or another, bigger firms are practically always bailed out by the government if they are threatened on the basis of their financial results. Enterprises in monopolistic positions—and there are many in these economies—especially can easily pass on cost increases in the form of increased prices. Under such circumstances, it would be logical to contain inflation by allowing import competition. But this is problematic in two respects, especially in the short term. First, taking into consideration the extremely strained current-account positions of these countries, import competition can only be allowed under conditions of very strict aggregate demand management. In other words, import competition can be a weapon against cost-push but not against demand-pull inflation. Allowing a significant deterioration in the foreign-trade balance in order to control the price level by increasing imports is not realistic in most of these countries. Second, as Béla Balassa states on the basis of the Chilean experience around 1980, free imports may not be a particularly effective weapon against rising price levels.[5] In Chile during that period, despite liberalized imports and a fixed exchange rate, wholesale prices (of tradeable goods) increased much faster than in the USA. Balassa's explanation is that in many sectors imported goods were not—and owing to differences in traditions, tastes, etc., cannot be—effective substitutes for domestic production. In my opinion, this holds *a fortiori* for today's Hungary, and very likely in the region's other countries as well, where in many fields (especially in consumption) the domestic market has until now been almost hermetically closed off from import competition. Therefore, domestically produced goods largely belong to quality, service, etc. categories quite different from those that are potentially importable from market economies.

The inflationary pressure on the wages' side is very intensive also. This is a corollary of the "property rights" problem: workers and bodies elected by them have rather broad self-management rights at enterprises. There is no "proprietor" who is strongly interested and able to contain wage increases. The solution of the problem is property reform—privatization—but that, of course, is not a short-term solution.

Under these circumstances, the "double or quits" paradox of restrictive monetary policy, formulated by Kaldor rather pessimistically for Britain, seems to be even more relevant for Hungary:

The . . . weapon at the disposal of the monetary authorities . . . is to keep on raising the rates of interest in the hope that there is some rate which is high enough—perhaps 50 or 60 percent—at which sufficient economic activity becomes unprofitable, or a sufficient number of business firms go into bankruptcy, to create a level of unemployment at which the resistance of trade unions is broken, partly because the nation will be in such a state of poverty that it will no longer be possible to afford social services such as unemployment pay, which undoubtedly stiffen trade union resistance at the present time. . . . Nobody knows whether the political disorders that will accompany the rigid application of this policy will (not) force its premature abandonment.[6]

Conclusions and Policy Implications

Given that in transition economies the possibilities of dampening inflation are rather limited in the short term, measures that are likely to accelerate inflation have to be avoided or postponed to the extent possible. The reduction of consumption subsidies should be cautious and gradual. Another crucial issue is the certainly unavoidable currency devaluation. The dilemma is whether to effect a large real devaluation—i.e., one that exceeds the difference between the domestic rate of inflation and price increases in the relevant foreign markets, as suggested by Balassa[7]—or to avoid this because of its inflationary impact, as recommended by Vissi.[8] Obláth's proposal (in Chapter 15 of this volume) of a relatively modest devaluation, combined with a complex set of measures that eliminate non-exchange rate systemic factors that hinder export expansion and boost imports, may be a solution.

Restrictive monetary policy may—and probably has to—be a device to contain inflation, but in the short term more can hardly be expected from it. The chances of a rapid "operation" aimed at stopping inflation through stringent aggregate demand management—as proposed, for example, by Kornai—seem to be rather weak. Kornai's blueprint is also problematic because he recommends against price, wage, and import liberalization for the state-owned enterprise sector,[9] which will remain the dominant sector in all these economies for some time. A combination of tight monetary policy with the rigidities of such administrative controls would lead to disturbances and significant falls in production, according to both historical experience and theoretical analysis.[10] This combination—applied not only to the state-owned sector but to the entire economy—might be a temporary solution, as part of a general, well-elaborated stabilization package, but it could not be a durable systemic option.

The recommended policy is not to "deliberalize" these economies or their state-owned sectors, either temporarily or semi-permanently. The liberalization within the given general institutional setting of the economy was certainly premature in Hungary and perhaps also in Poland. But instead of turning back, a better option would be to go ahead. The incongruency of the economic system and liberalization may be overcome by a rapid, decisive implementation of the systemic transformation toward a market economy. The stimulation of entrepreneurship, the de-monopolization of the enterprise structures, property reform, the strengthening of market competition, further steps in banking reform, the creation of the conditions for a more consistent application of bankruptcy rules—these are the most important elements of systemic transformation. At the same time, all these steps are important weapons in fighting inflation and will improve the efficiency of restrictive monetary policy in the struggle against inflation. Rapid systemic transformation is necessary if we want to succeed not only in containing inflation in the short run, but also in the medium and long terms. The elaboration of the real possibilities and details of such a program will require a substantial research effort and implementation, as well as political unity and leadership.

Notes

1. See joint Hungarian-International Blue Ribbon Commission, *Hungary in Transformation to Freedom and Prosperity: Economic Program Proposals* (Indianapolis: Hudson Institute, 1990, pp. 51-52.

2. J. R. Hicks, *The Crisis in Keynesian Economics* (Helsinki: The Yrjö Johnson Foundation, 1974).

3. For details, see K. A. Soós, "A propos the Explanation of Shortage Phenomena: Volume of Demand and Structural Inelasticity," *Acta Oeconomica*, Vol. 33, Nos. 3-4 (1984).

4. T. A. Wolf, "The Simultaneity of the Effects of Devaluation: Implications for Modified Planned Economies," *Acta Oeconomica*, Vol. 39, Nos. 3-4 (1988).

5. B. Balassa, "Policy Experiments in Chile," in Gary M. Walton (ed.), *The National Economic Policies of Chile* (Greenwich, Conn.: JAI Press, 1985).

6. N. Kaldor, *The Economic Consequences of Mrs. Thatcher* (London: Duckworth, 1983), p. 17.

7. Balassa et al., *Toward Renewed Economic Growth in Latin America* (Mexico City: El Colegio de México, 1986).

8. F. Vissi, "Infláció a gazdaság stabilizálásának időszakában" ["Inflation during economic stabilization"], *Gazdaság*, Vol. 23, No. 1 (1989).

9. J. Kornai, *The Road to a Free Economy: Shifting from a Socialist System—The Example of Hungary* (New York: Norton, 1990).

10. See, for example, Soós, *op. cit.*

20

Liberalization and Privatization

Márton Tardos

The transformation of the Central and East European planned economies to market economies is an unexpected development both for those who are in the midst of it and those observing it. The unforeseen and rapid weakening of Soviet power forced both the politicians of the earlier system and the new political personalities and parties who came to the fore during the transformation to face a new situation, both in the Soviet Union itself and in the countries of Central and Eastern Europe.

Economists in the West and in the East should be cautious about behaving in ways whose lessons are illustrated by an old joke. A farmer, upon seeing his geese dying, turns to the wise rabbi for advice. After adopting the rabbi's successive recommendations, the situation remains unchanged; the geese keep on dropping. Some time after all the geese have died, the farmer sees the rabbi and tells him about it. Instead of expressing regret for being unable to help, the rabbi says, "What a pity! I still have so many brilliant ideas about how to save the geese."

The tasks politicians and economists face today resemble those they faced during the old socialist party-state regime, but there are also differences. The common objective then and now is to make the national economy, ruined by socialist planning, suitable, in the interest of the people living there, for achieving significantly improved living conditions through hard and creative work.

Legacies
The difference between then and now has two important aspects. On the one hand, as late as 1989, those striving to transform the economy had to reckon with ideologically determined limits imposed by a weakening but still strong central power. On the other hand, the remains of the communist power meant that transformation had to be implemented from above.

255

The situation has changed drastically since then. The ideological constraints have eroded as a consequence of the central power falling apart. Nothing signifies this change more than the fact that the term "privatization," so fashionable these days, was forbidden to use in this region not long ago. Instead of changing the ownership system, one could speak only about the transformation of organizational arrangements. Similarly, the economic situation—however dire it might have been—could not be characterized as a crisis. Anyone daring to do so had to face serious attacks from the establishment. Changes in the political circumstances—the collapse of the old rule—have opened the floodgates of economic change. Instead of reforming the low productivity socialist economic system, the task today in almost all Central and East European countries is to manage the inherited economic crisis and to effect a deep-rooted transformation of the economic system.

The changed situation requires and facilitates solving the fundamental problems, but it also creates new difficulties. It is expressed more and more frequently that it is not possible to lead the country out of the crisis that is a heritage of the *ancien regime* under nice, calm circumstances. The economies of these countries can be characterized in varying degrees, as facing not only a critical deterioration in productivity, infrastructure, huge external and internal indebtedness of the central budget, and sharply declining propensities to voluntarily save and invest, but also situations in which the citizens' expectations concerning their standard of living surpass the capabilities of the economy to deliver those standards.

Is Liberalization the Solution?

These circumstances raise the question: What is to be done, and can the economic problems be solved through liberalization? Can economic stabilization be achieved and sustained growth be generated simply by eliminating government regulations on production, sale, pricing, and wage determination as well as by the full-scale liberalization of imports?

In my view, one can answer these questions in the affirmative only with considerable reservations. It is necessary to liberalize, but one can liberalize successfully only in those areas where the radical transformation of the ownership system has succeeded, and where privatization has already taken place; also, only monetary policy could exert a substantial control over the economy, which is as yet not the case. I believe that even to start the processes of stabilization and transformation requires that privatization and monetization decisively modify the behavior of private and institutional actors in the economy.

Sequencing of the Tasks

What should be done first? Is financial stabilization or privatization the priority task? It is, of course, true that it would be hopeless to try to jump-start economic growth with galloping inflation. But in my view, it is also true, as demonstrated by Poland's 1990 experience of stabilization via shock therapy, that as long as state ownership dominates in the economy, or at least until the requirement of a decent rate of return is enforced against public enterprises, and until large-scale privatization under rules that offer clear long-term perspectives to all economic agents is well under way, inflation cannot be brought under control. This is confirmed by Hungary's experience as well.

There has never been galloping inflation in Hungary. The acceleration of slow inflation was a consequence of the peculiar way subsidies were eliminated. It led to a speeding up of one-digit inflation to the 20-30 percent range all the while the government was pursuing restrictive monetary policy.

Since the mid-1980s, money supply has been increasing more slowly than the value of economic transactions. Nevertheless, even this monetary policy proved insufficient to exert adequate pressure on enterprises. Owing to the missing control of real owners, firms have found ways of comfortable survival even under difficult circumstances. Cross-indebtedness among companies (the so-called "queuing"), generating income from the sale of real estate, vacation resorts and other valuable assets, and the misappropriated use of cash-flows generated through amortization made it possible to ease the pressures exerted by tight money. These developments led to a situation where restrictive monetary policy could increase only marginally the efforts of the companies for higher profitability. The main impact has been to squander enterprise and national assets. From the above, it follows, in my opinion, that in the process of East European transformation, privatization and the establishment of monetary discipline must move on parallel tracks.

Towards the Solution

Privatization and the monetization of the economy are not only difficult tasks to complete, but are impossible to even begin efficiently without substantial political and public support. The economy cannot be brought into financial equilibrium under conditions of active resistance by the public. But open or passive resistance will not cease until companies continue utilizing production capacities even though they can be operated only at a loss. Resistance will not cease until people see not only the collapse of the old system, but the emergence of something new and positive.

Privatization is also not a popular task. Even though the successful transformation of the ownership system most probably will improve society's economic situation in the long run, during the process of its realization it will also increase differences in income and wealth. This will necessarily generate social opposition. If the government fails to give the highest priority to mobilizing all parties and organizations in behalf of privatization, then there is a great danger that the reconstruction of the ownership system, the establishment of private property, will lead to such tensions as to hamper the further transformation and development of the economy.

The process of privatization involves handing over public property to private individuals. This is troublesome even if we are aware that public property was no one's property in practice, or if we realize that property rights were de facto in the hands of managers and state bureaucrats who did not possess the constitutional right to do what they were doing. Privatization means that the state, as the representative of society, has to sell valuable assets to private individuals or groups of individuals. Even the best legal system would be unable to provide ready-made solutions to such large-scale transfers. Civil law provides only a legal framework to assure that when two citizens sign a valid contract of sale and purchase, the transaction will be implemented. However, even the best legal system would be unable to ensure that the price in the contract is a just one. Legal concepts do not even acknowledge the notion of a "just price." It leaves setting the price to the parties involved in the contract. The legal system refrains from seeking the answer to the question of how benefits should be distributed among the contracting parties. Should one suffer losses because of his improper evaluation of the situation, this is looked upon as a private matter. Society remains unconcerned also. Note, however, that in advanced market economies the prevailing price system enjoys widespread public acceptance. This, however, is not a consequence of the legal system, but of the successful operation of the market, working within the framework established by the legal system. The efficient functioning of the market is not in contradiction with the fluctuation of prices, the uncertainty of market values. This is especially true in the case of capital goods.

Stock market crashes occur even in the most developed countries. The social value of transactions in which large firms buy their partners frequently is often debated. But uncertainty concerning price setting will be much more characteristic in Eastern Europe, where markets are underdeveloped and the sale of capital is without tradition.

The absence of an unambiguous price system that is socially acceptable will constitute an especially difficult obstacle in the process of privatization, where the transaction is not between two citizens, but it is the state which offers for sale the "national patrimony." This is a transaction in which society is on one side and a private individual on the other. Inevitably, suspicions arise that the private individual, whether a local citizen or a foreign individual, obtains advantages at the expense of the community.

The conclusion one must draw concerning Central and East European privatization programs that they can be expected to be successful only if the privatization process itself is separated from government administration. Therefore, privatization should be privatized. This requires that the greatest possible number of private individuals should take part in the process. On the buyers' side, the saving and investment of private capital should be promoted. The appearance of foreign capital should also be supported. Possibilities should be given also for self-governing institutions, insurance companies, pension funds, mutual benefit societies, non-profit organizations and their foundations to acquire capital assets. Such a multifaceted approach would establish the demand side of privatization transactions.

It is also important that a great number of domestic and foreign companies should compete in the acquisition of public assets, under state supervision. Only the establishment of a capital market, the emergence of intense competition, can help society to manage successfully the social conflicts that will emerge as side-effects of privatization.

21

Systemic Change: Constraints and Driving Forces

László Csaba

As can be seen from the conceptual framework elaborated in Chapter 1, liberalization of the trade regime and the policy of opening up the national economy makes sense only in the context of overall economic and political liberalization—in short, "systemic change." Systemic change in the case of the ex-socialist countries is quite different from previous reforms. The latter were meant to preserve the underlying (power) structure via change, whereas the present policies aim at changing the fundamentals of the state socialist system. Therefore, if previous decentralization endeavors were more or less bound to founder as they reached the limits of the inherent features of the economic order, by the 1990s it has become a real possibility that liberalization of the external sector can take place as part and parcel of an overall—political as well as economic—liberalization of the state socialist system.

It may seem that, given the new overall historic context as well as the rationality postulates of economic theory, qualitative changes of the be-queathed systems will or should take place in one bold stroke. Influential political parties in the ex-socialist states as well as respected figures of the international community indeed repeatedly call for shock therapies—for the instantaneous introduction of the liberal order. The message of this essay is that such advice cannot be heeded. I will attempt to sum up the factors necessitating that the transformation to a pluralist economic order be a protracted one. Later on, the driving forces of systemic change are also surveyed to support the forecast: notwithstanding all the difficulties, the trend of evolution does point toward the market order.

Useful comments were made by the editors of this volume on an earlier version of this essay.

In formulating long-term expectations and forecasts, it is the historically unprecedented task of systemic change that is of paramount significance. Despite many analogies to various countries in various periods (most notably in wartime and its immediate aftermath), the task of transforming a practically fully nationalized economy into a market economy based predominantly on private property has no precedent in history.

Perhaps the most fundamental problem is that the middle class—the natural subjects and beneficiaries of such a transformation—has yet to be created. Today, 90 to 95 percent of the populations in these countries are chiefly or exclusively the employees of the socialist state. In other words, the capitalists to whom the property could be sold are yet to be created, for the most part. On the other hand, as Hungary's experience during 1988-1990 amply illustrates, the issue is not merely the proxy versus real proprietor conventionally postulated in the literature on reforms, but the legitimacy (social acceptance) of the entire process. If the new capitalist class will very closely resemble the old *nomenklatura*, the political shuttle is bound to move back soon in a populist direction. As is seen in experiences in Latin America, anti-Western and anti-capitalist governments (of the left or right variety) arise, and may halt in their tracks both liberalization and systemic transformation in the name of social justice. The same applies to other socially unaccepted forms of quick enrichment that the release of unbridled market forces may produce. Therefore, from the point of view of external liberalization, the time needed for profound and irreversible internal systemic change, and the political sustainability of the process (as well as its preconditions) are of decisive importance. So it is expedient to survey first the various factors conditioning the long march of the Central and East European countries toward the market—especially those hindering fast and radical change.

Sociopolitical Constraints

True, the once almighty communist party apparatus, the old-time major stumbling block to radical reforms, has mostly been pushed out of its former places of command. There are, however, governing parties for which there is always the temptation to "run" socioeconomic affairs directly with and for their clientele—"for the time being" and "in order to speed up transformation." More important, the state administration has not been substantially cut. And even when it is reduced, it has an inherent tendency to recover ("for democracy's sake"). From the branch ministries to municipalities and to various commissions, there are bodies eager to "arrange" things. Moreover, as in any system, political virtues deserve a reward. Thus, licensing procedures, "consultations," and various other sorts of political interference may well survive deregulatory legislation. De-bureaucratization is easy to declare but hard to carry out.

Bureaucratic coordination[1] takes place not only through the conventional channels of planning governmental priority projects and via the sectoral ministries. Particularly in the reformed socialist economies of Yugoslavia, Hungary, and Poland, a peculiar economic order had emerged during the 1980s. Decisions were made mostly in financial forms, often decentralized. Still, the predominance of bureaucratic coordination remained (and this explains to a fair degree the disappointing performance of these reforming economies). Although those economies were no longer centrally planned, they were monetized and decentralized, even though money, credit, and banking did not play the same role as in market economies. This is what the new governments have inherited and so the situation is quite the same today. Financial organs remain, for the most part, integral elements of the state administration and subordinate their way of functioning to it. Dismantling planning thus has not led to the market.

Although many of the reformist ideas stem from people working in the financial sphere, even in the reforming countries the fiscal and monetary authorities remain part of the state administration. Thus, as an institution they have a vested interest in preserving their management role: to remain the visible rather than the invisible hand. Therefore, in the reformed ex-socialist economies it is in the interest of the financial authorities and banks to maintain their discretionary power to decide, case by case, the fate of companies. This might turn out to be the most serious immediate barrier to crossing the Rubicon between the bureaucratically overdetermined and indirectly managed system on the one hand, and real market order on the other. Thus, contrary to the consensus of reformers that had emerged as far back as the 1950s, enhancing the role of money alone will not lead to the predominance of market coordination.[2] Most probably, only a long learning-by-doing process can lead to more and more ex-socialist economies crossing the Rubicon. The first liberalizing steps will probably transform them only to the intermediate stage of an indirectly managed economy.

The controversial role of the irregular, underground, or second economy is a crucial element in the overall process of systemic transformation.[3] In the second half of the 1980s, the conviction grew that the size and level of activity of the non-state sector is, in fact, a success indicator of systemic change.[4] In reality, however, the unofficial economy is a rather intimate bedfellow of the bureaucratically overregulated and coordinated formal/first economy (the public sector). In most cases, non-state activities are either integrated into the state-run ones (as in agriculture), or they operate under circumstances conditioned by the former. In services, the entrepreneurs often live on market imperfections, whose continued presence (e.g., effective barriers to entry) is secured by their active contribution (such as corruption money paid to the licensing authorities to keep out new entrants). Thus, they live in a symbiosis with the bureaucratic structures.

By correcting for some of the malfunctions of the state-run machinery, they do play a system-stabilizing role. If only for this reason, the second economy is anything but the forward bastion of free enterprise amidst an oppressive environment that it is sometimes considered in the West. On the contrary, many champions of the second economy are people who know how to get around in a generally nontransparent and arbitrarily bureaucratic environment. They therefore have a lot to lose if fair and free competition are to become the standard. In other words, the entrepreneurial stratum they constitute is just as much a foe of real competitive conditions as is the much-criticized managerial class of the large state-owned companies.

Let's not forget about the social implications of the expansion of the second economy. Because references to the market are usually made by the authorities at the time of major price increases, the population at large tends to associate these notions. Further concessions to market forces were customarily made when the expansion of the second/unofficial economy was allowed by the previous socialist governments. Therefore, in the eyes of the public, a rather pathological market behavior—on occasion, plain economic crime—is a phenomenon of what, to them, the "market economy" is all about. Precisely because it is an integral part of the outgoing bureaucratic system, the expansion of the unofficial economy (even when legalized) does not contribute to the social legitimation of market coordination. The outburst of hostility against the Soviet co-ops is but one example of our concern. In such an atmosphere governments are easily tempted to crack down on "profiteering," thereby constraining the expansion of the supply side of consumer goods and services as well as limiting the ways in which monetary overhand can be siphoned off.

In sum, governmental policy has a crucial role to play in finding a proper place for the informal economy within the strategy of overall economic liberalization. Only by cutting back the bureaucratic, ideological, and police harassment of private business and declaring the right to start and run a business as the constitutional prerogative of each citizen, and by creating favorable conditions for new market entrants and simultaneously following a tough line on monopolistic misbehavior, can the previously established norms of conduct change. Only then will the previously unofficial sector find its legitimate place in a market order. However, such changes don't come by themselves. Governmental policies bear a crucial responsibility for taking the necessary steps, in due course.[5] Only then will social acceptance legitimate the former underground sector as a valued part of the private economy.

Economic Constraints

One of the most paradoxical outcomes of the state socialist experiment is that the system failed most conspicuously in the areas where the comparative advantages of centralized decision-making could have been the greatest. These are the fields normally seen to be beyond the scope of profit-maximizing entrepreneurs: the social network as well as infrastructure, education, and environmental protection. It is important to face this unconventional feature of the East European crisis. Customary propositions of severely cutting back extra-economic outlays and simply letting the free market function (within the limits set by monetary policy alone) are out of touch with the nature of the very problem to be tackled by the twin strategies of systemic transformation and external liberalization. In other words, conditions for a liberal economic order are far from given in the region. The task of the transition strategy lies precisely in bringing them about.

What are the economic consequences of having imposed an artificially constructed theoretical model on a Central and East European landscape that was evidently unfit for it? The model was built on the presumption of uninterrupted high growth rates and, based on this, on an ever-expanding and ever more comprehensive state paternalism vis-à-vis the citizens—"supplying" them with housing (flats), catering, transportation, medical treatment, education, news, entertainment, foreign travel, and so on, all allocated through a benevolent central authority.

Though the idea was rather naive, the consequences are serious. The "expropriation of the expropriators" eliminated the interest in the return on capital. Consequently, the macroeconomic efficiency of growth remained rather low. This is illustrated by the internationally high rates of accumulation that were necessary to maintain world average growth rates during 1950-1980 and stagnation during the 1980s. Meanwhile, both standards and rates of social outlays lagged behind those of the most advanced nations.

An equally serious consequence of the application of the state socialist model has been the two-dimensional shortage of capital. This means that part of the social capital has been wasted on investments that never paid off, whereas another part was not accumulated for decades. Among the items of the first dimension are physical infrastructure, human capital (especially education and medical care), housing, and the neglect of the entire tertiary (service) sector (employing 60-70 percent of the population in the advanced countries). Among items of the second dimension are the sources for paying indexed old-age pensions, unemployment benefits, expenditures for re-training and resettlement, the substantial outlays needed to integrate a growing number of socially deviant or deprived groups, and the sizable sums needed to maintain the environment. In other words, the social welfare network criticized by standard economic theories as being overextended in the West is yet to be created all across Central and Eastern Europe.

What are the long-term economic repercussions of this state of affairs for the strategy of liberalization? First, growth performance of the region should be corrected downward both retrospectively and prospectively. The officially reported growth rates of the 1950-1985 period should be adjusted not only for measurement biases but also for the "omissions and delays" that must be made up in keeping residential areas inhabitable and pollution-free, schools functioning, and so on. The potential economic expansion of readjusting the structures is also limited by the bottlenecks stemming from infrastructural decay and environmental degradation.

Second, the state of the infrastructure and the structure of incomes renders the labor market rigid. Because wages normally do not contain the cost of housing, while the state has practically stopped building low-rent flats, and flat-leasing has become very limited and disproportionately expensive relative to wages, substantial labor mobility is inhibited. Due to the nature of the East European crisis, structural and even regional unemployment will be a long and costly socioeconomic problem, slowing down the speed of adjustment to market signals.

Third, poverty has grown into a serious problem by the 1990s, as Hungary's example shows. Old-age pensions and social transfer payments are not adjusted for the significant (double digit) inflation rates. The initial size of these payments was already so calibrated that only in an ever-growing economy with stable price levels could they deliver a decent living for the recipients. In reality, therefore, a truly frightening devaluation of these payments has taken place, which is proportionate to the time that has elapsed since retirement or starting to receive the transfer payment. In Hungary, for example, the purchasing power of the pension of a person having retired in 1980 was less than 40 percent of the original value in 1990, whereas additional income from property or private insurance was in most cases zero or negligible. Thus, 25 percent of the people live under and around the poverty level. Only for this reason is it obvious that the state's redistribution of incomes can't be cut back as much as conventional economic theory would require. This will be a very serious constraint on the actual speed and degree of internal liberalization, since in civilized societies pauperization is not tolerable. Moreover, these people are not normally in a position to react to market pressures by improved performance. Therefore, the sociopolitical pressure to put an end to nineteenth-century experimentation with "free" market forces will be irresistible unless this factor is properly reckoned with *a priori*.

Finally, outlays for environmental protection are anything but the luxury of the rich. Air and water pollution, and the way in which waste is being managed, have reached such a degree of decay during the decades of their having been a non-issue that the need for substantial action is urgent. Physical infrastructure, too, has to be developed to some degree; otherwise it will positively hamper economic recovery and transformation. And servicing large foreign debts implies a serious drain on the domestically disposable resources of most of the East European states.

Necessary spending for these three items—social safety net, the infrastructure, and the environment—add up to a single factor from the macroeconomic point of view—namely, that the availability of capital for economic modernization and structural readjustment will remain limited. It also implies that budgetary redistribution will remain larger, the level of interest rates higher, and consequently the expansion of the private sector substantially slower and the time needed for economic recovery much longer than optimal. Therefore, liberalization of the external sector and the move toward currency convertibility will probably remain gradual.

Driving Forces of Systemic Change

An egalitarian ideology no longer constitutes a barrier to a market-determined income structure. The economic crisis of state socialism, and the obvious inequalities and inefficiencies those arrangements have brought, add up to a mighty impetus to create market-conforming regulations in all walks of life. The social acceptance of remuneration according to performance has never been greater. There is a growing belief that there is no return to state socialism, property is legitimate, and savings in any monetary form will be melted away by inflation. Thus the propensity to invest and to start a new business, as an individual's way out of the ailing public sector, is bound to increase.

The collapse of the CMEA is an accomplished fact, as elaborated in the chapter in this volume by Köves. There is no return to previous normalcy. There is no easy way (soft markets) open to protected industries. It also implies that economic reorientation and the policy of export-oriented growth has no alternative. Unlike in previous years, this is not just a declaration of intent but an unavoidable fact of life. True, the shock effects of the immediate changes are considerable and the recession and unemployment they bring about will be substantial. Still, they did give the necessary first push to systemic and policy changes that otherwise might have been delayed. And if the road leads to the world economy, the need to create systemic congruity with the "outside world" has become immediate for all the Central and East European countries.

In all those countries that have opted for systemic change as defined in the introduction, there is now a social consensus on the need for bankruptcies, free prices, equilibrium exchange rates, and the necessity of balancing the budget by cutting back on the direct economic involvement of the state. In all these countries, as a consequence of one-sided priorities of socialist industrialization, there is an extreme concentration of employment in industry. Since the tertiary sector is underdeveloped, profitability in many of its sectors is usually high. This bodes well for the possibilities of job creation, as there are considerable incentives for people formerly employed in industry to switch over to the service sectors.

The reduction of the paternalistic economic role of the state will mean that more and more individuals will have to depend on themselves. The experience of Hungary, where during the last two decades there were growing pressures as well as opportunities to find new or additional ways to become economically active, suggests that there are considerable creative energies to be tapped in these countries. Given that in Hungary during the 1980s there was a steady fall in real wages in the public sector, people found ways to compensate for this by taking jobs in the second economy; 60- to 65-hour work weeks have become a standard for over 80 percent of the economically active population.

The five listed factors and their interaction make it probable that despite the constraints enumerated, systemic change and liberalization will emerge in the 1990s—though it may take longer than many believe.

Notes

1. J. Kornai, "Bureaucratic versus Market Coordination," *Osteuropa Wirtschaft*, No. 4, 1984.

2. For a detailed substantiation of this point using the contemporary Soviet reform debates as empirical evidence, see H.-J. Wagener, "Plan and Market in Perestroika," *Kyklos*, 1990/3; and A. Schüller, "Die Sowjetunion auf dem Weg zur Marktwirtschaft?" in H.-F. Wünsche, ed., *Marktwirtschaft im Sozialismus* (Stuttgart, New York: Fischer Verlag, 1990), pp. 33-68.

3. The non-state sector includes non-agricultural co-ops, auxiliary servicing activities of agricultural co-ops, work partnerships, and a large number of quasi-private activities, whose being truly private may be debatable, depending on the given form of activity. For a systematic overview of various forms and analysis of empirical evidence, see B. Dallago, *The Unofficial Economy* (Aldershot, Eng.: Dartmouth, 1990).

4. K. Mizsei, "Is the Hungarian Economic Mechanism a Model to Be Emulated?" *Eastern European Economics*, Vol. 26, No. 4 (Summer 1988); J. Kornai, "Affinity Between Ownership Form and Coordination 6, No. 4 (Summer 1988); J. Kornai, "Affinity Between Ownership Form and Coordination Mechanisms: The Common Experience of Reform in Socialist Countries," *The Journal of Economic Perspectives*, No. 3, 1990.

5. L. Csaba, "Some Lessons from Two Decades of Economic Reform in Hungary," *Communist Economies*, No. 1, 1989.

22

China's Industrial and Foreign Trade Reforms

Dwight W. Perkins

Economic systems reform in China, as in most other countries that have experimented with fundamental reform, was initiated with narrow economic goals in mind. But reforms as sweeping as those attempted in China can rarely be kept confined within the boundaries of economics and technology. Such reforms inevitably spill over into the political sphere. How the political sphere reacts profoundly shapes how the economic reform process itself evolves.

Why did China begin the economic reform process in the late 1970s? The principal answer is that Deng Xiaoping and most of the others who regained power in 1978 were dissatisfied with the pace of economic growth. By the standard of Eastern Europe and the Soviet Union in the 1980s, China's 4-5 percent a year GNP growth rate in the two decades prior to reform does not seem so slow. But compared with the 9-10 percent annual rates of China's East Asian neighbors, China was indeed falling further and further behind.

There was also little doubt that slow or negative productivity growth was at the heart of China's inadequate GNP growth performance. Accumulation as a share of net material product (NMP) had risen above 30 percent, an extraordinarily high figure for such a poor country. As the accumulation rate rose, the NMP growth rate stagnated and may even have fallen slightly. Certainly further increases in the rate of accumulation were neither feasible nor likely to lead to higher growth. By the mid-1970s, China had serious worker morale problems and stagnant wages. The unavailability of consumer goods was widely believed to be a major source of this low morale. A further rise in the rate of accumulation could only have made matters worse.

The goal was to increase productivity growth by reducing the waste and misuse of resources. But there was no roadmap for how this goal was to be attained. The Chinese were not lacking for advice or models of how reform should be done. The World Bank, which China was in the process of joining, saw export-led growth and market-oriented reforms as the key, with South Korea and Taiwan being the models. Others, including many economists in China, argued that Hungary's reform experience was the most relevant. In the agricultural reform sphere, China's own experience with a modified form of the "responsibility system" in the early 1960s was influential, although few were willing to cite this experience openly.

In short, there was a wide variety of models to choose from but no obvious criteria that could be used to make the choice. No systematic body of analysis could demonstrate conclusively that one or another model would inevitably accelerate the pace of development in the particular conditions that faced China. The Chinese leadership, therefore, was left with the task of trying alternative formulas until they found one that worked. Furthermore, there were significant differences of opinion among the leaders as to which course was likely to work best. Mao Zedong's mass mobilization campaigns may have been discredited, but the differences that remained ranged from those who wanted to tinker in only minor ways with the bureaucratic command system inherited from the Soviet Union, to others who were prepared to abandon many of the key features of that system.

This essay is mainly about the reforms in the industrial and foreign trade sectors. But one cannot fully comprehend the momentum behind economic reform in China in the 1980s without some understanding of what happened in the agricultural sector after the Third Plenum in December 1978. Reforms in agriculture initially began cautiously, with a decision to free up rural markets for subsidiary production by households. The result was an explosion of petty trading activity in the countryside. By 1981, the government was making a major effort to tie material rewards directly to the effort the farmers expended. The responsibility system initially attempted to make the collective production-team work-point system work better. But the poorer areas were allowed to experiment with turning land over to individual households to farm. Quietly, the system of household farming spread. By the end of 1983, most farm families were cultivating plots of land on an individual family basis.

The combination of new incentives led to a dramatic increase in agricultural production. Between 1978 and 1984, grain output averaged an annual rate of increase of 5 percent. The gross value of agricultural output grew at an even faster percentage. By 1988, the real per capita consumption of the average Chinese farm household had doubled. This contrasts with an increase in real income per capita in the countryside in the previous two-plus decades (1957-1978) of perhaps 25 percent. Per capita grain output in 1978 was the same as in 1957. If land reform and other means of income redistribution had greatly reduced the most abject forms of rural poverty in the 1950s, reforms in the 1980s lifted much of the countryside to un-dreamed-of levels of prosperity.

There was another noteworthy feature of these reforms in addition to their impact on farm production. The party leadership allowed one of the key pillars of party power—its control of the working lives of the peasantry—to be significantly weakened. There is at least some evidence that such party leaders as Deng Xiaoping and Wan Li clearly understood what was hap-pening and stepped in to push the process along whenever rural cadre resistance attempted to hold onto the collective system. The party, to be sure, did not completely lose its grip on the countryside. Contracts to deliver grain and other crops, for example, were used by rural cadres to retain some influence over farmer decisions on what to plant. But the degree of control was very different from when cadres directly planned work tasks.

Those associated with these rural reforms—notably, Zhao Ziyang—found their most optimistic forecasts of what could be accomplished by reform to be vindicated. Those who had resisted had little to offer as an alternative that could plausibly work as well, let alone better. In October 1984, after six years of successful rural development based on the reforms, the government announced the extension of an across-the-board reform effort to the urban industrial sector. Experiments with industrial reforms had been going on for several years, but the October 1984 document marked the clearest indication that the government wished to do for the urban areas what had succeeded so well in the countryside.

Opening a Closed Economy

One major element of reform that long predated the 1984 directive was the decision to open up the economy to foreign trade and investment. China, of course, had never achieved complete autarky, but during the early Cultural Revolution period, anyone who advocated importing foreign technology could count on being criticized. Exports plus imports in 1970 had fallen to 5 percent of GNP.

In the early 1970s, trade rose steadily as a share of GNP before falling as a result of the turmoil in 1976 surrounding the deaths of Zhou Enlai and Mao Zedong as well as the Tangshan earthquake. The upward trend began again in 1977 and 1978. With the purge of the Shanghai group around Jiang Qing and Zhang Chunqiao, enterprises were encouraged to go abroad for tech-nology, and they did so with a vengeance. One Hong Kong firm estimated that in 1977-1978, Chinese enterprises signed contracts and letters of intent to purchase imported products totaling some US$600 billion. Subsequently, the contracts were cancelled and the letters of intent allowed to lapse. Before China could expand imports rapidly, some means had to be found to earn more foreign exchange.

China's export drive, therefore, did not start as part of a conscious effort to emulate East Asian style export-led growth (described in Chapter 10 on South Korea and Taiwan, and Chapter 9 on Japan). The Chinese were aware to some extent of the many benefits gained by their East Asian neighbors from the exports of manufactures, but the immediate need was to generate the means to pay for more imports.

Initially, China hoped to gain much of the needed foreign exchange through the export of petroleum. The Chinese ten-year plan, put out immediately after Mao's death, indicated that China planned to develop in that period the equivalent of ten new Daqing oil fields, several of them presumably offshore. OPEC's 1979 price hike made this seem an even better idea. The only problem was that geologists had not managed to identify even one such new Daqing, each of which was to provide China with 50 million more tons of oil a year. In any event, the price of oil began falling in the 1980s and the hoped-for offshore bonanza did not materialize. By the end of the 1980s, there was much talk of China becoming a net importer of oil in order to help alleviate its severe and chronic energy shortage.

Another major step designed to alleviate the foreign exchange shortage was the decision to renew borrowing from abroad. China had borrowed funds from the Soviet Union in the 1950s, but those had been repaid in the 1960s, when China had resolved never to borrow again. This self-denial was reversed, however, when the new leadership began to gain access to supplier credits subsidized by foreign governments. Negotiations to join the IMF and the World Bank were begun, and the first World Bank loan was received in 1981. By the 1980s, the World Bank was lending China $1.5 billion each year. Total lending in the 1979-1982 period was $2.7 billion per year; by 1987 and 1988, this figure had risen to $5.8 and $6.5 billion, respectively. Later Chinese government officials were to come to appreciate the technical assistance the World Bank—and, to a lesser degree, other lenders—were capable of providing, but that had little to do with their initial decisions to borrow.

An even greater break with the past was the decision to allow private foreign direct investment (FDI). This decision was motivated by both a desire for foreign exchange through access to export markets controlled by foreign firms and a desire for technology not available through other means. The decision to allow FDI was characteristic of the approach to reform in the 1980s. First there was an announcement that joint ventures with foreign firms would be allowed, and then a joint venture law was promulgated. The law, however, did not begin to cover the many areas of concern to foreign investors. So as time passed, a whole body of commercial law began to emerge. China, it should be remembered, had for all practical purposes abolished the legal profession in the years prior to reform. Commercial law had to be recreated from scratch. It is likely that Chinese enterprises also benefited from having some of the new laws on the books.

Establishing the Special Economic Zones (SEZs) was another response to the perceived need to make China attractive to foreign investors. As numerous developing countries had earlier discovered, the pervasive bureaucratic controls characteristic of so many developing countries tend to discourage foreign investment. The solution, at least in the short term, was to provide special enclaves where the restrictions and controls characteristic of the rest of the county did not apply. However, export-processing zones—the more common name for what China called SEZs—did not generally have that much impact if they remained isolated enclaves. Their real impact was when the rules that applied to the special zones began to be applied beyond the borders of those zones. In the case of Taiwan, for example, over time the whole island became an export-processing zone. In the late 1980s, the same kind of phenomenon could be observed in Guangdong Province, which borders on Hong Kong and Shenzhen, the largest of China's SEZs. In the late 1980s, many of the vestiges of central planning and bureaucratic control still existed in Guangdong, but the degree of such control was far less than in the rest of the nation. Some of the loosening of restrictions was the result of conscious policy emanating from Beijing designed to treat Guangdong as an experimental area for further reforms. Other aspects were unplanned and resulted from pressures emanating from Hong Kong and Shenzhen that the Chinese government was less and less able to control.

It is worth noting that for all of the publicity given to the joint venture law, the great bulk of FDI into China came from Chinese investors in Hong Kong who were setting up small, labor-intensive operations throughout Guangdong but not in the rest of China. Total investment by Hong Kong investors in 1987 amounted to 69 percent of FDI, much of it taking place in forms not encompassed by the joint venture laws. American and Japanese direct investment were 11.4 percent and 9.5 percent, respectively, of the total. Most of the Hong Kong investment was motivated by a desire to use cheap Chinese labor to produce goods that could be exported to Europe and North America through marketing channels in Hong Kong. Most of the U.S. investment, in contrast, was motivated by oil exploration or by a desire to gain access to China's domestic market with its billion potential customers. The Chinese were interested in access to foreign markets and high technology. This lack of concordance between American and Chinese interests had already created some disillusionment among American investors and prompted decisions on their part to cut back on commitments in China.

For all of the publicity surrounding joint ventures, oil, and World Bank loans, the real story of China's turn outward was the rapid expansion of the export of manufactures. Between 1978 and 1988, total Chinese exports rose from $9.75 billion to $47.5 billion, at an annual average rate of 17 percent. Of this total increase of $37.8 billion, $28.6 billion was accounted for by a rise in the export of manufactures. This performance was not far below that of South Korea and Taiwan during the same period and well above the average of the developing countries as a group.

What explains this high growth rate of manufactured exports? There is little evidence that urban industrial reforms had much to do with what happened. Nor did the promotion of joint ventures with foreign firms contribute that much. Accelerated export growth occurred long before either the joint ventures or the urban reforms had much opportunity to take hold. Some of the exporting enterprises were allowed to keep a share of the foreign exchange they earned. There was also a decentralization of control over foreign trade, away from the Ministry of Foreign Economic Relations and Trade's FTE monopolies. Provincial trade corporations were allowed to make their own deals and many, particularly those in coastal provinces, took full advantage of the opportunity. There was also some direct contact between the producing enterprises and their foreign customers, but this was not common enough to explain much of the export performance.

The history of how China managed to increase its export of manufactures has yet to be written. The core of the government's effort to promote exports in the 1980s involved several key elements. One was the expansion in the number of organizations authorized to deal with foreign trade—from a handful of FTEs at the beginning of the period, to 800 a few years later, to roughly 5,000 by 1989. These new trading units were under the authority of the provinces, other localities, and ministries; there were also producing enterprises that could deal abroad directly. The net result was to narrow greatly the distance between producers and foreign markets.

The government also introduced direct financial incentives to the exporting enterprises. Initially firms were allowed to keep a percentage of the foreign exchange earned. This percentage rose to 25 percent, to be shared by the FTE and the producing enterprise. Later the system was modified so that the firm could keep up to 55 percent of foreign exchange earnings above the agreed export target. There was a rebate of indirect taxes on the goods that were exported. There were also efforts to simplify and speed up the processes involved in getting hold of these foreign exchange payments and tax rebates, processes that earlier could take a year to complete.

Finally, from early on the government began to set the exchange rate at levels designed to encourage exports. Initially they created a dual rate, with that applying to exporters being substantially devalued. Then the two rates were combined and the renminbi was twice devalued. Later still, a swap market was created where firms could sell and obtain foreign exchange at whatever rate the market set. With inflation, the gap between the swap market rate and the official rate, initially only 20-30 percent, rose to around 80 percent by 1989, indicating that the renminbi became increasingly overvalued as a result of the inflation in China.

Another major influence on China's exports, but one that is difficult to quantify, is the impact of Hong Kong and overseas Chinese. In Southeast Asia, North America, Hong Kong, and Taiwan there are tens of millions of people of Chinese descent. Many of these people are among the world's most knowledgeable international traders. A large proportion of them still have some family ties to the Chinese mainland. As already mentioned, the impact of the Hong Kong Chinese on neighboring Guangdong Province is readily apparent. But overseas Chinese contracts go far beyond Guangdong. By the late 1980s, Taiwan businessmen were also becoming a force in China both as investors and traders. And overseas Chinese probably had more than a little to do, directly and indirectly, with why the United States was China's third largest trading partner.

Whatever the explanation, there is little doubt that the expansion of foreign trade had much to do with why China's GNP growth rate averaged 9 percent a year in the post-1978 decade. With a 1988 foreign trade ratio ([exports + imports]/GNP) of 27.6 percent, China could afford to turn to imports to overcome bottlenecks, such as the shortage of steel and road transport. It could also spend substantial sums on imported high-quality equipment not available domestically.

But opening up to the outside world also brought with it powerful influences outside the sphere of economics and technology. In the first half of the 1970s, China was as closed a society as one finds anywhere in the world in the twentieth century. Few Chinese had traveled abroad, and information about what was happening elsewhere was confined to publications such as the *People's Daily*. The party and government elite did read something called "Reference News" (*Cankao Xiaoxi*), but this publication dealt mainly with foreign affairs, not how people outside of China were living their daily lives.

In contrast, by 1989, China—at least urban China—had had ten years of considerable access to information about the outside world. Trips by China's academics and sports team leaders to Japan, Korea, and the West, reported on television, gave onlookers a view of how others live; so in a way did Western television programs shown on Chinese TV. Citizens from the industrial countries, from tourists to teachers of English, are now scattered across the country. Books and articles including numerous translations of Western works have been readily available. Internal passports for foreign travel were abolished for most cities and many rural areas several years ago. Tens of thousands of Chinese students and visiting scholars have spent a year or more in North America, Europe, and Japan, and perhaps 20,000 or so are now back in China.

China's communist party and government have not completely given up the effort to control the flow of information and confine it as much as possible to science and technology. These efforts, however, have been partial and incomplete at best. In places such as Beijing and China's Southeast Coast, there is little effective control whatsoever of the information flow. The result has been a revolution in rising expectations in both the economic and political spheres.

Increasing the Role of Market Forces

There was some connection between the opening of the economy and the effort to increase the role of market forces. The boom in the economy of Guangdong Province in the latter part of the 1980s that spilled over into the export sphere would probably not have been possible if key inputs such as coal and steel had been available only through application to the central planners. But to a substantial degree opening up and increasing the role of market forces were not directly connected.

There were five elements to the effort to increase the role of market forces, and China made some reform progress on all five fronts. But the degree of progress on each front was highly uneven. And there were vigorous debates throughout the latter half of the 1980s over which elements deserved the greatest emphasis.

The five components necessary to make a market system work are:

1. Intermediate and final goods must be available for free purchase and sale on the market. All products including critical inputs cannot be the monopoly of the central planners and allocated through administrative channels.

2. The prices of these goods must reflect relative scarcities or prices will give the wrong signals to both producers and consumers.

3. Decision makers in producing units must behave in accordance with the rules of the market; specifically, they should maximize profits by increasing sales or by cutting production costs. Maximizing gross value of output is not what is required. Nor does behaving according to the rules of a perfectly competitive market mean to maximize profits by generating more subsidies or monopoly rights from the government bureaucracy. Violations of this basic requirement are prevalent in socialist economies but also in the majority of the world's developing economies. China is both a socialist and a developing country.

4. There must be competition among enterprises. It is, of course, possible to have a market without competition, but one of the principal reasons for increasing the role of the market is to stimulate enterprise productivity. Planning through bureaucratic commands heavily favors monopoly of markets because competition makes it difficult to plan. Markets, in contrast, work best when there is a great deal of competition.

5. There must be a degree of macro stability if markets are to function well. In theory, one can have a rapid increase in the money supply and in

prices, and markets can continue to allocate goods efficiently. But in the real world of political economy, money is not a veil and the rate of price increase does matter. In China in 1988 and 1989, inflation more than any other single element fostered a political climate that pushed the government back toward controls and away from the market.

In the early 1980s, China experimented in certain localities and within particular enterprises with reforms that had the effect of enhancing the role of market forces. But there was no consensus in the early 1980s in favor of a major role for the market. The view of many was that planning should dominate and that the market should play only a supplementary role in such key areas as the distribution of intermediate goods. The change in emphasis to moving toward a dominant role for the market came about not so much because of the influence of specific economic events as because of the increasing influence of Zhao Ziyang and the many reform-minded people around him.

The key document was the State Council directive of October 1984. The content of the document itself is not remarkable. It calls for reform but is full of words such as "guidance planning," which were not easy to interpret even for those who helped write them. In the four years that followed, however, the direction of reform efforts was quite clear. The role of the market in the distribution of both intermediate and consumer goods was steadily expanded, particularly in the coastal provinces.

The share of industrial inputs distributed through the market rather than through administrative channels expanded steadily, although we only have published data for 1984 and 1985. The expansion of small-scale industry—what the Chinese call township and village enterprises—would have been far less dramatic in the absence of this particular reform. Between 1985 and 1988, township, village, and other collective enterprises expanded at a much faster pace (28 percent) than large and medium-scale state industrial enterprises. Of the total industrial growth during these four years, the various collective and other township and village enterprises accounted for 41 percent. Not everyone cheered, though. There was the view that many of these enterprises wasted raw materials and energy; that view became the dominant one after June 4, 1989, at least among planners at the center.

Price reform was hotly debated from the outset, both over how to go about it and over the priority to be given to one kind of reform over others. The effort to change prices began initially as a bureaucratic exercise in which prices were changed one by one. That process, begun in the early 1980s, made little headway as every price change inevitably became a political battle between those who gained from the change and those who lost.

The major innovation in the latter half of the 1980s was to downplay the effort to change state prices for intermediate goods and instead institute a dual pricing system. The state continued to set prices on goods allocated by administrative means. For products distributed through the market, however, prices were allowed to float up to their equilibrium level, at least in those provinces where the system was fully implemented.

The dual price system went part of the way toward meeting the need for more efficient resource allocation. Marginal decisions by enterprises were increasingly being made on the basis of market prices rather than on the basis of prices fixed by the state. Political resistance to specific price changes was difficult to mobilize because the state did not directly control those prices. By this relatively simply device, the state appeared to be on the way to solving the problem of rationalizing prices.

But economic reforms are rarely as simple as they first appear. To begin with, prices on the secondary markets rose by a large amount in the case of intermediate goods. In the case of some consumer goods as well, price increases were sometimes substantial. To be sure, high prices for certain agricultural products usually led to a supply response that brought prices back down, at least initially. Not so with intermediate goods, where the "input hunger" of socialist firms kept prices up. Because this "input hunger" reflected enterprise actions not in accordance with the rules of the market, the high prices were not really the efficiency prices of a perfectly competitive or even a monopolistically competitive economy in the Chamberlinian sense, but the "spillover" effects of excess demand caused by the well-known behavior patterns of managers in centrally planned economies. Still, those prices were a considerable improvement over the state prices, most of which had been frozen for over two decades.

Dual prices, as it turns out, were one source of another problem that had a direct bearing on the events of June 4 in Tiananmen Square. The dual price system created very large rents which, potentially at least, could be captured by enterprising individuals with access to the government's allocation system. The method was simple enough. Obtain an allocation of goods at state-set prices that is greater than one really needs to fulfill state obligations and sell the extra quantity at the market price. If one can get hold of goods at state prices without having to produce anything, so much the better. Everything can then be sold at market prices. In China, firms proliferated whose primary purpose was to play this middleman role. In actuality, Chinese enterprises really needed middlemen to smooth out the inefficiencies inherent in any planned distribution system. But many of the enterprises created for this purpose did not really search the country in order to transfer surplus goods in one area to deficit areas where they were needed. Some of these firms were part of the problem because they used their political influence to divert goods to themselves that otherwise would have gone directly to the producing enterprises.

How many of those intermediary enterprises were providing a socially useful service and how many were mainly grabbing rents will probably never be known accurately. What is clear is that many, perhaps most, Chinese saw what was going on as corruption—a point that Csaba made also for the "second economies" in Eastern Europe in Chapter 21. The dual price system was not the only source of corruption. The levers that give officials discretionary control over the allocation of everything from steel to passports create the potential for corruption. But the really large rents were there because of the dual price system. In a country where people thought of a 10,000-yuan-per-year household as enormously wealthy, individuals were earning 100,000 and even a million yuan a year. Much of what was going on was technically legal, but the public, imbued with strong egalitarian values, didn't see it that way.

The logical answer to the problems created by the dual price system was to eliminate state-set prices and leave only market prices. But that solution ran up against the fact that a large number of enterprises would have had to pay far more for needed inputs. Many would have been forced into large losses, which in turn would have led them back to the government for loans at below market interest rates—loans they might never repay. The banks would be pressured by the political authorities and would in turn go to the central government for injections of deposits that would allow them to keep on lending. Money would flow from the government to the banks to the enterprises to the workers in these enterprises to consumer markets, and the result would be accelerated inflation. Even without getting rid of the dual price system, this process was well under way by the late 1980s. Enterprises, both large and small, were in the midst of an investment boom that was larger than the economy could sustain without inflation.

The problem was, in essence, the kind of investment hunger that is characteristic of most socialist command systems. The principal source of this hunger is that neither the producing enterprises nor the banking system faces a real budget constraint. Nor were these firms maximizing profits in the appropriate way. Chinese enterprises had, to a substantial degree, switched over from gross output value objectives to profits. But profits were earned as much by getting access to subsidized credit and physical inputs as they were by raising sales and cutting production costs. The solution was to make enterprises truly independent and dependent on their own resources. To do that one had to break the numerous ties that connected the enterprises to the government bureaucracy. China in the late 1980s was full of experiments designed to do just that. The interest in selling shares of enterprises, for example, was one of several steps. It was in part an effort to create enterprises that obtained their capital from investors independent of government ministries and central planners. The capital would come from other enterprises rather than individuals in the case of the larger firms.

There were various other efforts to break the connection between the state bureaucracy and enterprises, and there was much discussion of new experiments. But by 1988 and early 1989, the typical enterprise budget constraint was still quite soft and ties to the government bureaucracy still quite strong.

As controls over prices and the allocation of inputs relaxed and enterprise independence remained illusory, inflation began to accelerate. For nearly twenty years prior to the 1980s, the Chinese people had been used to a world in which overt inflation was nonexistent. The official cost of living index did not rise at all after 1962 until 1979. In 1987 the rate rose to 8.8 percent; in 1988, to 20.7 percent. These were not high rates by international standards but they were a shock to the Chinese people who were lacking in experience with inflation, except for those old enough to remember the Kuomindang inflation of the 1940s. Those most worried were residents of the urban areas and, in particular, those in government and other salaried occupations who were not in a position to profit from the inflation, as was the business sector.

Efforts to control inflation by tightening up enterprise credit ran into another feature of the reforms. For a high percentage of the total number of enterprises, it was the local government that mattered, not Beijing. Enterprise control had been effectively decentralized and it was in the interest of the locality to keep it that way. The localities, on the other hand, had no incentive to do their share to control the national macro imbalance. Only the center was willing to control excess investment demand, but it lacked appropriate levers for doing so smoothly. In effect, its main level was its capacity to freeze credit, but an across-the-board freeze on credit was highly disruptive of production; hence any freeze was bound to be partial. The rate of inflation did come down by early 1989, but it was still higher than what many considered politically acceptable. Only enterprises with hard budget constraints and a more developed financial system would make macro control effective in both controlling inflation and maintaining efficient markets.

Conclusions

For all of the troubles China faced in 1988 and 1989 as a result of the reform effort, the bottom line was that beginning in 1979, China had managed to break out of the "moderate growth and low efficiency" pattern so characteristic of a command economy. China in the 1980s achieved the kind of performance that its successful East Asian neighbors had enjoyed since the early 1960s.

The reforms, however, also contributed to the political tensions that erupted in June 1989. But were the reforms really to blame for these tensions, or was it the incompleteness of the reforms? It was the continued existence of centrally allocated goods at low state prices that created the opportunity for gain. Eliminating the dual price system would have lowered the profits obtained by gaining access to goods at controlled prices. But that would have meant continuation of the mutual back-scratching or back-door deals that are the inevitable characteristic of the common system, only the profits to be gained would have been lower. Only a return to Maoist-style repression that makes it impossible to enjoy the fruits of higher incomes would eliminate payoffs as long as discretionary bureaucratic levers continued to operate.

But eliminating the strains of China's recent reforms, if attempted through greater and greater controls, will bring about tensions of other kinds. The likely result will be a markedly slower growth in output, exports, and employment. With a work force that is growing by fifteen million new entrants a year and a rural population where many more tens of millions are redundant, China can ill afford a slow growth policy. The country thus faces a major dilemma.

The path that China will choose is not now clear to either those responsible for its economic policy or to outsiders. In early 1990, the dominant position belonged to those who called for greater administrative controls over the economy. But virtually no one advocates a return to autarky and the centralized command system of the 1950s. The question is whether the inevitable compromise between market forces and bureaucratic commands will arise out of a thoughtful debate and purposeful experimentation or be imposed by officials determined to hold on to bureaucratic power without challenge and without much concern for the economic costs to the nation.

Index

About the Book
and Editors

This groundbreaking volume combines theories of economic liberalization with a wide variety of case studies from market and socialist economies. Internationally regarded scholars and Eastern European policymakers have collaborated to evaluate the dramatic economic changes taking place throughout the world.

The opening essays contribute to the theoretical debate by showing that foreign economic liberalization goes beyond reducing import barriers to policies on investment, financial liberalization, convertability, and export promotion. Case studies compare successful and unsuccessful liberalization attempts world wide. The disintegration of the CMEA and the policy dilemmas facing Central and Eastern Europe are examined in great detail, as the authors explore the pitfalls and opportunities inherent in the transformation from a centrally planned economy.

This up-to-date text will be invaluable for courses on the history and transformation of socialist economies, comparative economic systems, and international trade and investment.

András Köves is deputy director, Institute for Economic and Market Research and Informatics in Budapest, Hungary. **Paul Marer** is professor of international business at Indiana University, Bloomington.